D1220314

In this book Gary Goertz analyzes different ways states interact with their environments; he also examines some specific environments that influence state behavior. Three substantive contexts especially important in affecting decision-making are history, system structure, and international norms, and Goertz discusses the theoretical, methodogical, and empirical dimensions crucial to understanding them. The ways these contexts matter are explored by viewing context in turn as cause, as changing meaning, and as barrier. Goertz engages the literature on structuralism and international regimes, and uses rational actor and diffusion models as theoretical references. To show how different contexts influence behavior in different fashions, several empirical studies are provided, including oil nationalization, USSR–East European relations, enduring military rivalries, and decolonization.

CAMBRIDGE STUDIES IN INTERNATIONAL RELATIONS: 36

CONTEXTS OF INTERNATIONAL POLITICS

Cambridge Studies in International Relations is a joint initiative of Cambridge University Press and the British International Studies Association (BISA). The series will include a wide range of material, from undergraduate textbooks and surveys to research-based monographs and collaborative volumes. The aim of the series is to publish the best new scholarship in International Studies from Europe, North America and the rest of the world.

CAMBRIDGE STUDIES IN INTERNATIONAL RELATIONS

36 GARY GOERTZ
Contexts of international politics

35 JAMES L. RICHARDSON
Crisis diplomacy
The Great Powers since the mid-nineteenth century

34 BRADLEY S. KLEIN
Strategic studies and world order
The global politics of deterrence

33 T. V. PAUL
Asymmetric conflicts: war initiation by weaker powers

32 CHRISTINE SYLVESTER
Feminist theory and international relations in a postmodern era

31 PETER J. SCHRAEDER
United States foreign policy toward Africa
Incrementalism, crisis and change

30 GRAHAM SPINARDI
From Polaris to Trident: The development of US Fleet Ballistic Missile technology

29 DAVID A. WELCH
Justice and the genesis of war

28 RUSSEL J. LENG
Interstate crisis behavior, 1816–1980: realism versus reciprocity

27 JOHN A. VASQUEZ
The war puzzle

26 STEPHEN GILL (ed.)
Gramsci, historical materialism and international relations

25 MIKE BOWKER and ROBIN BROWN (eds.)
From Cold War to collapse: theory and world politics in the 1980s

24 R. B. J. WALKER
Inside/outside: international relations as political theory

23 EDWARD REISS
The Strategic Defense Initiative

Series list continues after index

CONTEXTS OF INTERNATIONAL POLITICS

GARY GOERTZ
University of Toronto

Published by the Press Syndicate of the University of Cambridge
The Pitt Building, Trumpington Street, Cambridge, CB2 1RP
40 West 20th Street, New York, NY 10011-4211, USA
10 Stamford Road, Oakleigh, Melbourne 3166, Australia

First published 1994

Printed in Great Britain at the University Press, Cambridge

A catalogue record for this book is available from the British Library

Library of Congress cataloguing in publication data available.

ISBN 0 521 44070 X hardback
ISBN 0 521 46972 4 paperback

TAG

CONTENTS

LIST OF FIGURES

LIST OF TABLES

ACKNOWLEDGMENTS

I would first like to thank Paul Diehl, friend and colleague, with whom much of the empirical research presented in this volume was conducted. In addition, Paul has read the whole manuscript; his comments and suggestions have been invaluable. Others have read or heard, and criticized parts of this book: my thanks go to Lars-Erik Cederman, Douglas Dion, Scott Gates, Harvey Starr, Ray Taras, John Vasquez, Keith Webb, and Dina Zinnes and the folks at the Merriam Lab. Jon Solem and Nathan Adams were intimately involved in the researching of chapters 7 and 8. Their contributions made the section on barrier models much clearer and theoretically coherent. Thanks go to John Bailey who constructed the index. I would also like to mention Caryl Flinn whose remarks about social science style incited me to make the book more readable than it was originally.

Various portions of the book appeared in earlier versions in various journals. I would like to thank *International Studies Quarterly*, *The Journal of Conflict Resolution*, *Comparative Political Studies*, *International Interactions* and *Paradigms* for permission to use this material.

I would like also to thank Steve Smith, John Haslam, and the people at Cambridge University Press for making the production of this book a pleasant process.

1 INTRODUCTION

Everything should be made as simple as possible,
but not simpler.

Albert Einstein

Over the last twenty years the concept of context has had wide currency throughout the social sciences and the humanities. In art and literary history it has meant attempting to understand the social, political, and intellectual environments in which various masterpieces of Western culture, from Shakespeare to Renaissance art to Machiavelli, were produced. These attempts have emphasized that human action is not understandable ripped out of its sociological, cultural, and historical nexus of reference. These calls to context have been made to stress the variability – if not the capriciousness – of human behavior; they attempt to "de-universalize" knowledge and meaning.

In contrast, the social sciences in their more behavioralist and positivist modes have sought laws of behavior and generalizations independent of culture and historical accident. After years of effort one may come to the conclusion that simple context-free laws of behavior do not exist. Researchers have often found that relationships may be positive in one period and then negative in the next or changing from one country to another (e.g., Singer, Bremer, and Stuckey 1972). From the empirical literature in world politics the conclusion imposes itself: simple bivariate hypotheses have no simple answer.

Just as the meaning of words cannot be completely specified by dictionaries, so simple laws of international behavior may not exist. To understand the meanings of words we need a theory of pragmatics, so in international relations we need a theory of context. This book examines some contexts and how they influence the way states act. For example, the relation of the individual state to the structure of the international system has occupied scholars of international relations over the last few decades. Some have argued that the structure of the system – be it bipolar or multipolar – determines in large part how nations act (Deutsch and Singer 1964; Waltz 1964). At the same time most believe that governments have some freedom of choice. A largely uncharted area is the character of the relationship between structure and individual: To what degree does system structure *determine* individual state behavior? Or, conversely, how much room does system structure *permit* for individual differences? The problem of the mechanisms connecting the international environment to individual states – or rather, from my point of view, their interaction – is one focus of the problematique of context. One goal of this book is to construct some contextual tools that facilitate the construction of theories about how states relate to their environments. Like all tools they work better for some purposes than others, but I suggest that they are tools scholars of world politics might want to keep handy.

Depending on the theoretical perspective the environment is accorded more or less weight in determining behavior, its impact is variously described as "cause," "factor," "determinant," "influence," "constraint," "intervening variable," etc. A perusal of *Roget's thesaurus* or the literature of world politics might suggest that these words are synonyms. Even though "influence" suggests less impact than "cause," it is not clear whether this is a theoretical claim or just modesty on the part of the author (not to mention the bad influence of the generalized passive voice in social science writing). Nevertheless, in the final statistical wash these concepts appear to be little different because they all tend to be formalized in regression models with the corresponding causal interpretation. One important part of developing a contextual tool box is considering the different ways – what I shall call "modes" – that individuals and environments interact. It is important to understand how the environment can "cause" behavior, but this does not constitute the only possible kind of impact it can have.

This book is also about some contexts of world politics. International power structures are one important context but there are others; regime theory points to normative structures. One fallout of regime analysis is the recognition of the plethora of rule contexts within which nations operate. Between global contexts and individual states there is a wide range of middle-level contexts that affect regions and issue areas. Through the emphasis on plural contexts I suggest that states live in multiple environments.[1] These contexts often overlap but at the same time may be quite distinct. Even within the standard power politics mode of analysis this is the case. For a world system theorist the nineteenth century is one of British hegemony, but a specialist on European politics finds this century to be the archetype of a multipolar balance-of-power system. Likewise the post-World War II period is one of US hegemony for international economists and a bipolar one for security analysts. This book discusses several substantive contexts, norms, power structures, and history, providing concrete applications and examples of each.

In order to address the complex of problems related to individual–environment relations, the concept of context provides the key overarching concept. One aspect of context is the *relationship* between a state and its surroundings or history. I discuss three *modes* of context in this book:

1 Context as cause. This is the default category. Though different terms may be used, they all mean cause as contributing to a globally sufficient condition for the outcome: the context is neither individually necessary nor sufficient, but in conjunction with other factors it explains the outcome or makes it more likely.

   Though the issues are rarely discussed as such, most empirical studies using system or group variables treat them as just ordinary variables, implicitly giving them the same causal interpretation as the individual-level variables. As such system-level variables have no different theoretical status; they are just part of the laundry list of possible causes. Depending on the problem cause may be the appropriate interpretation, but due to the lack of alternative ways of thinking about individual–environment relations contextual effects are virtually always interpreted as causes.

2 Context as barrier. The Sprouts' (1965) notion of "environmental possibilism" means that options open to governments are limited; states have a certain degree of freedom of maneuver, but external constraints block many desirable goals. Barriers exist which prevent decision-makers from achieving desired ends.

[1] The emphasis on the multiplicity of contexts raises the question of the relation between contexts. When I speak of contextual theory I refer to individual–context relations, but a theory to be developed is one about intercontext relations (I return briefly to this in the Postface).

Once attentive to metaphors such as barrier and constraint it is striking how frequently they arise in the discussion of world politics. It is somewhat surprising that there appear to have been no serious attempts to develop methodologies and theories that move beyond the metaphorical. Barriers have characteristics that significantly differentiate them from positive causes. (Deterrence theory is an element of the class of barrier theories.) In fact, barriers are "counteracting causes" – they *prevent* actions – and as a result have a different epistemological status.

3 Context as changing meaning. Just as words mean different things when uttered in different sentences or social situations, so can the relationship between cause and effect vary according to the surroundings in which behavior occurs.

This is probably the most subtle contextual mechanism. The potential importance of this mode of context can be seen by noting how frequently the correlation coefficient between two variables changes with spatial-temporal domain. The correlation between two variables may be strongly positive in one century and negative in another: the two factors are important in both centuries but in different ways (this may be true even when controlling for all relevant variables). This rather simple, but abstract, concept of context turns out to have a variety of interesting consequences for theory, research design, and modeling.

In addition to these three modes of relationship, I discuss three *substantive* contexts that influence state behavior:

1 The structure of the international system. This has long been studied as a "cause" of war. However, I think that the contextual approach provides new insights in this overmined vein of research. By far the most important context, at least in the number of pages devoted to it, is the power structure of the international system. This literature has most often centered on system polarity, expressed either through alliances or geographic power configurations. What is curious about this work, which now seems a bit passé (though see Mansfield 1993), is that analyses were virtually always performed at the system level. There was the implicit notion that since the independent variable, say, system polarity, was a system-level variable so too should be the dependent variable –

the amount of war in the whole world. There were arguments why individual behavior should aggregate to certain system-level sums, but there was little about how system structure affects individual behavior and dyadic relationships, the across-level impact of systems on individuals.

2 The historical context of behavior. One commonplace notion is that history is important in understanding world politics. However, beyond the mode of historical narration, there is little theoretical or empirical work on *why* or *how* past actions are related to present behavior. What are the mechanics of the relationship? Is there more that we can do than to provide convincing narratives?

In spite of the putative importance of history, a glance at the quantitative research on international conflict reveals its virtual absence. Normally each event is considered a separate case, torn from its historical context. A simple indicator of this is the lack of historical variables in statistical and formal models. With the exception of concepts such as arms race, lateral pressure, and power transition, it is not at all clear how yesterday is related to today and tomorrow. History forms an important context, since even though in many respects nations find themselves in the same situation, their historical development and experience mean that they may act differently: an idea succinctly expressed in the concept of path dependency.

3 The normative environment. Many realists have generally ignored, at least until the resurgence of interest in "international regimes" (Krasner 1983b), that states exist in an environment of rules and norms that influences their calculations and their goals. The usual realist claim is that international norms, often in the form of international law, have little impact on state behavior. But this leaves puzzles unexplained: Why does the demand for elections form a part of US foreign policy? Why does apartheid affect policies toward South Africa?

The merit of regime theory is to have signaled the existence and the importance of the normative context. But the regime literature offers little guidance on conceptualizing and formalizing *how* this context influences behavior. With the important exception of Kegley and Raymond (1990), there have been few attempts to measure norms, to empirically and rigorously assess their impact, and to chart their evolution over time. In particular there is great unease and uncertainty about how these rules (which after all have no material existence) can "cause" behavior. Again, the problem is the relation between a system-level variable – norms – and individual state behavior.

Diffusion and rationality

Two constant theoretical companions throughout this volume are rational actor and diffusion models. The former is already quite familiar to students of world politics through the work of Bueno de Mesquita and others who have applied decision theory and game theory to problems of international conflict. Diffusion models also are present in the literature – though not as prominently – in the work of Starr, Siverson, and Most. These two frameworks represent two different visions of individual–environment relations. Diffusion models are "causal" focusing on the past, while rational actor models are "intentional" emphasizing the future (Elster 1979). Diffusion models emphasize the role of the environment in determining behavior, while rational actor models focus on the decision-maker whose beliefs and desires determine her behavior. Diffusion models are "top-down," while rational actor models are "bottom-up." Their intellectual homes differ as well, rational actor models come from economics, while diffusion models originate in anthropology and geography. Since contextual theory is about the interaction of the bottom with the top these two theories are natural points of orientation.

Rational models also serve as a "null hypothesis" for a number of problems raised by the emphasis on context. The focus on context raises questions about the interconnectedness of events across time and space. One problem that reoccurs is that phenomena are not evenly or randomly distributed in space or time; they appear in clumps or clusters. From a rational actor point of view this clustering, be it oil nationalization, decolonization, or repeated conflict, is an epiphenomenon of repeated or changing rational calculation.

Stressing context also highlights aspects of rational actor models normally taken as exogenous, in particular the goals and preferences of decision-makers. Explaining why a state has certain goals, why its preferences change, and what is legitimate in the international system are often just as important as the discussion of the means of efficiently arriving at a goal. An analysis of the normative context of state behavior emphasizes that goals and values must not be assumed but investigated, that they vary over space and time. In addition rational models usually take the "feasible set" as given; the concept of context as a barrier suggests that changing systematic constraints are fundamental in explaining why certain phenomena occur.

Diffusion models provide one framework for explaining changes in preferences and the feasible set. How are we to explain that environmental protection has become part of the values (at least the publicly expressed values, e.g., George Bush) of many leaders? Diffusion models provide one answer, through forces such as social pressure and imitation individuals acquire new desires. Most and Starr (1980) have used diffusion models to understand the spread of war; part of their argument is that the existence of wars in a region changes the feasible set of decision-makers ("opportunity" in Starr's terms 1978).

Diffusion and rational actor models emphasize different aspects of the individual–environment problematique and hence will appear regularly in the discussion of these issues.

Is context less important than individual-level factors?

Depending on one's basic theoretical position nation-level variables are put forward as more important than system-level variables (Bueno de Mesquita and Lalman 1988), or vice versa (Waltz 1979), in explaining international behavior. For rational actor models the priority goes to individual-level preferences and power relationships. The environment may influence rational behavior because it is, for example, more or less uncertain – or more accurately knowledge about it is uncertain – but these aspects play a secondary role. Structural theories take the opposite view, the debate about system structure and war implies that these factors are primary in understanding world politics. (Hollis and Smith (1990) give a philosophically informed discussion of the relative importance of different levels of analysis.) The theory of context presented here focuses on the *interaction* of the two rather than arguing for structural determinism or methodological individualism.

The level of analysis concept (Singer 1969) is part of the conceptual tool kit of world politics scholars. Influential textbooks such as Russett and Starr's (1992) are organized on its principles. At the same time, it is extremely difficult to find analyses that actually employ two levels of analysis simultaneously. Both theoretically and empirically the case studies in this volume attempt to integrate environmental and individual-level variables in various ways. The Sprouts (1965) explored in very general terms the man–milieu relationship, but never gave it concrete shape. It is easy to say that contexts are important but it is difficult to say how and why.

Many aspects of individual–environment relations that have exercised social scientists have also been central to natural history. The explanation of evolution by the theory of natural selection is exemplary in this regard. Natural selection theories assume that there is variation within species (and between species for some, e.g., Eldredge 1985) which is then selected upon by the environment (see Mayr 1982 for a description of how the two interact). Natural selection is a theory of interaction between individuals and their environments. For Darwin the mechanism producing variation was a black box much like the black box that system theorists use to describe decision-making processes. And like international relations researchers, biologists tend to choose one level or the other for research, biology being divided between naturalists and geneticists until a synthesis of the two was achieved in the 1930s and 1940s. The evolutionary biologist uses the terminology proximate and ultimate causes (Mayr 1988) to explain animal and plant characteristics: genes are the proximate cause of much animal behavior, but ultimately these behaviors are selected because changes in the environment choose (allow to survive) the best genetic program. Similarly, a complete theory of world politics will require adequate linking of domestic and bureaucratic processes with changing international environments.

One of the essential aspects of an emphasis on context is to rid us of the idea that structural or individualistic paradigms are universal panaceas. There are situations where structures are quite constraining and others where individual choice has a large field of action. In part this is an empirical question to be answered by the estimates of different parameters in contextual models. These models contain parameters that represent system-level, individual-level, and interaction variables. Statistical estimates can help answer the question of relative importance. It seems fruitless to argue about these issues in general; what we need is a framework that allows data to provide an appropriate response to the question. Nature can only answer a question if it is posed. If a model has only system-level or individual-level variables nature cannot add the missing elements.

Metaphors and theories

One subtheme that runs throughout this investigation of context is how metaphorical theoretical language is. This does not come as a surprise to post-structuralists (Der Derian and Shapiro 1989) who look at theories and the world as texts (that is their metaphor!). Metaphors can be quite useful in thinking about the world, but all metaphors carry theoretical baggage with them. Much of this volume can be seen as an analysis of some common metaphors of world politics. Some I shall find hinder understanding, e.g., war as a contagious disease; others I find useful, e.g., system structure as a barrier. I have chosen the word "context" to represent a certain way of viewing a central problem of human behavior, but there is a whole list of related terms that illuminate various facets of the phenomenon:

individual–environment
level of analysis
micro–macro
structural realism (Waltz 1979)
situational determinism
constraint
market
structuration (Giddens 1984)
willingness and opportunity (Starr 1978)

All these expressions, and others, imply a certain relation between an individual and its context. It is, unfortunately, often not clear what they really mean. Phrases like "system structure constrains ...," "in this situation a certain behavior is more likely," or "market pressures forced ..." are common but what is often lacking is an explicit mechanism or story linking states and environments. What is a "constraint?" How does one model it? Do markets "cause" certain behaviors? I too will use these expressions, but I shall try to be explicit as to what they mean. For example, Rosenau (1990) refers to micro–macro issues, but it is never clear *how* many micro decisions add up to macro phenomena. For him the result is often macro "turbulence"; the mechanisms that link the two are explained via metaphor and analogy. One common metaphor comes from the conflict literature in which war is described as "contagious." I argue in chapter 5 that when a mechanism for war contagion is provided the metaphor breaks down (though not without providing some important insights into the phenomenon of war expansion). Context with its many implications appears best suited to weave the methodological and substantive threads I use. Careful attention to language highlights the ambiguity which lies just below the surface of much theoretical discourse.

Methodology

Developments in the philosophy and history of science associated with names like Lakatos, Kuhn, and Feyerabend have changed widely held views of natural science. There has been a realization in the "hard" sciences that there is no longer any privileged position; observers interact with the observed, there is no Archimedean point. This has been a move toward relativism, to views more often thought to be particular to the study of man. It is the realization in an important sense that all knowledge is local knowledge.

Philosophical judgments about what is possible or not, about the correct form of an explanation (e.g., methodological individualism) are futile because they depend on the course of actual scientific research. This does not mean it is not important to reflect on research approaches, but rather that such reflection should be motivated and tied to current research practices. Many of the big problems in the social sciences like man–environment relations, norms and regimes, measurement theory, and the scope of international relations theory will be treated below, but in the framework of particular theories and models, and in the application of them to empirical cases.

The emphasis of context has important methodological implications. It results in new ways to try to integrate state and system levels of analysis. Rare are studies that deal simultaneously with both levels. The emphasis on the interaction between a state and its environment leads to models quite different from the usual linear regression analyses. For example, if context is considered a barrier, one of the immediate implications is that the relationship is no longer linear.

One unifying thread of my empirical and theoretical approach is the state as the fundamental unit of analysis. In statistical terms the dependent variable is the action of individual states or pairs of states. The international-system-level factors, both as created by the action of states through norms, alliances, etc. and as represented by more static aspects such as power structures, are used as an explanatory factor, but I am not usually concerned with explaining the evolution of the system as such (i.e., as a dependent variable). Nevertheless, in examining international norms and barriers contexts are partially endogenized, since individual choice cannot be understood without a theory of changing contexts, and context change frequently results from the action of many individuals.

Vade mecum

Chapter 2 introduces the three different modes of context that form the methodological heart of the book. The following chapter discusses context as changing meaning, using simple issues such as how war is defined in order to illustrate that contextual analysis is important from the first definitional stages of research. Chapter 4 proceeds to apply this contextual mode to indicator construction and measurement issues. Here I show that the meaning of "overallocation" to the military depends dramatically on the spatial and historical context.

Chapter 5 introduces two important alternative views on the importance of the environment that will reappear regularly throughout the rest of the book. One is the rational actor position associated with scholars like Bueno de Mesquita (1981) which argues that states act in order to achieve conscious goals and maximize their power. The other position is that conflict "diffuses," that events are related over time via "addiction" and over space by "infection" (Siverson and Starr 1991). According to the latter the environment plays a very large role in explaining who gets the war disease; the former argues that preferences and beliefs of leaders determine their behavior. I use the problem of war expansion to illustrate the differences between these two approaches.

Context as barrier is investigated in chapters 6–8. I argue that nations face an environment that constrains them to act in certain ways. But, as the environment changes states *learn* about these changes and alter their goals and behavior. As a consequence they are not passive *vis-à-vis* their environment as many structuralist arguments imply. Chapter 6 discusses theoretically the issues and develops a dynamic equation model for studying these kinds of events. Chapter 7 follows with a discussion and a statistical estimation of a model of oil nationalization 1950–80. Chapter 8 is a case study of East Europe–USSR relations, particularly the democratizations of 1989, using this conceptual framework.

Chapter 9 discusses how we can conceive of the importance of the historical context in explaining international behavior. I propose a definition that distinguishes between historical and ahistorical theories of behavior. I then discuss several approaches to how the past influences the present (where conflict diffusion theories make another appearance). I examine popular metaphors like "inertia" and "momentum" as possible explanations for historical continuity. Chapter 10 shows why the historical context is crucial to understanding international conflict, using the concept of "enduring rivalries" – repeated military conflict between a pair of nations. I show that a large proportion of interstate disputes and wars occur in the context of enduring rivalries. Thus much international conflict cannot be understood ripped from its historical context.

Integrating all the contextual threads together, the last two chapters discuss international norms. The contextual modes as well as the substantive contexts are all central to an understanding of norms and regimes. Norms are slowly put into place over time as the result of actions and conflicts involving the major players on the world scene. These rules exist in a sense independent of any given state but exert a real impact on all states of the international system. In addition to proposing the beginning of a theory of international norms, I discuss how the normative context is related to the two other substantive contexts of the manuscript, system structure and history. Methodologically, I discuss how the three modes of context – changing meaning, cause, and barrier – are relevant to the understanding of normative contexts. In chapter 12 I use this theory of international norms to develop a behavioral measure of the norm of decolonization, and then argue that even controlling for self-interest this norm had an impact on the transition of dependent territories to independent nations.

Conclusion

The three contextual modes and the three substantive contexts are the subjects of a six-part fugue that is the heart of this project. The book is a working out of these themes in various combinations. Some chapters such as chapter 6 on barrier models and chapter 9 on historical factors develop theories about substantive contexts. Others like chapters 7, 8, and 10 apply these theories to particular problems such as oil nationalization, East European democratizations, and enduring military rivalries. The six subjects make repeated appearances in different ways throughout. For example, the historical context appears as an important factor in the constitution of the normative environment of state action, because rules and norms are gradually put into place over time and one cannot understand their current importance without a knowledge of their historical evolution. It also appears as crucial in constructing valid indicators of military allocation ratios over the long time period, 1816–1980, frequently used in conflict research. Finally, it forms a major topic of discussion in the study of enduring rivalries as a context of international war.

I have tried to tread that fine line between general theoretical discussion and specific empirical analysis. Most of the book can be understood without much quantitative, mathematical, or statistical background. I firmly believe that unless a theory is useful in explicating specific cases it is not of much value, hence following each theoretical chapter I apply the theory to a specific problem(s). The book can be read then in various ways, either as a book on international relations theory or as one treating some important specific problems of international politics, such as oil nationalization, democratization in Eastern Europe, decolonization, war expansion, military allocation ratios, and enduring rivalries.

2 MODES OF CONTEXT

> Unavoidable mention of causality is a cloak for ignorance; we must appeal to the notion of cause when we lack detailed and accurate laws. In the analysis of action, mention of causality takes up some of the slack between analysis and science.
>
> Donald Davidson (1980, p. 80)

Introduction

A central debate in international relations has been which level of analysis is most important in explaining nation-state behavior. Some like Waltz (1979) argue that system structure plays the largest role in the explanation of war. Others (Bueno de Mesquita and Lalman 1988) claim that explanation must come at the state level of analysis. In contrast to this classic opposition I would like to begin by asking not which level is most important but *how* contexts matter – what I call the modes of context.

Usually this "how" is not an issue, the objective is to get as quickly as possible to the central substantive issues: the independent and dependent variables. All-purpose causal glue cements the independent variables – at whatever level – to the dependent variables. Context is just another element of an explanation, either an independent or dependent variable. The contrast between context as cause and the other modes of context forces us to specify what we mean by cause. The major thesis of this chapter is that there are different types of conceptual glue which we can use to build contextual models. We do not need to use the Elmer's glue of cause for all purposes – although of course it is sometimes very useful.

It is perhaps helpful to compare my procedure with that of Most and Starr who propose an individual-level variable "willingness" which interacts with system-level "opportunity":

> We have used opportunity and willingness (which can also be interpreted as structure and decision or macro- and micro-factors) as a "pre-theoretical" structure that allows us to link context/contextual, environmental or structural variables to decision making/process variables. (1989, p. 20)

The substantive contexts, history, system structure, and norms correspond roughly to different types of opportunity. Sometimes the opportunity and willingness structure fits well with my discussion of context, for example how the environment acts as a barrier. In other cases, such as context as changing meaning, my approach does not match up well with their theoretical structure.

In addition to the substantive elements of opportunity and willingness Most and Starr provide a mechanism for joining them. Opportunity and willingness are *joint necessary conditions*. This chapter on contextual modes is analogous to their discussion of necessary and sufficient conditions. In contrast to the requirement that the opportunity–willingness relationship be a necessary condition, context as cause proposes that contexts can be sufficient conditions. It is context as barrier that functions as a necessary condition. The concept of modes of context implies that multiple relationships can exist between opportunity and willingness: necessary conditions are one, but there are others.

In this chapter I shall examine three modes in which the relations between states and their environment can be envisaged. The most common mode of analysis is context as cause. For example, the structure of the system may increase the likelihood of war; though many different expressions can be used to express this increased likelihood I shall use cause to embrace them all. The second mode of analysis is context as barrier. Context as barrier contrasts with context as cause because instead of producing an effect it prevents the effect: barriers are "counteracting" causes. If causes increase the likelihood then barriers decrease it. The third contextual mode is context as changing meaning which argues that basic structural elements vary in their relation to each other according to the circumstances. In other words, the variables in the bivariate relationship are right, but the relationship is not constant (i.e., the β's vary). This aspect of context is perhaps the most different from context as it is often used in the social sciences, but it is at the same time the one with perhaps the most interesting methodological, philosophical, and theoretical implications.

Context as Cause

The most common way to view context is as some sort of cause. It is often the case that some higher-level factor, such as system structure, is said to "cause" some lower-level state behavior, such as interstate war. Frequently the brutal language "cause" is not used but more equivocal expressions such as "constrains," "influences," and "helps determine" replace it. It is not clear in what sense these variants really mean something other than cause since, if the study is empirical/statistical, it probably uses a regression model with its implicit causal interpretation. Figure 2.1 gives a common graphic illustration of the relationship, where the arrows indicate, as is the convention, a causal relationship. Higher-level factors (e.g., system structure) are the context and the cause of the outcome. Diagrams such as figure 2.1 are generally referred to as causal(!) models, and there exist methodologies that translate these figures into systems of regression equations (Asher 1976). Unless otherwise explicitly stated, arrows between boxes can be assumed to express some sort of causal relationship.

Durkheim provides a classic sociological view on social structure as cause. In his *Rules of sociological method* (1937) he describes social structure as *coercion*. If structures permit no choice, one is forced to act in a certain way, and those structures can be called the causes of action. In economics this is referred to as "situational determinism" (Latsis 1972; Machlup 1974). In a perfect market an individual firm has no freedom to set prices since these are determined by the market. Though not usually thought of in this fashion, the market is an important causal context of behavior.

One way to view context as cause but different from other causal variables is to relate it to what is called in the philosophical literature the "causal field" (Mackie 1974). This causal field is the set of circumstances and background conditions that are important or necessary in explaining a phenomenon. In economic theory this would be the assumptions like those about institutional arrangements for private property or for enforcing contracts that define the context within which the economic calculus takes place. This is partially a matter of emphasis; for example we can say that the lighted match caused the fire when someone put it to a pile of paper, but we also say that the gas leak caused the explosion when someone struck a match. Strictly speaking the match caused the fire in both instances. But since a lighted match does not commonly produce an explosion but gas leaks do, the latter gain the role of cause. An image commonly used to describe the pre-World War I period was a "powder keg" waiting to be set off by some

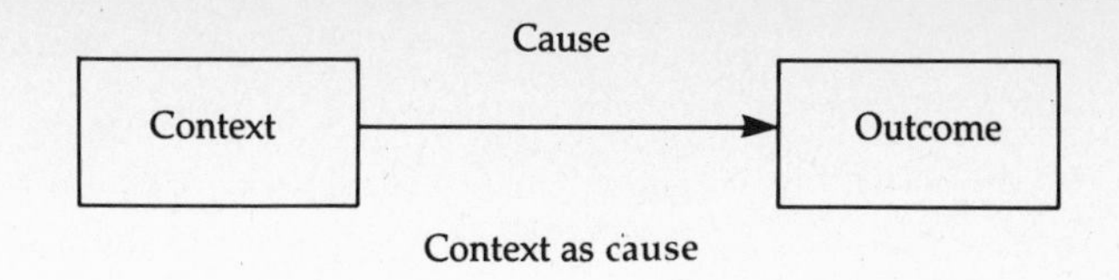

Context as cause

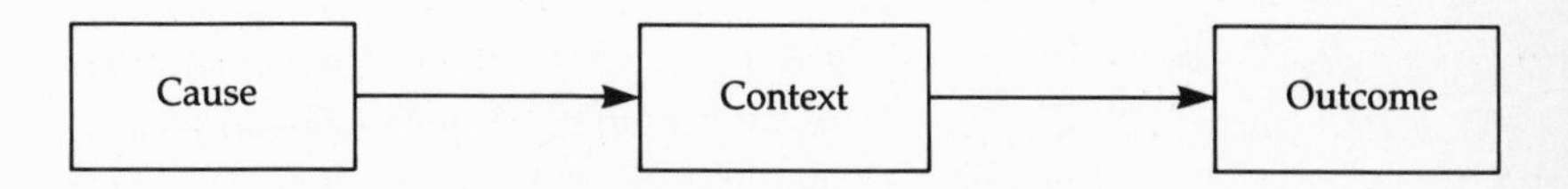

Context as an intervening variable

Figure 2.1 Context as cause

event (like the assassination of Archduke Ferdinand). Or, many feel uncomfortable calling geographical contiguity a cause of war. It may well be correlated with war (Bremer 1992; Vasquez 1993), but theoretically it is something else than a cause. There appears to be no consensus on what this "something else" is or should be called. I suggest that gas leaks, lit matches, geographical contiguity, system structure can all legitimately be called causes.

But after all what is the *definition* of cause? Rarely do students of international politics define what they mean by cause (or its metaphorical cousins, factors, influence, etc.), but my reading of the literature, plus the widespread use of regression models, lead to the conclusion that a cause is something (state-of-affairs or act at any level of analysis) that contributes to a sufficient condition for the outcome:

> A factor *X* is a cause of another factor *Y* if and only if *X*'s existence contributes to *Y*'s existence. (Humphreys 1989, p. 9)

X may not be sufficient in itself, but does increase the likelihood that *Y* will occur (all other relevant variables being controlled for): the existence of a gas leak is not sufficient for an explosion but makes it more likely. A cause is thus a factor which increases the likelihood of *Y*. This probabilistic definition of cause matches very well the standard interpretation of regression models, fits well with commonsense intuitions about cause, and stands up well under philosophical analysis (Humphreys 1989; Eells 1991). For this reason when I speak of context as cause I shall mean this kind of cause.

Regression models are basically sufficient condition models: if the sum of

X_1, X_2, ... is large enough then Y occurs (this can be extended to sufficient interaction terms, see Ragin (1987)). None of the X's is necessarily sufficient alone, it is the sum that is sufficient. Since each X contributes to the occurrence of Y it can legitimately be called a cause. For example, the model of what Most and Starr (1989) call "foreign policy substitutability" fits a sufficient definition of cause. There are many different policies that have the same function. A country can deter an enemy through alliances (X_1), arms purchases (X_2), or military conscription (X_3), or some combination of them all. If the "sum" of these is great enough then deterrence (Y) is achieved.

Simple additive regression models follow J.S. Mill's principle of the composition of causes (1859): if different causes act on an object the result is the sum of the causes (with the major proviso that there are no interaction terms). This is the way classical physics deals with forces: the total force on an object is the sum of the individual forces. Balance-of-power theorists tend to view alliances in much the same fashion: the power of the alliance is the sum of the power of the individual countries. Generally speaking, with the important condition about the independence of the causes, sufficient causes are additive.

One consequence of this definition is that a cause may be present without producing an effect. This may be due to various reasons. The cause may increase the likelihood of the outcome but not enough for it to occur. Or, for the cause to be effective other causes must be present; this is the case with interaction terms or stories like the gas explosion one. Or, there may be counteracting causes (see below) which prevent the cause from taking effect, like medicine prevents disease.

An important question is how it is possible to call the system structure or geographical contiguity a cause if it does not change over time. How can geographical contiguity be a cause of war if between time $t-1$ and time t X (contiguity) is not changing but from time $t-1$ to time t Y goes from a no-war to a war state? The gas leak story above provides part of the answer: the presence of gas is constant throughout but along with the lighting of the match an explosion does occur. In one possible scenario environmental factors remain fixed and lower-level factors change. This is the pre-World War I powder keg waiting to be set off. Opportunities are constant and nothing happens until there arises the willingness to act (e.g., with a change in government). Or conversely, the willingness exists but cannot be exploited until the opportunity arises. Most and Starr (1980) argued that war changes opportunity structures thus possibly leading to war diffusion. Though we tend to think of system-level phenomena as more stable than individual-level phenomena (encouraged in this by language like "structure") the opposite may also be the case. In fact, a classic assumption of realism is that governments have a *constant* desire to increase their power; they await opportunities to do so. In the section on barrier models I shall present an example of this kind of argument: I shall assume that goals are relatively constant but that changes in system structure carry a large part of the explanatory load.

This concept of sufficient cause is much weaker than the definition of a cause as a necessary condition.[1] If Bueno de Mesquita (1981) is correct and there are necessary conditions in international relations, this does not contradict the sufficiency definition of cause. A positive expected utility increases the likelihood of war and in conjunction with other X's can produce war. There may be single or joint, necessary, or necessary and sufficient conditions for particular phenomena in world politics; all these would count as causes under this definition.

A misleading, but common, conception of context is as relevant but less important as causal factors. (Proponents of methodological individualism tend to put forth this view.) In non-statistical analysis the causal language used often reveals the weight the author gives to various aspects of her analysis, e.g., "cause" implies more weight than "influence." How are we to determine the relative weight of different causal factors (Sober 1988)? In a regression equation it is the size and significance of the coefficients that determine which variables have more impact than others. If some variables

[1] One important issue is the different techniques suitable for testing necessary or sufficient condition theories. Most and Starr (1989) argued that case selection based on X (no $-X$ cases) was a sufficient cause research design and case selection on Y (no $-Y$ cases) was a necessary condition design. However, if the underlying mode of analysis is regression then this is misleading, because simple regression is a model of sufficient conditions. From a regression point of view situations where Y is present but not $-Y$ are not of interest since statistically it is *impossible* to get estimates unless there is variance in Y: if Y is constant there is no variance to explain. If X is constant (no $-X$) then it equals the intercept which is not frequently of theoretical interest. What happens is that in practice there is a range of Y values (e.g., more or less war) but no cases of $-Y$ (no war), this permits statistical estimation, but the result is that *inferences* based on these results apply only to situations where war is *already* underway. Thus the research design is not faulty per se but faulty only if inferences about non-war situations are the goal. As Most and Starr note, this is frequently the case. For example, Paul Diehl and I (1992) examined military conflict and territorial change. An important limitation to that research was that we only studied successful territorial changes and thus could not infer anything about territorial problems in general. Starr and Most in their research on war diffusion do not have this problem because they are by definition interested in what happens *given* that there is an ongoing war, hence their research design is able to answer the central question. Their discussion of research design issues remains valuable, but care must be taken in transferring the analysis into regression or causal terminology.

are contextual and others are individual it is hard to argue a priori that the coefficients of the contextual ones are smaller or less significant than the coefficients of the individual-level variables.

Related to context as cause is context as an intervening variable, illustrated as well at the bottom of figure 2.1. A common feeling is that intervening variables have a special kind of causal status. For example, Krasner (1983a) argued that one way regimes matter is as intervening variables. He illustrated this as in figure 2.1, replacing context by regime as an intervening variable (I shall return to this issue again at length in chapter 11 on international norms). But it is not at all clear how an intervening variable differs from other kinds of causes. I suggest that intervening variables are fundamentally just other causal variables where the causal links are made in a more detailed fashion. For example, we say that Smith killed Jones by shooting him. At a more detailed level the bullet damaging Jones's heart "intervenes" between Smith and Jones's death, but since we can trace the causal chain back to Smith we can also say he caused the death. Chains of causes remain causes.

For Krasner there are no other conceptual tools than cause for thinking about how regimes and contexts matter in international politics. The result is that context is treated like other causal variables. Although different expressions may be used, in the final wash these all come out as sufficient, probabilistic cause. This may be appropriate, but the following sections are devoted to two different ways of thinking about individual-context relations which suggest other ways of relating states to their contexts. I began this section with a quote from Davidson suggesting that we resort to causal language when we do not have a very clear analysis of the phenomenon; the next two sections provide means of analyzing more clearly individual-context relations.

Context as barrier

The second contextual mode is context as barrier. It differs from context as cause, because states are not positively incited to do something, but rather the menu of choice is limited. Due to power configurations or simply because of geography – physical distance – certain options are not available or very costly. The Sprouts (1965) refer to this as "environmental possibilism," but beyond the notion that not all is possible the working of environmental constraints in world politics has not been systematically investigated.

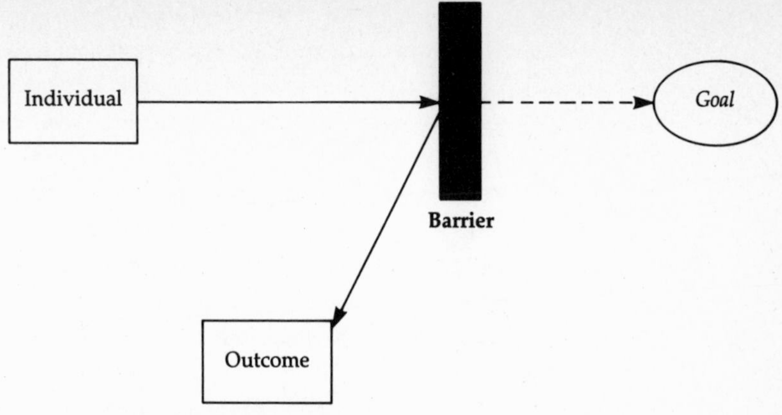

Figure 2.2 Context as barrier

Barriers are *negative* forces, they keep events from occurring. In this sense they are the opposite of a cause:

> A factor X is a barrier to another factor Y if and only if X's existence contributes to the *non-existence* of Y.

Contrast this with the definition of cause given above: causes *make* things happen; barriers *prevent* them from occurring. This distinction has important theoretical and methodological consequences.

One way of visualizing this is illustrated in figure 2.2 where the solid arrow represents attempts to attain a goal that are not successful because of the existence of the barrier. Nations often have preferred outcomes they cannot achieve due to the existence of constraints. In Most and Starr's terms they have the willingness but not the opportunity. As a consequence, the outcome will not be the achievement of the goal but some other less desirable outcome. But, as the world turns, barriers break down and constraints loosen resulting in new situations with new possibilities. The barrier prevented numerous states from achieving their goals, but now a previously unobtainable end can be achieved. Once it was clear that the USSR had changed its policies, Eastern Europe democratized itself rapidly. The peoples of Eastern Europe had repeatedly tried to change the existing state of affairs in Poland, Czechoslovakia, and Hungary. This desire for change was repeatedly frustrated but the peoples of these countries kept coming back. (This case is examined in detail in chapter 8.)

State behavior is constrained by factors such as the structure of the international system but at the same time barriers are not eternal. Nations by their actions continually create and destroy barriers. Just as the constant pressure of water on a dam contributes to the weakening of the dam, so do attempts to achieve goals contribute to the weakening of constraints. Essential to the concept of context as barrier is the interaction between the barrier and pressure on the barrier for change. We know barriers exist because they are tested from time to time, we know barriers are disappearing because tests of them are more frequently successful. Once again, the emphasis as with all contextual models is on the interaction between individual interests and the structures of the world they live in. Individuals interact intelligently with their environment and by their actions create the environment of the future.

An interesting example of the ambiguity of interpreting context as cause when perhaps it is better seen as a barrier is the status of borders and contiguity in the literature on international war. Starting already with Richardson (1960b) the number of borders and geographical contiguity have been explored in a variety of connections with war. For Richardson the question was the relationship between the number of boundaries and the amount of war. Borders and contiguity are important in the literature on the diffusion of war (see chapter 5), because wars are more likely to spread to contiguous states. They have also been widely used in studies on the likelihood of disputes escalating to war (e.g., Diehl 1985) since military disputes between contiguous countries are more likely to escalate to war. Borders and contiguity have thus been closely associated with a number of important aspects of war. Most and Starr explicitly refuse a causal interpretation: "we recognize that a border does not necessarily *cause* either conflictual or cooperative interactions" (the emphasis is the authors', 1989, p. 30). What then is the theoretical status of contiguity or number of borders?

Two plausible options seem to be that contiguity and borders stand for some substantive cause or that they are viewed as a constraint. If they are merely stand-ins for other substantive causes then borders and contiguity play *no* theoretical role, but perform a role in some measurement model (as an indicator of something). If borders and contiguity are in themselves important it seems that we need some way to think about them that is not causal. One way to think about borders and geography is as a constraint on the use of military force. Instead of using the default concept of cause it is perhaps more useful to view this relationship in other fashions.

I have argued that context as cause and context as barrier are two different ways of understanding state–environment relations. An important question is whether the barrier view can be subsumed as a special case of context as cause. Methodologically there is frequently little difference since causal and barrier variables are thrown helter-skelter into regression models. But I claim that the two are really different types of explanations and that therefore it is important not to confuse context as cause with context as barrier. The images do point in different directions; cause is normally seen in a positive sense of *producing* change (Blalock 1961), while barriers *prevent* or *counteract* change. This corresponds to the distinction between positive and negative power or between compellence and deterrence.

One characteristic of sufficient positive causes is that they are transitive, i.e., if A causes B and B causes C then A is also a cause of C. Frequently B is referred to as an intervening variable and A as an indirect cause (figure 2.1). This transitivity is at the heart of causal models of all sorts.[2] However, if this relationship is not one of cause but one of counteracting cause then transitivity no longer holds. This can be seen from the simple example of a balance where on one side there is a 10 kilogram weight. This can be counterbalanced by the addition of a 15 kilogram weight on the other side (B counteracts A), but if we counteract this 15 kilogram weight with a 5 kilogram weight (C counteracts B) we do *not* have the situation where the 5 kilogram weight is counterbalancing the 10 (C counterbalancing A) but rather C combining with A, the exact opposite of counterbalancing. For example, we think of power-balancing and alliances in the same fashion. Counteracting causes do not have the property of transitivity[3] but act like logical operators, i.e., $-(-A) = A$; a counter-cause to a counter-cause is a positive cause. But barriers are just counteracting factors. They do not positively influence the course of events but rather prevent events from taking certain courses.

In figure 2.2 the barrier prevents the state from achieving its goal: in order to attain it the barrier must be removed:

> A necessary condition for the occurrence of an event E is the non-occurrence of events that would prevent E from occurring. (Sober 1983, p. 202)

A necessary condition for the goal to be attained is the non-existence of the barrier. If causes are sufficient conditions, barriers are necessary ones.

[2] While transitivity appears an intuitive part of most concepts of positive cause, if cause is taken in the probabilistic sense (as I have done here) transitivity is not guaranteed. In chapter 9 I shall give a counter-example and discuss this issue in more detail.

[3] Another relation that is non-transitive is "to be near," 1 is near 2, 2 is near 3, etc. but 1 is not near 100.

The additive sufficiency view of cause suggests that a dam can be made stronger by adding more dams (adding more X's), putting more dams behind the original one. However, if the dams all have the same strength and the water pressure is strong enough to break through one then it can break through all: the extra dams add *nothing* to the strength of the whole.

Similarly, the strength of one barrier itself is not determined by adding the strength of its component parts: *A chain is only as strong as its weakest link.* Each link of the chain is necessary for the whole to work: the links do not add up to give strength. If one part goes then the whole barrier is likely to collapse. It may not matter that 99 percent of your car works perfectly if an important part breaks down. Kahneman and Tversky (1982; see also Cohen, Chesnick, and Haran in the same volume) have shown that psychologically we are not well equipped to deal with conditions with interacting probabilities. I shall argue that this failure contributes to the surprise factor when barriers do break down (e.g., collapse of communist regimes in Eastern Europe).

The components of the barrier thus interact in a multiplicative fashion (as opposed to the additive relationship typical of causes). The strength of the whole is the product of the strength of the parts. If any one part breaks down (has a value of zero) then the whole product equals zero. The weakest link metaphor expresses well this relationship of the parts to the whole. For example, the barrier mode illuminates the structure of deterrence. There may be numerous sufficient conditions for one nation to attack another, but deterrence focuses on one (are there others?) necessary condition: the likelihood or costs of success. By putting a barrier at this point the whole process is stopped.

Another difference between context as cause and context as barrier is that counter-causes often depend on particular causes. The use of a wide variety of useful medicines does not usually result in a higher likelihood of cure because of the additive effect of the drugs. A chain is of no use if not to prevent something from happening: there is no need to a chain a dog who never leaves home and never attacks anyone. A counteracting cause may only be effective if the appropriate cause is present, otherwise it may have no effect at all. It is not useful to put a dam where the river does not flow. Barriers are not barriers unless they change the direction of flow; the effect of the barrier is dependent on the flow being in a certain direction. Thus barriers and counteracting causes are frequently linked to particular causes. Causes can exist without counter-causes, but certain counter-causes have no impact without their appropriate, original cause. In the post-Cold War era the question arises: Who is the US deterring with thousands of nuclear missiles? Deterrence assumes an adversary to be deterred. The Department of Defense needs a real threat to justify its existence. ("Defense" is a *blocking* move, if it were still the War Department – leaving "offensive" options open – the justification of its existence would be less of a problem.)

Thus there are four conditions that fundamentally distinguish context as a cause from context as a barrier:

1 Barriers are not transitive.
2 Barrier strength is determined multiplicatively not additively.
3 Barriers are necessary conditions.
4 Barriers are linked to particular causes.

My brief analysis indicates that each member of the pair represents a very different causal mechanism: the differences between necessary and sufficient conditions, additive versus multiplicative interactions, and transitively versus intransitivity are not minor. Positive–negative pairs like compellence–deterrence are common in the literature of international politics. These pairs correspond to the distinction between context as cause and context as barrier.

Once attentive to the barrier family of metaphors examples crop up frequently. For example, discussions of deterrence often employ barrier metaphors: "Did Israel's leaders anticipate a challenge to deterrence? ... Did Israel's leaders consider the possibility that deterrence was buckling before it visibly collapsed?" (Jervis, Lebow, and Stein 1985, p. 60). Chapters 6–8 examine in some detail one way barriers function and apply that theoretical framework to the oil nationalizations of the 1970s and the history of Soviet–East European relations after World War II. These were two events virtually impossible to describe without recourse to this family of metaphors.

Context as changing meaning

Concepts, definitions, and indicators are sometimes viewed as having a fairly hard core that allows them to be expressed in a few words and that permits layman and specialist alike to converse without undue pain and confusion. For this "hard core" the classic recourse is to the dictionary. However, for many ideas that are intuitively understandable an – not to speak of *the* – exact specification or definition turns out to be quite difficult to formulate. In fact, no hard core may exist but rather something more like a family resemblance is the appropriate metaphor.

Simple bivariate hypotheses are like these words with constant meanings. A constant relationship between the independent and dependent variable is assumed to hold regardless of the context. The clearest expressions of this constancy are the fixed parameters (β's) of the model. These do not vary and express the timelessness of the hypothesized relationships. For example, in military conflicts and war we are quite certain that power plays a central role, but what may well be the case is that it does not play the same role in all conflicts. There is a potentially changing relationship between war and power, or power has different implications and meanings in different conflicts. More generally Most and Starr argue:

> While scholars are trained to search for generalizable patterns that hold through time and across space and often seem to believe that the isolation of such associations is the sine qua non of the systematic analysis of international conflict, the existence of such patterns seems unlikely. While patterns may still exist, they are not likely to be of the variety – or even *appear like* the variety – of patterns for which analysts have been exploring. (1989, p. 98)

Most and Starr deal with this possibility with what they call "sometimes true laws," which are not universally true but are true in some specific context. In other words, laws that are context sensitive.

Why do relationships vary over time and space? One possible response is that these relationships are embedded in different contexts. The context influences those relationships just like contexts mediate between words and their meanings. Using this basic insight the concept of context as changing meaning can formally be defined as:

> A factor(s) that influences the relationship between two (or more) other variables.[4]

This is graphically illustrated in figure 2.3. To take the example of words, the two boxes "Independent Variable" and "Dependent Variable" can be replaced by "word" and "meaning." A quite stable relationship often exists between the two that permits an answer to the question "What does X mean?" without any given context (this is what dictionaries do). Nevertheless, this relationship can easily vary depending on linguistic, social, historical, and cultural contexts. It is not essential to my argument

[4] A common definition of "group selection" reflects the same idea: "group selection exists when groups vary in fitness, and the fitness of an organism depends on the sort of group it is in" (Sober 1984, p. 267). Sober gives a philosophical analysis of the concept of cause in the "unit of selection" problem in biology (which corresponds to the level of analysis problem in international relations).

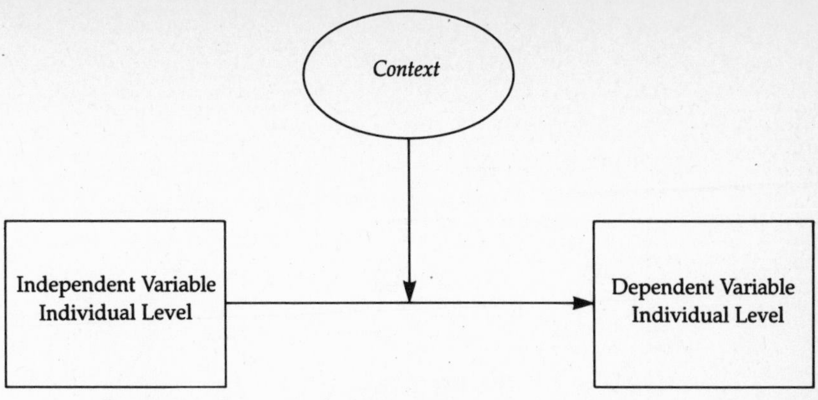

Figure 2.3 Context as changing meaning

that there be an *unchangeable* core meaning, however the above definition does imply certain meanings are more central, which accords with certain philosophical positions (e.g., Lakoff 1987). For example, in chapter 4 I will show that a given level of military spending can have different implications depending on the context within which that spending takes place. This occurs since how states *interpret* the military spending of their adversaries depends on what is *normal* for that period. Bueno de Mesquita's expected utility model (1981) also illustrates how this can work. He proposes that governments make standard expected utility calculations in order to determine whether to initiate a war. These calculations involve the standard elements of belief in the success of a war initiation (the relative power of the two countries) and the degree of antagonism (preference) between the two parties. In figure 2.3 the "Independent Variable" is the expected utility calculation and the "Dependent Variable" is a war initiation. Bueno de Mesquita also argues that the relationship between expected utility and war initiation varies according to the uncertainty of international environment (see the next chapter for a longer discussion of this).

Many acts gain their meaning by reference to existing norms and institutions. The form of exchange "theft" depends on the cultural institutions of property (private). Such an "interpretive" stance in a volume driven by a positivistic view of social science may surprise, since these aspects of human behavior are frequently used to demonstrate the impossibility of a positivistic approach (e.g., Winch 1958). But if there are patterns to the ways meanings are generated then I see no reason why these patterns cannot be investigated in a positivistic fashion. In the next chapter, devoted to this mode of context, many central issues of comparative politics

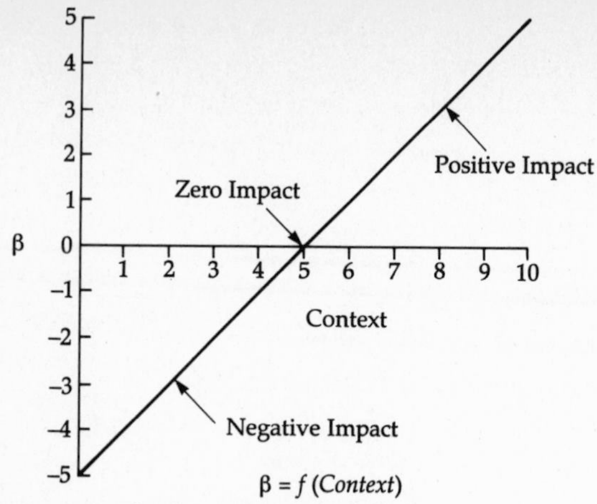

Figure 2.4 The changing impact of context

arise. A fundamental issue is how to make legitimate comparisons between different societies. How can contexts be taken into account in order to compare different countries?

An important aspect of the changing meaning mode of context is that it is "triangular"; it involves three entities. The basic X causes Y model is now embedded in some context. Context plays a radically different role than that played by cause and effect; context does not cause X or Y but affects how they interact. For context as changing meaning the arrow from context does not lead to a box but to another *arrow*. For this reason context as changing meaning is a hierarchical notion. The hierarchy integrates two levels of analysis into one model. It is a way to think of the interactions between states and their environments.[5]

Is context as changing meaning just a specific form of context as cause? Yes and no. In some environments there may be no relationship between X and Y, yet in another context this relationship is positive; hence by the definition of cause the contextual factor is a cause. But still in other contexts X is a barrier, preventing the outcome from occurring. This variation is not necessarily capricious but can be quite systematic, as illustrated in figure 2.4. This shows that when "context" is greater than five then it increases the likelihood of the outcome (i.e., $\beta > 0$) but when it is less than five it decreases the likelihood of the outcome. Thus context as changing meaning cuts across the context as cause–context as barrier contrast. When I discuss

[5] These three elements recall the distinction made by French structuralists between the *signifier* (independent variable), the *signified* (dependent variable) and the signification (how context gives the two a *meaning*).

military allocation ratios (chapter 4) we shall see that the same allocation ratio is high in the nineteenth century and low in the twentieth.

Often we must determine what an act "means" before assessing what kind of impact it will have. An extended hand may be a signal of peaceable intentions in one culture and a hostile act in another. What kind of response this act provokes depends *first* on understanding its meaning. Context as changing meaning addresses a different kind of problem from the other modes of context which look at causal issues. The two issues are closely related but one cannot be collapsed into the other.

Context as changing meaning is a different *kind* of contextual mode. Contexts in this sense do not directly act upon Y and for this reason should not be called a cause. They are an important part of the explanation but with their own particular role. The context may increase the likelihood of the outcome: there are situations where it falls under the definition of a cause. (I argue in the Postscript to the next chapter that this is the usual interpretation in contextual voting models.) But context as changing meaning states that the relationships between X and Y vary. There are reasons for this variability but we may not want to call these reasons causes.

Context is usually viewed implicitly as a cause. This contrasts with context as a changing relationship since in a regression model (context as cause) the exogenous variables are usually defined *independently* of each other: a regression analysis is usually a set of dyadic hypotheses. It is best to keep the concept of cause for situations where this is a direct link from cause to effect. For this reason the rules of drawing causal figures are important. Causes are indicated by arrows from cause to effect. Context as changing meaning is an arrow to a relationship: it is simply a different explanatory mechanism.

I would however like to emphasize that the definition of context as changing meaning does accord with general notions about what context is. For example, context is often taken to mean that people in the "same situation" act differently because they have different histories. Words mean different things because they are uttered in different sentences. Sentences mean different things when uttered in different social environments. The changing meaning mode of context captures these different intuitions about the impact of situational factors on behavior and meaning.

Much could be said about this definition of context, and the philosophical and more abstract methodological questions are quite interesting. This is however not my purpose. A discussion of the relevant philosophical, linguistic, and social scientific literatures would be fascinating, but that leads away from another goal which is a quite practical discussion of this problem in terms of actual research strategies. The next chapter is devoted to a discussion of the theoretical and methodological implications of this mode of context. Chapter 4 uses this mode to analyze military allocation ratios, where we shall see that contextualizing variables is vital in valid indicator construction.

The zero degree of context

The various modes of context have interesting differences when confronting the possibility as well as the interpretation of what it means – or if it is even possible to say – that there is "no context." To use a linguistic analogy, if the context is the sentence then no context may be what the dictionary says a word means. In this way it may be possible to discuss the "zero degree" of context.

For context as barrier, the image is quite clear; it is the "natural" course of affairs that occurs. If context is a force keeping things from happening then already built into the theory is what would happen in a different context (see the Postscript to this chapter on counterfactuals). When I discuss barrier models in later chapters this becomes quite clear. For example, once the USSR as a barrier to change is removed in Eastern Europe these societies move in directions in which they had been trying to move for the previous forty years.

The zero degree of context in the causal mode is also frequently quite obvious. When a particular influence on behavior is absent this usually means that the independent variable has a value of zero. This is not to be confused with when context is not important, signaled by the regression coefficient being near zero and statistically insignificant. When I consider the influence of a norm in chapter 11, the zero point will be when that norm is completely absent, the implication being that nations are completely driven by self-interest.

In context as changing meaning the situation is ambiguous, since it depends on how context is specified and considered. In a simple model of changing context the zero point may be when the contextual variable has a value of zero, or it may be the intercept value of the contextual equation. In either case it is likely that this zero context condition is of substantive importance. It may correspond to a situation that never occurs in practice but which may have theoretical importance, something like the importance of the concept of absolute zero temperature. It is also possible that an action has no meaning outside its institutional or societal context, the action may only be comprehensible in certain contexts: contexts may be an integral part of the phenomena. For example, there is the old nature–nurture debate, but it is impossible for nature to exist without nurture: genes if they are to survive need some nurture (Sober 1988). One may ask about the relative importance of the two, but we cannot observe genes without an environmental context. There is much speculation in the history of political philosophy about "human nature"; but of course we cannot observe humans except in societies (statistically this is the problem of collinearity).

Conclusion

In summary, three modes of context shall concern me in the pages to come: context as changing meaning, context as cause, and context as barrier. Context as changing meaning is probably the most faithful, yet rarest in positivistic social science, to the ordinary language meaning of context. Yet this notion is at the heart of comparative research. Basic issues of indicator construction, definition, standardization, and data gathering all have at their core that contexts must be eliminated (standardization) or limited (spatial–temporal domain) since these factors would otherwise invalidate the research design. The next chapter is devoted to a discussion of these issues. By contrast, context as cause is the most common way to view context. Most problems with this mode arise from lack of clarity about the definition of cause. While there is a huge philosophical literature on cause, I believe that the analysis presented here corresponds to a reasonable interpretation of social science practice. Context as barrier poses a contrast to context as cause. Barriers are counteracting, negative, necessary conditions while context as cause is a positive, sufficient condition. Context as changing meaning and context as barrier are the subject of whole chapters because these concepts depart from the common view of context as cause. Although thinking about the environment as a cause is not unproblematic – hence the importance of alternative modes of thinking about context – I will not discuss it further in detail.

The kind of cause that interests a researcher also depends on her purposes. This becomes particularly important if one purpose is to discover means for changing the world. For those interested in preventing war the best strategy may be to focus on necessary conditions; if one is found then a focused attempt to change policy at this point may prevent war. Attempting to prevent sufficient conditions requires an attack on a much wider front. This aspect of causes is what Collingwood (1940) called a "handle" because we can *control* the event by its means. A policy analysis might focus on human actions that are necessary conditions as a strategy for eliminating war.

Postscript: context and counterfactuals

The modes of context permit the clarification of a number of issues surrounding the status of counterfactuals.[6] I limit myself to a discussion of those aspects relevant to contextual analysis (for more see Lewis 1973b; Elster 1978).

Fearon's (1991) otherwise admirable account of the use of counterfactuals in world politics is flawed because he is not clear about the definition of cause. A counterfactual analysis depends for its effectiveness on the definition of cause as a necessary condition (Lewis 1973a). The counterfactual proposition states that if the cause had not occurred then the effect would have been different: the cause was necessary for the effect. If cause is understood in this sense then counterfactual propositions arise quite naturally. This is the case with context as barrier. Part of the concept itself is a proposition about what an actor *would have* done had the barrier not existed. In the chapters on oil nationalization and USSR–East European relations part of the analysis consists in trying to demonstrate the validity of this counterfactual proposition. Early tests of the barrier are important because they support the counterfactual condition necessary for the validity of barrier models.

If, on the other hand, cause is defined as a sufficient condition then counterfactual analysis loses its value. In this case the cause being absent does not allow us to conclude anything about the occurrence or non-occurrence of the effect. There may be other sufficient causes so that the effect would have occurred anyway. Or the cause may only contribute to an overall sufficiency, in which case the effect might not have occurred to begin with. If different foreign policy options have the same functionality then we have to consider all possible sufficient conditions in making a counterfactual analysis. For example, one way to view Van Evera's (1984) counterfactual analysis of World War I is to interpret the cult of the offensive as a necessary condition for the outbreak of the war. All his arguments are designed to counter competing sufficiency positions. Thus counterfactual analysis is not easy or natural in the context as cause mode.

[6] I would like to thank Lars-Erik Cederman for impressing on me the connection between the two.

Part of counterfactual analysis are hypotheses about "possible worlds" (Lewis 1986), usually about worlds similar to our own but with small, maybe crucial, differences. But this is very much the notion of context as changing meaning. The "same" (see chapter 9 for an analysis of the theoretical weight carried by this word) individual transported into another context may act differently. Or the relationship between two variables in another world is different from the current one. Many of the contexts that concern us are not possible worlds but different parts of our real world – just like an experimental scientist tests a counterfactual by creating a new world in the laboratory with the counterfactual conditions. Nevertheless a general theory of context as changing meaning leads to counterfactual hypotheses about individuals in non-existing contexts.

It may be problematic to transport an individual from one context to another. In practice the "same individual" means another individual with the same causally relevant traits, e.g., education, income, profession, etc. In comparative analysis we can examine how this same individual acts in two different contexts. But it may be that part of the individual's causally relevant traits are some that tie him permanently to one context; if being French is causally relevant then we cannot find a counterpart in England. My understanding of the argument for the impossibility of comparative politics (MacIntyre 1973) is that it depends crucially on these kinds of variables being causally important. Put in this fashion one cannot make an a priori philosophical case against comparative politics since the issue becomes one of evaluating competing theories, and what's more the result of this evaluation probably depends on the phenomenon to be explained (it would be odd if it were otherwise – a phenomenon-independent argument would be based on "human nature" or cross-cultural universals?).

3 CONTEXT AS CHANGING MEANING

For some years now, the word *context* has been fashionable in article titles as genuine contextual analysis has been missing. In general, the specification of context and its treatment as either an exogenous or endogenous *variable* remains vague.

Heinz Eulau (1987, p. 256)

Introduction

Eulau's remarks illustrate the common view of context as a cause or an effect. In this chapter I suggest another alternative: context can influence relationships. The causal arrow from the context is not directed to or from another variable but at another arrow. Using this model of context makes international relations look much more like comparative politics, which has always been concerned with how the same variables can have different effects in different societies. In comparative politics national boundaries separate systems, thus there is a natural concern for the variability of relationships in different societies. But there is no such obvious dividing line between systems at the global level. In general there are many potential useful criteria for defining different contexts; ultimately each individual is unique (and even she may have multiple selves, Elster 1986). Context as changing meaning emphasizes how similar the theoretical and empirical problems of international relations and comparative politics really are.

This chapter develops some of the ramifications of the concept of context as changing meaning for the study of international politics. "Contextual" models are familiar to students of American politics but not to those who study international relations (see the Postscript to this chapter for a discussion of the "American" contextual literature from my perspective). Much of the statistical methodology is readily available in works such as Boyd and Iverson (1979) and the literature that volume has spawned. In addition to being a tool for conceptualizing how state–state relations are environment dependent, context as changing meaning is a general research design tool. It provides a way of thinking about many problems that all researchers must face: indicator construction, choosing a spatial–temporal domain, standardization, and concept definition. One reason why this is a book on context and not one on level of analysis or agent–structure relations is that context reaches beyond these frameworks and touches other research concerns. In the sections that follow I briefly sketch out some of the theoretical, methodological, research design, and conceptual issues the idea of context as changing meaning raises.[1] I shall focus on the literature on international war and conflict, in part because it is central to the study of international relations, in part because it is an area of personal interest and expertise.

Contextual definitions, data, and indicators

Contextual issues arise at the very beginning of a research project. When examining possible operational definitions context sensitivity is an issue. An example of this is the Singer and Small operational definition of a "war" as a militarized conflict producing 1,000 or more military casualties (this is not the complete definition, see Small and Singer 1982). Its advantages are simplicity and that it generates an intuitively acceptable list of wars. The definition is invariant with regard to the states involved, the period, the consequences, and declarations of war. Because of its spatial–temporal invariance it is an example of a "context-free" definition of war. In terms of figure 3.1 the relation between indicator (1,000 battlefield deaths) and phenomenon (war) is fixed and independent of any context.

One of the earliest and most obvious criticisms of this definition is that given the boom in world population over the last 200 years, 1,000 battle deaths becomes a much smaller percentage of total population or of military forces as one moves toward the present (Job 1976). This criticism implies that there are important *outside* factors determining if a militarized conflict is to be defined as a war. As figure 3.1 illustrates, the Singer and Small definition implies a constant relationship between the 1,000 casualties and war. If, however, one argues that war should be defined as the percentage of total population lost on the battlefield then the national demographic context determines whether a conflict is a war or not. The number of

[1] I shall use context in this chapter to refer to context as changing meaning, the other modes of context, cause and barrier, will be referred to by name.

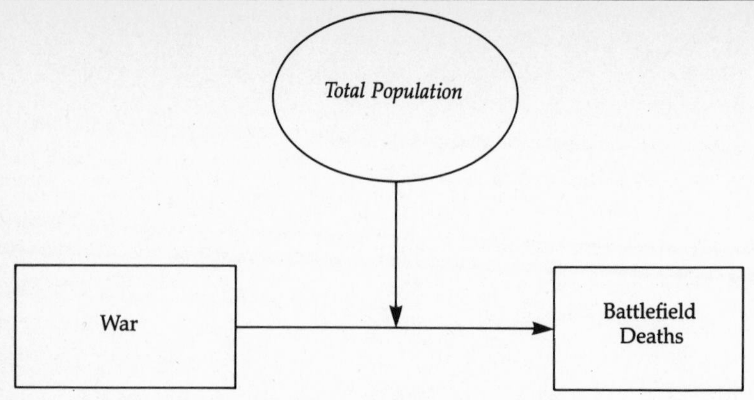

Figure 3.1 Contextual definition of war

casualties is intimately related to whether a conflict is a war, while the total population of the countries involved is not. If one were to argue for an increasing threshold that followed world population growth then global population trends provide the relevant context. Another argument for increasing thresholds involves improvements in technology that allow for more people to be killed more rapidly in more recent times. Here the relevant context is industrial know-how. The important point is that factors outside strictly war-related ones are influential in determining what is and what is not defined as a war. In terms of figure 3.1 population, size of military, or technology level fills the context ellipse.

This "outsideness" characterizes one aspect of contextual variables. The theoretical status of the indicator and that of the context are quite different. The nature of this "outsideness" can vary from problem to problem. I use "outside" in order to avoid the frequent connotation of context as "higher." Outside really means to play a "different" theoretical role. The nature of this difference depends on the problem and the theory.

The multiple indicator approach provides one common way of measuring many-faceted concepts like war. The complete Singer–Small definition of war includes alternative clauses for the "odd war" that the 1,000 casualty criteria does not catch. One of these clauses is troop involvement; if 1,000 of its troops see action then a nation is considered a party; for example this clause is necessary to include the US in the Gulf War. Motivating multiple indicator approaches is the intuition that no one indicator can adequately define or capture a many-sided concept, but that constructing a measure from many indicators produces a more valid one. This approach and methodology differ, however, from those generated by contextual indicators: more complex does not necessarily mean more contextual.

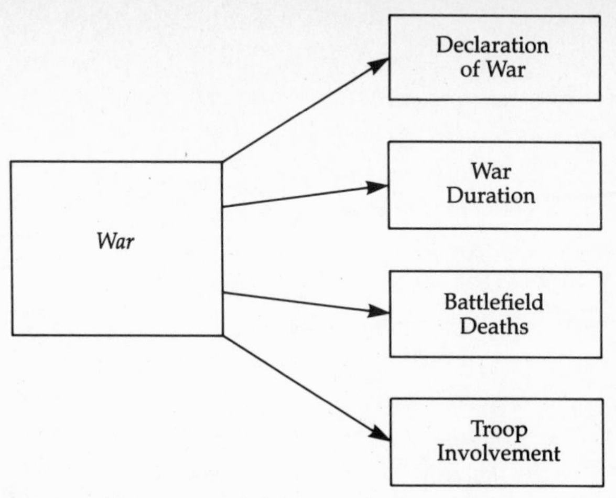

Figure 3.2 Non-contextual definition of war

It is possible to develop a multiple indicator model of war containing only non-contextual indicators. If one takes the framework of confirmatory factor analysis (LISREL) – under which many multiple indicator models can be subsumed (Jöreskog 1979) – the latent, unmeasured variable "war" may have a variety of different indicators, such as number of troops involved, number of casualties, declaration of war, length of conflict, and intensity of conflict. All these are indicators of different aspects of war that can be measured, but do not involve factors outside the war itself. So the latent variable is a non-contextual measure of war. In spite of the multiple indicator approach, the concept of war is not context sensitive (compare figure 3.1 to figure 3.2). Whether there be one or many indicators of a phenomenon is irrelevant, the issue is the stability of those relationships in changing environments. The concept of intensity (battle deaths/total population), where the relationship between battlefield casualties and war is affected by the total population of the nations involved, could for example be added to the measurement model as well as other contextual indicators. By adding more contextual indicators the latent variable war becomes more sensitive to various contexts, e.g., national, regional, or global. (I do something like this in chapter 12 where the measurement model of the international norm of decolonization is measured via multiple indicators, some of which include the domestic political context in the different colonial powers.) One might propose a "test" of the two kinds of models; the next chapter provides such a test of different indicators of military allocation ratios, some of which are more contextual than others. In general it may be that certain concepts are more environmentally sensitive than others; for these concepts the importance of contextualizing indicators becomes correspondingly greater.

The difference between contextual and multiple indicator approaches follows closely the contrast between context as cause and context as changing meaning. The arrows in figure 3.2 mean that the phenomenon "war" has various manifestations; war is the independent variable and its visible characteristics are the dependent variables. It is no accident that the language of LISREL models is full causal images (Bollen 1989). The latent variable causes its manifestations much as intelligence causes one to answer test questions correctly. The linguistic analogy also holds: the multiple indicator approach is like word definition via synonyms (or antonyms), but contextual aspects of word meaning do not always appear in dictionaries – they belong to the "pragmatics" of meaning. In different terms, figure 3.2 says that the manifestations of war remain constant from war to war while figure 3.1 states that these manifestations vary from war to war.

Contextual issues can arise in rather subtle ways beginning even in the data generating phase of a research project. As the discussion of the Singer–Small war definition showed, the operationalization of a concept can be more or less contextual, but the importance of context can change even within a coding scale. An example of this is the militarized international disputes data set from the Correlates of War Project which contains data on serious militarized conflicts and wars since 1816 (Gochman and Maoz 1984). To code the seriousness of the dispute a "level-of-force" scale is used consisting of six levels (a collapsing of a more detailed scale, see Leng and Singer 1977) going from 0, no response, to 5, war. These levels divide themselves rather naturally into two categories: (1) symbolic and verbal acts, showing the flag and verbal threats, and (2) actual use of military force.

Assuming the scale is a reasonable one,[2] it is interesting to consider the information and coder judgment required – both a priori and in fact – to code various incidents as legitimate serious militarized disputes. The information needed to code a use of force is minimal, just the fact that the military of one state took action against the territory, property or ships of another state. On the other hand, consider a "serious, explicit" threat to use

[2] There seems to be no strong objection to considering the magnitude of military force to be unidimensional. This seems implicit in the majority of the strategic literature on the use of nuclear weapons for example. There are actions that perhaps do not fit on the scale such as economic sanctions and closings of embassies. But it can be argued that these actions are off the scale on the zero side, since states unwilling to undertake military responses act in this fashion.

military force. Clearly this requires more judgment on the part of the coder, but also requires more information about the conflict, for example, who issued the threat, and the general state of relations between the two states in order to decide whether a threat was a serious, explicit one. Threats are slippery things. Consider Khrushchev's famous remark "We will bury you." Does this constitute a serious threat to use force? Hindsight and consideration of the situation allow its elimination, but it requires considerable information about the context in which he made the statement to understand that what he meant was only that marxism would outlive capitalism.

The use-of-force level being based on physical acts makes the coding easier, but at the same time permits the inclusion of possibly inappropriate cases. For example, the seizure of fishing boats is counted as a use of force. There are a number of militarized disputes between the US and Peru because the Peruvian navy seized US fishing boats. These conflicts do not fit everyone's understanding of militarized disputes but are included. North Korea also seized fishing boats. The "same" action may mean different things (see chapter 9 for an extended discussion of this problem), it may be a military action in one context and a police action in another.

In the militarized dispute data set there seem to be fewer anomalous cases involving a threat than for the use-of-force level, the reason perhaps being that a wider range of factors are implicitly taken into account when coding them. Almost by definition the coding of a threat involves the evaluation of the meaning of the action, while the physical nature of force permits the issue of meaning to be eluded. In short, these two levels require different amounts of information about the incident and interpretative analysis in order to arrive at a coding decision. The relative reliability and validity of the two levels remain to be studied, but they may vary depending on the amount of contextual information used to code the data.

The converse of an action with multiple possible meanings is the situation where different policy options all *mean the same thing* (foreign policy substitutability); they are different ways to achieve the same goal. In indicator construction we tend to assume that a concept must be represented by the same thing in all situations and countries. Once it is clear that different policies are functionally equivalent, indicators can consist of several quite different actions (e.g., searching for allies, increasing military expenditures, etc.), all of which may be appropriate responses to the same situation. Conversely, the same action may need to be coded differently; military spending may be the result of domestic pressures or the response to a foreign threat. Thus it is possible for two different actions to mean the same thing or for the same action to mean different things. Context in both cases determines the best interpretation.

All these problems of indicator construction, definition, and data gathering are essentially those of comparative research. In a deep sense international relations is comparative:

> Comparative research requires a strategy for establishing equivalence. The models of measurement based on inference provide a means to remove the multiplier effect of hundreds of social systems and thereby measure properties in terms free of the context of particular systems. The strategy proposed here in effect holds the social system constant by adapting the bases for inference so that the impact of the social system can be removed. (Przeworski and Teune 1970, p. 111)

Equivalence expresses what I refer to as "constant meaning." Przeworski and Teune want to measure properties "free of context," while I want to measure properties in context. The methodology is identical but the theoretical optic is different. Context is not something to get rid of, it is an integral part of the phenomena being compared.

Przeworski and Teune are concerned with the problem of standardization. They want to remove the effects of systems to be able to compare individuals. We frequently standardize data without realizing the profound methodological implications of the operation. It is so habitual and mundane an operation that it is rarely treated in statistical or methodological textbooks (outside "statistical" standardization which is quite different). Yet when one standardizes, as in inter-nation comparisons by population, the implicit goal is to *de-contextualize* the data. The problem is that there is some aspect of the situation that invalidates comparison per se. We do not consider it acceptable to say that one country is richer than another because it has a larger total GNP; we consider the fact that countries are of different sizes invalidates that comparison. GNP per capita is a valid way of comparing nations because we have removed the invalidating size factor. Sometimes this is not enough since the cost of living is much higher in some countries than in others, hence GNP per capita must be adjusted. The point is that to make *valid* comparisons there are important contexts that have to be included. The simple operation of standardization is already an implicit theory about contextual factors and their importance.

Contextual models and theories

By using the term "contextual theories," I shall refer to two related aspects of theory building. One is the theoretical notion of context as changing meaning, the second is how this notion gets translated into regression models. The thesis is that potentially contextual theories are often formally modeled as simple linear regressions. Part of the problem is due, I believe, to some uncertainty on the theoretical level as to what context is or how system structure interacts with state-level variables. The other part of the problem is the general use of regression models where independent variables are interpreted as cause. The concept of context as changing meaning provides a tool for thinking theoretically about the relations between levels of analysis, but these ideas need to be translated into models that can be checked with data. Thus an important part of the discussion is how this may be done starting from the framework of regression models. As a point of departure I shall take the simple multiple regression model[3] (my remarks apply basically to this model, but since they focus in particular on model parameters they can be applied to dynamic and non-linear models):

$$Y = \beta_0 + \beta_1 X_1 + \beta_2 X_2 + \epsilon \quad \epsilon \sim i.i.d.\ N(0, \sigma^2)$$

This is an example of a basically non-contextual model, thus, from the perspective developed here, the basis of many problems in understanding multi-level models and context. If one starts with the simple regression equation, the argument is generally that X_1 causes Y in some sense. Normally X_1 by itself does not explain all the variation in Y so other causes, X_2, X_3, ... are adduced to explain it. In the best of all possible worlds the independent variables are orthogonal (there is no collinearity, a situation which normally exists when the experiment can be controlled) so that the relative importance of the independent variables in explaining Y can be unambiguously attributed to the various X's. Regression models are often a series of dyadic hypotheses between the X's and Y. Each dyadic hypothesis does not mention other X's and they are not relevant. Thus each X is hypothesized to have a fixed relationship with regard to Y (represented by the β_i's), and that relationship does not depend theoretically on the presence or absence of other variables: the context of the other X variables has no import (statistically, collinearity will affect the estimates, but this is a data

[3] This is the standard textbook regression model where the ϵ's are *i*ndependently, *i*dentically *d*istributed random variables with mean 0 and variance σ_2.

problem). The relationship is that depicted in figure 2.3 between "Independent" (X) and "Dependent" (Y) variables with β_1 being the arrow linking the two. Now, if the X's and Y's are contextual indicators then the model is in part sensitive to changing environments via the indicators; nevertheless, structurally the model is not context sensitive.

A simple way of thinking about contextual effects is through stochastic parameter models. β_1 represents the context-free fixed relationship between X and Y. Including context makes this fixed relationship variable:

$$Y = \beta_0 + \beta_1 X + \epsilon, \quad \epsilon \sim i.i.d.\ N(0, \sigma_2^1) \tag{3.1}$$

$$\beta_1 = \alpha_0 + \alpha_1 Z + \mu, \quad \mu \sim i.i.d.\ N(0, \sigma_2^2) \tag{3.2}$$

Equation 3.2 indicates that the assumption of a constant β_1 has been removed. The impact of X on Y as measured by β_1 is not constant, but varies depending on the level of context Z, where α_0 represents the effect of X on Y if the contextual factor Z is completely absent – the zero degree of context – and α_1 measures the importance of the context Z in mediating the relationship between X and Y. This formulation has all the characteristics of a contextual model. It is triangular in that X, Y, and Z are all related to each other, but at the same time the status of Z differs from that of X and Y producing the hierarchical effect typical of contextual models. The "outsideness" I referred to in the discussion of contextual definitions receives expression in a separate equation for the context variables.

One can substitute for β_1 in equation 3.1 and get the reduced form:

$$Y = \beta_0 + \alpha_0 X + \alpha_1 Z X + \mu X + \epsilon \tag{3.3}$$

α_0 represents the main effect of X on Y and α_1 the multiplicative interaction effect of the individual level X and context Z.[4] This reduced form is in fact a simple regression equation (not quite since the error structure is different) with interaction terms. Equation 3.3 has a rather thin theoretical structure, but the original structural equations (3.1 and 3.2) provide a richer understanding of the relationships between X, Y, and Z. Contextual models of voting behavior typically report the reduced form of the equation, not the

[4] In addition, the μX term means that the variance of Y changes, not according to the context Z, but according to X itself. Thus the variance of Y can be broken down into two components, one the "direct" effects (i.e., σ_2^1) and the other due to contextual effects (i.e., σ_2^2 from the μX term). There are techniques for estimating these variance components (see Judge *et al.* 1985) and the relative magnitudes of these can indicate which part of the model may be in need of refinement. See Entwisle and Mason (1985) for an example of such a model and Tate and Wongbundhit (1983) for a comparison of stochastic versus non-stochastic parameter models. Boyd and Iverson (1979) discuss in detail different ways parameters can change, although the change is always assumed to be non-stochastic, i.e., no μ in the context equation.

structural equations (see the Postscript to this chapter for further discussion). This illustrates the very important point that no particular modeling technique is by definition contextual, but rather many techniques can be if a contextual theoretical approach to the underlying relationships is taken.

Other variations on the general linear model can be subjected to this reinterpretation. It is the conceptualization of the underlying relations that is important not the statistical techniques used. These models and their reinterpretation are a first step away from the fundamental belief that it makes any real sense to talk about *the* effect of X on Y; rather one must talk about their relationship in a meaningful context. There is a tendency in the social sciences to include indiscriminately interaction terms in regression models. Often they are included without any strong theoretical motivation in order "to see what happens." One advantage of the contextual approach is that simple interaction terms can be motivated by viewing the context as having an impact on fundamental relationships. The basic statistics remain the same, but the theoretical coherence of the model increases.

For example, relative power considerations are often important variables in models that try to explain war initiation. Assume for the sake of argument that the greater the relative superiority of A over B the more likely A is to attack B (see Siverson and Sullivan (1983) for a review of the large literature on whether war is more likely under conditions of preponderance or parity). Also assume that this is a linear relationship and that β_0 is the "grievance" – to use Richardson's term – that A feels toward B which would incite A to attack no matter what. Then we may start with the model (the basic sort of analysis of the preponderance/parity literature):

$$\text{War} = \beta_0 + \beta_1(\text{Power of A/Power of B}) + \epsilon$$

As it is this model has no particular spatial–temporal limits, but a theory of spatial–temporal domain is an implicit theory of context. One argument about the exceptionalness of the nuclear era concerns increases in the destructiveness of weapons and the general growth in military technology (Kegley 1991). One can ask how this element might be put into the equation and what the consequences are. For example, β_0, the attack-no-matter-what term, may go quickly to zero as destructive potential increases. Or, it may be necessary to have a greater superiority in order to induce a state to attack in periods of greater destructive potential. In low destructive potential systems marginal superiority may incite attack since there is little potential for major damage, like warfare between primitive tribes. Greater destructive potential requires that a nation have a larger superiority in order to attack, in other words, β_1 is getting smaller. The relationship stabilizes at a low level with modern industrial technology and nuclear weapons. In general the relationship between relative power and war initiation may be time–space dependent.

One might well ask if there exist examples of contextual theories. The model Bueno de Mesquita develops in *The war trap* (1981) provides one example, in particular his operationalization of decision-making under uncertainty. He uses changes in the international system – or to be more precise the potential coalitions for a given conflict – to indicate the degree of uncertainty in the environment. The basic decision-making calculus of the model changes depending on decision-maker's uncertainty. Which decision rule to use depends *operationally* on the international context (Tversky and Kahneman (1981) discuss how different "frames" – contexts – influence decisions). Uncertainty in his theory is in the heads of leaders (the *world* is not uncertain, it knows what it is doing) but this is operationalized as changes in the international environment. (Here we have the somewhat peculiar situation where a mental state – uncertainty – is measured by characteristics of the international system!)

Although the context is usually thought of as some larger encompassing framework, one can also speak of the lower-level context. A crucial context of international politics is domestic politics and structures. For Bueno de Mesquita the relevant subnational context is the decision-maker's propensity to take risks.[5] The decision-making calculus is then altered depending on the "personality" of the actor and its preference for risk. Examples like this show why viewing context via the micro–macro or agent–structure framework misleads. Context is not necessarily some larger environment.

Bueno de Mesquita's model takes changes in the international environment as a measure of uncertainty, but beyond this system structure has often been viewed as quite influential in determining nation-state behavior. Instead of being viewed as a cause as is often implicitly the case, there are occasions when it is better understood as changing patterns of behavior. The debate on the relative war-proneness of bipolar versus multipolar systems takes on a different hue if the structure of the international system is conceived of as context. For example, it seems to be agreed on by both sides (Waltz 1979; Deutsch and Singer 1964) that multipolar systems allow for greater freedom of action than bipolar systems. Their differences lie on

[5] A more common characteristic of the domestic context that has been thought to influence war is the type of governmental regime. The hypothesis is that democratic regimes or dyads are less war-prone than authoritarian ones.

the implications of this flexibility for war and conflict. From a contextual view, whether more or less war occurs depends on how polarity interacts with causal variables. One hypothesis is that a nation which has more interaction opportunities (to use the Deutsch–Singer terminology) is more variable in its behavior. Multipolar systems may allow personality and domestic politics to play a larger role than in bipolar systems.

One story that illustrates this hypothesis is about the impact of the preferences of government leaders for the use of armed force. The constraints of the international system have made the behavior of recent US administrations more similar in the more bipolar parts of the world (e.g., Europe) than in areas less subject to these constraints, where individual differences are more likely to appear. Reagan's preference for military force is allowed expression in places like Grenada or Libya, whereas under a different administration one might have expected different reactions. In some circumstances the *variability* of behavior may be greater than in others.

Structural realism has a contextual flavor to it. This framework contains arguments that are contextual. But when it comes to estimating a model, regression techniques are chosen. The rather methodological character of the discussion in this section indicates that it need not be so. The structure of the model should reflect the theoretical arguments, at the same time attention to formal structure often reveals ambiguities in theoretical foundations.

Context and control variables

Another way to understand higher-level variables as independent non-causal variables is via the concept of control variables. "Multi-level" models often include macro variables such as the state of the national economy although the focus is on the individual or the firm. If these variables were not included cross-national comparisons of individuals would be invalid (the problem leading to the inclusion of control variables is basically the same that leads to standardization of individual variables). The concept of control variables sometimes expresses itself in the concept of "partialing out" the effects of "extraneous" variables. The study is interested in the relationship between Y and X but Z is known to be closely related to both. The effect of Z on the relationship between Y and X is removed so that their "true" relationship comes to light. In both cases the result is formally the same as context as cause, the regression equation includes another independent variable (Z).

Often the use of control variables is a matter of theoretical emphasis; the important issues are the individual-level relationships. From my perspective this is an attempt to remove context from the model, and basically a case of going two steps backwards to move one step forward. There may be nothing unequivocal that can be said about *Y* and *X*, but this is not necessarily bad. The chimera of a true relationship between two variables may not be worth chasing and leads down a path away from concepts more suitable to the complexity of social situations.

For example, a central issue in my study of international norms is their relation to self-interest. I argue in chapter 12 that a norm can only easily be seen to have an impact when it diverges from self-interest. One way to state this is that international norms (context) only have an impact when controlling for self-interest (individual level); the converse of the situation above. I could argue that even when controlling for self-interest the norm variable is statistically significant, which is the natural temptation. Yet, I think that it is not an either/or situation and that self-interest interacts with normative values, that there are compromises where each side gives some. The control approach is to argue that norms cause behavior, but self-interest must be controlled for; the contextual framework focuses on the interaction of the two.

From a contextual point of view the concept of control variable has limited usefulness. This is not just true of theories but exactly the same issues have arisen in the discussion of indicator design where it is easy to talk about removing contextual effects. Przeworski and Teune (see the quote on page 45) want to "remove the impact of social systems"; the concept of controlling for variables has the same goal. Controlling is an attempt to remove context (ironically, by adding it) instead of incorporating it into a theoretical framework.

Conclusion

The ideal of the untainted bivariate relationship comes to us from the laboratory. The laboratory ideal is to remove all contextual effects; by having only *X* and *Y* present it is possible to ascertain if *X* causes *Y*. In an experimental setting if *Z* is also considered important it may be included, but in a fashion to make *Z* and *X* independent of each other (thus statistical analysis will give the same value to the coefficient of *X* whether *Z* is present or not). This procedure has guided much thinking about the nature of human relationships.

Przeworski and Teune (1970) suggested a variation on this approach for comparative research. If the coefficient relating X and Y is constant across nations – with X and Y being individual-level variables – then there is no need to introduce nation-level variables Z. This constant relationship – sort of a cross-cultural universal – is context independent. This is the comparative politics equivalent of the search in world politics for simple answers to simple hypotheses. My reading of the world politics literature is that these simple answers have not been found. One should not infer from this that the Przeworski and Teune research strategy is inappropriate, it would be silly to build a complicated model when a simple one works. The proper inference is that one should be prepared to include contextual variables.

Not only do system characteristics need to be introduced but there needs to be a methodology for introducing them. The default solution is a causal or control variable, but another option is to model how relationships change systematically. The system-level variable may not be a cause, it may be that relationships *are* just different.

Crucial to a complete understanding of context as changing meaning is that it be kept distinct from micro–macro, individual–environment perspectives. Context is *not* necessarily some higher-level factor, it can be active at any level. Thinking about context in this way inhibits some of the reflexes that dichotomies like agent–structure provoke. Likewise the existence of an alternative to context as cause forces the researcher to ask more clearly about the nature of the individual–environment relation. Is cause always the most appropriate conceptual category? These are fundamental reasons why I have chosen to use the word context throughout this volume. I do not want to prejudice unduly the interpretation in terms of level of analysis.

Context as changing meaning is probably the most interesting methodologically and philosophically of the three modes of context. I have tried to illustrate that this mode provides a tool for thinking about the basic questions of theory, and research and indicator design. Unlike a statistical treatment à la Boyd and Iverson (1979) I have placed the larger theoretical, methodological, and research design implications in the forefront. In particular, this contextual mode addresses one of the central problems of social research, making cross-sectional and cross-temporal comparisons. The next chapter illustrates that intuitively reasonable indicators are not necessarily valid in long temporal domains and that the spatial context provides a crucial point of comparison.

I have tried to show some simple ways in which the relationships between basic variables can systematically vary. Many social scientists think in terms of peculiar little diagrams consisting of circles, boxes, and ovals with arrows between them. Context as changing meaning shows that the arrows do not have to go from box to box but can go from box to arrow. Simple.

Postscript: contextual voting models

Context as changing meaning has been widely used in models of voting and electoral behavior. This literature is quite large, my goal is not to summarize it but rather to examine it in the light of the distinctions between context as changing meaning, context as barrier, and context as cause. To do so I shall take the work of Huckfeldt (1986) and Sprague (1976, 1982; Huckfeldt and Sprague 1987) as representative and typical of the best work in this domain.

The central problem addressed by these studies is the impact of the environment (context) on the individual voter. In this regard it is directly analogous to problems of the impact of the international system on states. However, the focus on this one kind of "contextual situation" has a number of important theoretical and methodological consequences.

The research question is frequently one like: What is the influence on a person's vote of living in, say, a working-class (and hence Democratic) neighborhood? If she lived in the Republican (affluent middle-class) neighborhood would her vote change? Now, in practice we cannot expose the same subject to different treatments, but if we look at the same type of person – according to socio-economic-cultural traits – and find her voting differently from one context to another then this is evidence for a "contextual effect." This fits exactly the definition of context as changing meaning: the relationship between individual characteristics and voting varies according to the neighborhood political context.

The political context (e.g., the percentage of Republicans in a neighborhood) has an impact because the probability that an individual will talk to and interact with a Republican in a Republican neighborhood is higher than in a Democratic one. In part, it is an "interpersonal influence model," or what Huckfeldt and Sprague (1987; Sprague 1982) call a "social interaction model." I emphasize the *interpersonal* because that is more precise than the ambiguous "social"; it is interpersonal as opposed to person–environment. One central question is whether there is a contextual effect beyond the number of interpersonal contacts with members of the neighborhood. In other words, could the model be reformulated, at least theoretically, as a completely individual-level model? Przeworski gives this interpretation:

"The influence of the context on an individual is conveyed through the interactions [interpersonal] which result in a change of behavior" (1974, p. 29). A real contextual effect however would be one where interpersonal contacts are controlled for. Huckfeldt found that even controlling for interpersonal contacts or friendships there was still a contextual effect due to the political characteristics of the neighborhood: "It would appear that the social context [degree working class] ... demonstrates a relationship to political loyalties even when intimate associations and class loyalties are controlled for" (1986, pp. 129–30). At this point however the theoretical argument is not clear: what is the effect if not through contacts with working-class people? Social interaction is measured by the political loyalties of close friends, but perhaps it is important to consider more informal and infrequent contacts. It is possible then that "context may become influential through a more generalized milieu effect that occurs because individuals are embedded within distinctive social and political worlds. Such an effect is impossible to measure *independently* of context" (emphasis is Huckfeldt's, p. 130). I take expressions like "generalized milieu effect" to mean that it is hard to conceive of context as having an impact outside of interpersonal influence models.

Huckfeldt states in the Conclusions to his book (1986): "Finally, how is the neighborhood social context translated into political influence? The social context becomes politically influential by structuring social interaction at two levels: (1) personal, primary group interactions between friends, and (2) the casual, impersonal interactions that inescapably occur among an area's residents. Both are important to politics and political behavior, and both are subject to variations in the social context" (1986, p. 149). The problem is that context stands *both* for the opportunity structure for contacts *and* the actual extent of interpersonal contacts (borders and contiguity in the war literature have this same ambiguity). The latter is not what I mean by context while the former is. Instead of considering the percentage of Democrats in a neighborhood as a measure of the number of contacts with Democrats a contextual approach argues that the socio-political characteristics of a neighborhood structure the opportunities for interpersonnal contacts. Local structures determine how hard or easy it is to contact members of the Democratic party, not how many Democrats are contacted. If there is little choice then Durkheim is right, contexts coerce (context as cause). If there is more slack then perhaps the Sprouts are closer to the mark with environmental possibilism (context as barrier).

In spite of these substantive problems, there are the more epistemological ones concerning the nature of context *vis-à-vis* other variables in the model. Generalizations are hazardous, but it appears that context is interpreted as cause. One bit of evidence for this conclusion comes from the language used to describe context, words like "factor" and "influence" which tend to be generic synonyms for cause, plus the fact that these same synonyms are used for other variables in the model.

Methodologically, this is clearer from the regression models used and how they are reported and presented. The contextual variables are usually given in a table along with individual-level variables. When researchers present their results they do so using the reduced form of the contextual model. There is nothing in the presentation of the results which suggests that contextual variables receive a different interpretation from individual-level ones. So although the model is often one of context as changing meaning, context is in fact interpreted as a cause. By way of contrast, economists virtually never publish the reduced form of their equations – which are merely used for estimation purposes – but give the structural form since it is the theoretically relevant one. Context as changing meaning is about how context affects individual-level relationships, there is no direct connection to the dependent variable; but if the reduced form is reported then there is a direct link between context and the dependent variable through the parameter estimate for the contextual effect. This would be clearer if the model reported were illustrated by a figure, as is customary in causal modeling.

The local political context is often operationalized as, say, the percentage Republican vote.[6] Here there is the additional problem that individual-level variables may well be highly correlated with characteristics of the environment. In contextual voting studies in particular, this potential problem is aggravated by the fact that the environmental–contextual variables are virtually always the same as the individual-level ones aggregated at the neighborhood or county level. This procedure has serious methodological problems since the context measured as a group mean is correlated with the individual-level variable. But it should be emphasized

[6] The implicit or explicit hypothesis is that the likelihood of voting Republican is directly proportional to the percentage of Republicans in the neighborhood (with the additional possibility of an interaction term). Is it mathematically certain that if you did the same analysis but using percent Democrats you would get the same result? Assuming the simple case that percentage Republican vote is equal to one minus percentage Democrat vote, it is not clear that the analysis will produce the same results since contextual models usually have non-linear factors (interaction terms); regression coefficients are invariant only under linear transformation.

that there is no a priori reason why context should be correlated with other independent variables.

Boyd and Iverson's solution to the methodological problems of collinearity that almost by definition arise in this case are interesting. Their proposal for "solving" the collinearity problem involves centering the individual variable around the relevant group mean. This preserves the slope and intercept of the individual-level variable, but makes the group, individual, and interaction terms uncorrelated. This centering implicitly redefines the context of reference. If, for example, the individual-level variable is income then one can compare incomes *across* groups (since income is measured in dollars). The centering changes the frame of reference to the subgroup. Once centered, income is income *relative* to the subgroup and thus comparisons across groups become impossible: centering *contextualizes* the measure. Since Boyd and Iverson (and their critics as well) have not considered the wider implications of the notion of context they do not realize that, ironically, their solution to a technical problem of collinearity is in fact an application of the contextual method in its larger sense. Tate (1984) can justly criticize and dismiss in short order the Boyd and Iverson technique because he too focuses narrowly on methodological issues. While he is absolutely right in stating that the centering technique produces new variables, he does not realize that maybe these are better! We shall see in the next chapter that taking absolute measures and contextualizing them is a way to make them more valid, in ways quite analogous to Boyd and Iverson's centering technique.

Boyd and Iverson focus mainly on context as changing parameters, in this sense they define context as changing meaning. However, it is clear that they do not understand the theoretical consequences of their approach. They are, in fact, almost exclusively concerned with context as defined by group means, and while they provide a nice survey of the different ways parameters can change, their approach is a very nuts and bolts statistical one. One result of this emphasis on statistics is that the relatively mechanical application of their techniques makes a model "contextual." As we have seen the concept of context as changing relationships has much deeper and wider-ranging ramifications than Boyd and Iverson's statistical treatment implies. Their volume is really devoted to modeling parameter change and not to the theoretical notion of context.

4 CONTEXTUAL INDICATORS

> But isn't *the same* at least the same?
>
> Ludwig Wittgenstein (1953, p. 84e)

Introduction

One of the eternal problems of behavioral social science is the creation of indicators that satisfy two often contradictory conditions, local validity and global relevance. To the extent that we create general theories we also by implication need indicators that can be applied to a relatively wide variety of situations. But as this variety increases so do the risks that the connection between indicator and concept weaken. For example, the manifestations of power may change over time; what is perhaps suitable in the nineteenth century is no longer so in the nuclear era. Since we would like to apply the concept of power to various circumstances, this may mean using indicators that reflect its changing nature (Stoll and Ward 1989). Indicator construction is a balancing act between idiosyncratic models designed for particular cases and models of general applicability. The research design may englobe dozens of countries over many decades as the research from the Correlates of War Project typifies, frequently covering all nations from 1816 to 1980; others such as Levy (1983) and Thompson (1988) use the period from the end of the fifteenth century to the present. If an indicator must be valid over the period from the musket to the atomic bomb this places extraordinary demands on indicator construction.

The indicator–concept relationship can change in various ways. One is that the same variables are important but their relative importance changes from group to group or period to period. More dramatic is when one must specify idiosyncratic factors in order to increase the local validity of a model. These aspects of indicator construction are closely associated with the general problems of comparative research. Much of the behavioral

Table 4.1 *Context and indicator construction*

		Concept: Same	Concept: Different
Indicator	Same	Default	Context dependency
	Different	Comparativism	Relativism

literature on international war shows no explicit concern with comparative analyses per se, but if the sample of cases is split into different groups or into different periods parameter estimates can be quite different: it means estimating the same measurement model and getting quite different results. Research designs that include many nations over long time periods run the risk that the connection between indicator and concept is variable according to the environment.

Table 4.1 gives the possible relations between indicator and concept as they vary over time and space. "Same" means that the concept or indicator does not vary; "different" means that the concept or the indicator used to measure the concept changes from one situation to another. The default assumption is located in the upper-left cell; the "same action" performed by different actors or in different epochs still means the same thing, such as the 1,000-casualty definition of war. The same indicator of war (1,000 casualties) is used to measure the concept "war" over the period 1816 to 1980. By assumption the concept of war measured by this indicator does not change either over this period: a "war" in the nineteenth century is the same as a "war" in the twentieth. This, after all, may be the case, but it cannot be assumed so, some justification is necessary. This cell's partner is in the lower-right cell, which signifies that face differences correspond to real differences: different words mean different things, synonyms do not exist. According to this view a war is different in the nineteenth century than in the twentieth, there are no uniform criteria that can be applied to make wars comparable. The extreme relativists take the position that equivalence relations across space and time are impossible; each war must be considered in its own terms.

The goal of indicator construction is to find oneself in the first column; whether the same indicator or different indicators are used the essential issue is that the concept being measured remains constant. For example, if military expenditures are used to indicate military capabilities it is important that what counts as military expenditure does not differ from country to country or over time. Much of the data creation effort goes into defining what should count as a military expenditure and then modifying each country's data in order to make it conform with this uniform definition. The "same" indicator is constructed for each country and the assumption is that since the same procedures are used for all countries and all time periods the concept of military capabilities being measured also does not vary. This is the standard procedure in virtually all data gathering efforts, be they COW data, GNP data, regime type data, etc.

The off-diagonal cells correspond to situations where context plays a crucial role. The lower-left cell represents the classic problem of comparative politics: to use a variant of MacIntyre's example (1973), does "courage" in English mean the same as *courage* in French, or more problematically, does "virtue" in English equal *virtú* in Italian? MacIntyre (see also Winch 1958) argues that contexts are always so different that identical meaning is impossible (poetry is what is lost in the translation). MacIntyre's argument is that it is impossible to move from the "relativism" cell to the "comparativism" cell. On the contrary, the comparativist (Przeworski and Teune 1970) argues that different measures can be created, that there is sufficient correspondence between cultures and nations so that indicators tapping the same concept can be created for each society. In comparative politics it may be impossible to have the same indicators since the indicator does not make sense outside of a given society (e.g., questionnaires must be translated into different languages).[1]

The argument for impossibility of comparative politics consists, in fact, of two independent points: one, that we are in a situation where the same action has different meanings, and two, that it is impossible to slide down the diagonal to make meanings equivalent. I grant the first point but not the second. Context as changing meaning is the road from where we frequently are to where we want to go.

The upper-right cell is one that has not received much attention. The issues surrounding the problems of comparative methods and the arguments for and against relativism have been widely debated. I shall concern myself with the problem of the upper-right cell, the possibility that the same action

[1] In the philosophical literature the concept of "supervenience" is used to express a concept which may have no fixed representation in physical reality (Kim 1978). This problem arises in the relationship between mental phenomena and their physical substructure (Fodor 1979; Davidson 1980) where the biochemical locus of the same mental process may vary. The same point has been made about the concept of "fitness" in biology (Rosenberg 1984; Sober 1984) since what determines the fitness of an organism varies widely from species to species.

(e.g., spending 5 percent of GNP on defense) may mean different things in different historical periods. The problem posed by the same indicator/different meaning cell is one of context dependence.

This chapter examines the natural and common assumption of the same indicator/same concept cell and finds it not to hold in one particular case. This puts us in the upper-right cell where we do not want to be, since the goal of indicator construction is found in the first column not the second. The concept of context as changing meaning allows us to move along the off-diagonal to the different indicator/same concept cell restoring the validity of the indicator. I suspect that the world frequently places us in the upper-right cell rather than in its neighbor to the left. In other words, the goal is context-sensitive indicators which remain valid in a wide variety of settings, for large countries and small, for recent as well as remote times. This chapter is an investigation of how the concept of context as changing meaning can inform theoretical thinking about this problem. To give substance to the notion of contextual indicators I empirically examine several indicators of the concept of military burden, the relation between them, how they vary on the continuum of contextualness, and how they perform in a standard hypothesis.

The military burden, or what I shall more neutrally call a "military allocation ratio," is the portion of a nation's resources that a country allocates to the military. In order to study international war a number of different indicators have been constructed to measure this concept, e.g., military expenditures divided by GNP. These indicators vary significantly in their context sensitivity. One question is whether the contextual indicators measure the same thing as the non-contextual ones. Another query is whether the contexts that are incorporated into the contextual indicators influence the validity of the other indicators. The final question is whether in a typical hypothesis contextual indicators perform better than non-contextual measures.

Theory always informs measurement approaches in the social sciences, which vary according to the purposes and preconceptions of the individual researcher. Rather than assess all possible measurement approaches to military allocations I choose to concentrate on those related to the study of war. In making such a choice I bypass those indicators of military allocations designed to study economic costs; instead I focus on those that have actually been used in order to study the impact of military burden on conflict escalation.

This is not simply a methodological exercise, there are important substantive issues at stake. Like arms races, military spending at high levels is closely related to war. Both as cause and effect it is part of the nexus of factors leading to war. In principle (and surely in propaganda), military establishments exist in order to protect a nation from its enemies. All countries, with the possible exception of Costa Rica and Iceland, have a standing army or militia ready to fight. In order to maintain that readiness a state utilizes economic resources, be they human or capital, for military purposes. Many think that military allocations play a prominent role in national decisions about war. First, high military allocations may be an early warning indicator of conflict escalation. Nations may be reluctant to fight unless adequately prepared. In addition, high military allocations could foster the growth of militarized movements or strengthen their public appeal (Noel-Baker 1958). For these reasons the use of force might become a likely policy choice during a serious confrontation. The probability of war may also be affected if one nation seeks to bring its opponent's economy "to its knees" through protracted arms competition. Some argue that a strategy of increasing military allocations to unacceptable levels could lead one side to back down. Another school of thought states that the overallocating protagonist could launch a preventive war before it falls behind its less encumbered foe in the future (Lebow 1983).

Prior empirical research on military allocations and conflict using a variety of different indicators has yielded varied and often inconsistent results (Weede 1977). Newcombe and Wert (1973) discovered a positive relationship between high allocations and conflict involvement. Rummel (1972) found a similar but weaker relationship. In contrast, Kegley, Richardson, and Richter (1978) discovered high allocations were positively associated with external conflict only in the relative absence of domestic conflict. Choucri and North (1975) reported wide variation in the military allocations ratios of the major powers prior to World War I.

The indicators

Military allocation ratios in conflict research usually consist of a comparison of some portion of a nation's resource base with the resources devoted to the military. The majority of studies use military expenditures to represent resources devoted to the military. Variation in measurement approaches tends to center on the choice of an indicator for the nation's resource base and the technique of construction.

With respect to existing techniques, approaches can be divided into two categories: those based on a simple ratio and those that use data about other countries in the system. Simple ratios imply a constant relationship between indicator and concept. They fix neither spatio-temporal limits nor is the behavior of other states relevant; they are not context sensitive. Indicators that depend on the behavior of other states or time period are context sensitive. I shall first discuss the non-contextual indicators.

Non-contextual indicators

Military expenditures divided by gross national product (ME/GNP)

Perhaps the most common indicator of military allocations is a simple ratio of a nation's military expenditures to its Gross National Product, henceforth referred to as "ME/GNP" (Russett 1964; Weede 1977; Kegley, Richardson, and Richter 1978; Reisinger 1983). The rationale for this approach is that GNP indicates best a nation's total resources. Consistent with most other measures of military allocations, military expenditures are believed to be the best available measure of resources devoted to the military. Military expenditure figures generally include a wide range of items – from research and development to military hardware – and therefore accurately reflect what a nation actually allocates to its military establishment.

Another approach to measuring military allocations substitutes national income for GNP as an indicator of a nation's resource base (Nincic 1983). The advantage of national income relative to GNP is that it does not include indirect business taxes and allows a capital consumption allowance. Thus national income presents a more accurate picture of national resources. This indicator varies little from ME/GNP and has severe data availability problems, not to mention the controversial problem of defining "capital consumption." Given its similarity to ME/GNP and these data problems I will not consider it further.

Military expenditures divided by government budget (ME/GB)

Another indicator is military expenditures as a percentage of government budget (Rummel 1972; Haas 1974; Choucri and North 1975; Cusack and Ward 1981). Here the assumption is that a national government can only use or only has access to resources represented by its budget. Government budget data have the advantage of being readily available for an extended time period, though only sporadically for various closed societies such as the People's Republic of China. Nevertheless, this indicator has important limitations. Government budgets are not very comparable given the great range of items found in different types of economies and historical epochs. Socialist economies tend to channel a greater share of their economic resources through government budgets than do market economies, thereby making military allocations of socialist nations appear smaller than those of societies where the government plays a more modest role. This plus the historical changes in the role of the state – the development of the welfare state – make comparisons problematic.

This kind of problem arises frequently in comparative research. Since different societies assign different roles to their governments, comparing, for example, Sweden and Switzerland, would not be fruitful: government expenditures in these two countries measure different things. The problem is resolved by making a list of items that define "government expenditures" and then modifying each country's expenditure data to fit this definition. In the language of table 4.1 one tries to move into the same indicator/same concept cell by making the indicator identical for all countries.

Military personnel divided by total population (MP/TP)

Rather than focus on monetary resources, another approach to measuring military allocations concentrates on human resources devoted to the military. Andreski (1968) developed the idea of a "military participation ratio" to signify the proportion of individuals in the population occupied – directly or indirectly – by the military (Richardson (1960a) also developed a similar measure). In conflict research this has been operationally defined as the number of military personnel of a nation divided by its population (Stoll and Champion 1977; Rummel 1972; Russett 1970). The reasoning behind this indicator is that those individuals in military service cannot contribute to a nation's production of goods and services and therefore are a burden on the economy. Benoit and Lubell (1967) carry this one step further operationally: they multiply the number of men in the armed forces by the average civilian wage, labeling the result "lost production" due to military service.

The major problem of this indicator is its lack of sensitivity to the changing nature of war. The importance of manpower in warfare has declined greatly over the last century as a result of the increasing importance of industry. Success in war has become more dependent on weaponry, hence industry, than on increases in troop strength. Also the nature of the military has changed; by 1946 virtually all major powers maintained large standing armies. This change in the nature of human resource allocation means that intertemporal comparisons become problematic. For the previous indicator it was the changing nature of governments that makes intertemporal comparisons difficult, here it is the changing nature of warfare.

Contextual indicators

Regression strategy

A more sophisticated approach developed by Newcombe and his associates uses a regression model of GNP and military expenditures (Newcombe 1969; Newcombe and Wert 1973; Newcombe, Newcombe, and Landrus 1974). The size of a nation's military establishment is postulated to be largely a function of the size of its economic base. Therefore military expenditures are regressed on GNP for a large number of nations over a three-year period. After deriving the regression equation they apply it to yearly GNP figures in order to obtain a state's predicted military expenditures. The observed (actual) expenditure is then divided by the predicted value and multiplied by a hundred. Scores that deviate significantly from one hundred indicate over- or underallocation to the military relative to other countries.[2]

The simple ME/GNP ratio, on the other hand, provides no systematic method of defining which nations are over- or underallocating. It cannot, since the whole concept of overallocation itself is implicitly a relative one. The question is what should be the appropriate context of comparison. The regression strategy defines the context to be the military spending activity of all states in the international system. It is not merely a state's own ME/GNP but also the behavior of the system as a whole that defines a state's allocation level. The relationship between ME/GNP and the concept

[2] Biologists use the same technique to answer questions about the relative intelligence of species. The problem is that brain weight varies according to size, e.g., women's brains weigh less than men's. A regression line determines the average brain size for a species of a given average weight. For example, humans have much larger brains than they should based on this regression equation. On the other hand, *within* species there is no relationship between brain size and intelligence; women are as intelligent as men. (For an elegant presentation of this see Gould's (1980) "Were dinosaurs dumb?".)

of the military allocation ratio depends on the military spending behavior of all states in the system.[3]

This regression technique constructs a reference point but does not take into account the temporal aspects of the problem. Newcombe's studies are cross-sectional in nature. It is not clear that the relationship he finds for a given three-year period is constant over time. He considers the spatial context but not the temporal one.

Stratified epochs

All the indicators discussed above are "ahistorical," there is no reference made to any historical period or to previous spending patterns of individual states. They are timeless measures of military allocation ratios. The "stratified epochs" indicator takes into account that overallocation can be period dependent (Diehl 1985).[4]

This approach assumes that military personnel are more significant than other aspects of the military in determining military effectiveness for the early and mid nineteenth century. The stratified epochs indicator allows for the changing nature of warfare by using military personnel until 1860 and then military expenditures thereafter as measures of resources devoted to defense. Because of the problems with GNP, national income, and government budgets, the indicators of national resources are total population for the pre-1860 period, and energy consumption and iron/steel production thereafter.

In addition to taking into account the temporal context it utilizes the regression strategy – a variation on the Newcombe technique – to allow for the spatial context as well. For the period 1816–60 military personnel are regressed on total population. For the period after 1860, military expenditures are the outcome variable and the two industrial indicators serve as separate predictor variables. The post-1860 regressions are stratified by historical epochs (1861–1913, 1919–38, 1946–80) corresponding to observed changes in the baseline. This indicator illustrates the strategy of the different indicator/same concept cell of table 4.1: the indicators change

[3] Some might argue that a minor power's foreign policy has less scope and thus spends proportionately less than a major power. By including all powers the technique risks overestimating the value for the major powers and underestimating it for the minor. Newcombe does not seem to have tested this assumption of his technique.

[4] In chapter 9 I shall define "historical theories" of international relations as those that take explicitly into account the historical past, by consequence the stratified epochs indicator qualifies as a historical indicator.

over time reflecting changing systems but the concept measured remains the same. It explicitly takes into account the changing character of warfare.

The yearly population and industrial data are used in the estimated regression equation to calculate expected values for military personnel and military expenditures. The actual personnel and expenditure values are then divided by the predicted values and the quotient is multiplied by 100. The scores using the industrial indicators are averaged to form a composite measure. A score of 100 indicates the "normal" number of troops or level of military expenditure for a particular-sized nation.

This approach has the advantage of adjusting for parameter changes over time; thus different historical epochs can be easily compared with each other. As opposed to the regression strategy, it takes into account the temporal aspect of change. Also the calculation of the baseline using data from more than just a few years of each epoch means that a nation's score is not only determined by current spending levels of other countries but also by the recent spending behavior of all countries in the current epoch.

One empirical limitation of this approach is the weaker fit of the regression line for the 1919–38 period. Because the fit of the line is rather imperfect, the discrepancy between predicted and actual expenditures is quite large, leading to greater variation in the military allocation scores for this period than others. The outlying scores exaggerate the actual allocations of countries and distort the results when used in analyses of conflict.[5]

This approach has been attempted thus far only on major powers, and its applicability to minor powers remains uncertain. It appears that some adjustments relating to military aid and the technological development of minor powers would be necessary before the measure could be useful in this domain. Finally, there is a serious problem when analyzing the slopes and intercepts of the regression lines. Because the dependent variable is monetary (for the post-1860 period), inflation will exaggerate the actual ratchet effect or changes occurring across epochs; though this problem can be solved with suitable deflators.

System percentage

Another approach (Wayman, Singer, and Goertz 1984) is a variant on the Singer, Bremer, and Stuckey (1972) power index. Wayman, Singer, and Goertz begin by calculating the major power subsystem totals for military

[5] See the postscript to this chapter for how this can be a factor in the problem of "the disappearing .400 hitter" in baseball.

expenditures and two industrial indicators (energy consumption and iron/steel production). Then they determine the percentage of the total system capabilities that each major power has on each of the three dimensions. The underlying assumption of their next set of operations is that a nation should have approximately the same percentage of the system's military capabilities as it does of industrial capabilities. For example, if Nation A has 10 percent of the industrial capabilities of the system it is expected to have 10 percent of the military capabilities: values over one signify overallocation to the military. This assumption provides an *a priori norm* for military allocations and as such is not empirically testable.

This approach has some attractive features. It establishes a baseline by which the researcher is able to identify military allocations in excess of the norm, thus permitting analyses of the effects of overallocation. The baseline is defined a priori and hence there is no problem with it changing over time as is the case with empirical baselines. By using percentage shares instead of raw data, the approach is not subject to problems of inflation. Finally, the data required are readily available and the authors conducted a set of analyses on a period extending back to 1816.

Like the regression approach, the system percentage indicator depends on the spatial context: the ratio depends on the behavior of other states in the system. This indicator does not, however, take into account trends in military spending. A finding that all major powers are overallocating simultaneously is impossible. If there are large concurrent increases in military expenditures for all major powers then this measure does not adequately reflect them. Unlike the stratified epochs indicator, there is no temporal dimension to the comparison. Each nation could triple its military spending without any increase in industrial capability and yet retain basically the same military allocation ratio.

Summary

These are the main approaches to measuring military allocations in the conflict literature; though by no means an exhaustive list of the *possible* measurement approaches, it is almost an exhaustive list of *actual* approaches. Table 4.2 summarizes the indicators that I include in the empirical analysis that follows and their characteristics on a number of criteria.

Figure 4.1 illustrates graphically the difference between non-contextual and contextual indicators. Notice that the contextual indicators try in different ways to take into account the possibility that the indicator–concept

Table 4.2 *Allocation indicators and their attributes*

Indicator	Military resources	Resource base	Norm or baseline	Spatial context sensitivity	Temporal context sensitivity	Contextual indicator
System %	military expenditures	energy iron/steel	yes (a priori)	yes	no	yes
Stratified epochs	military expenditures	energy iron/steel	yes (empirical)	yes	yes	yes
ME/GB	military expenditures	govt. budget	no	no	no	no
ME/GNP	mil. exp.	GNP	no	no	no	no
MP/TP	military personnel	total population	no	no	no	no

relationship varies according to historical epoch or depends on the behavior of other states. The non-contextual indicators are all simple *constant* bivariate relationships between concept and indicator, completely independent of historical period or the current allocation activity of other states.

Comparing the indicators

In empirically assessing the various measures of military allocations, I focus on the major powers for the years 1861–1980.[6] The Correlates of War Project provided data on military expenditures, military personnel, energy consumption, iron and steel production, and total population. Government expenditure data are taken primarily from Banks (1971) supplemented by Mitchell (1978), and the US Arms Control and Disarmament Agency (1983). Bairoch (1976) provided Gross National Product figures and also graciously provided some unpublished estimates. Because the GNP data are for ten-year intervals I ran a polynomial regression for each country (all R^2 values over 0.99) in order to obtain yearly estimates. It must be pointed out that these estimates represent basic trends and do not reflect fluctuations due to the business cycle. Additional GNP data were taken, when necessary, from

[6] The major powers for this study are those identified by Small and Singer (1982): United States (1899–1980), United Kingdom (1861–1980), France (1861–1940, 1945–80), Austria-Hungary (1861–1918), Germany (1861–1918, 1925–45), Russia/Soviet Union (1861–1917, 1922–80), China (1950–80), Italy (1861–1943), Japan (1895–1945). Inasmuch as the participants' military allocations during major power wars are all but impossible to measure since nations completely devote their economies to the war effort, I bypass the analysis for the World War I and II years, i.e., 1914–18, 1939–45.

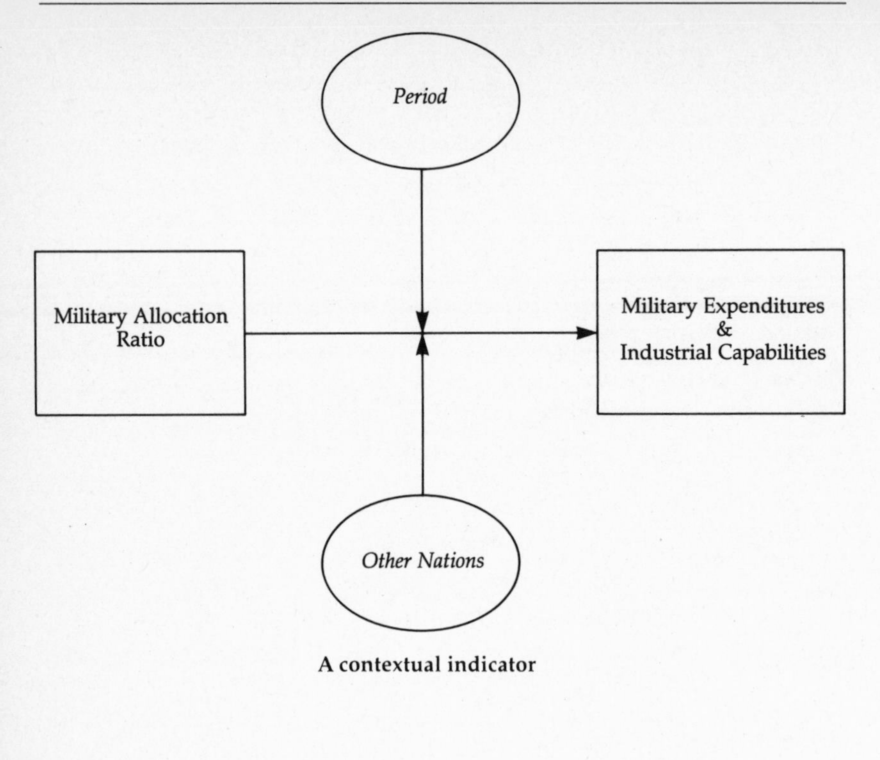

A contextual indicator

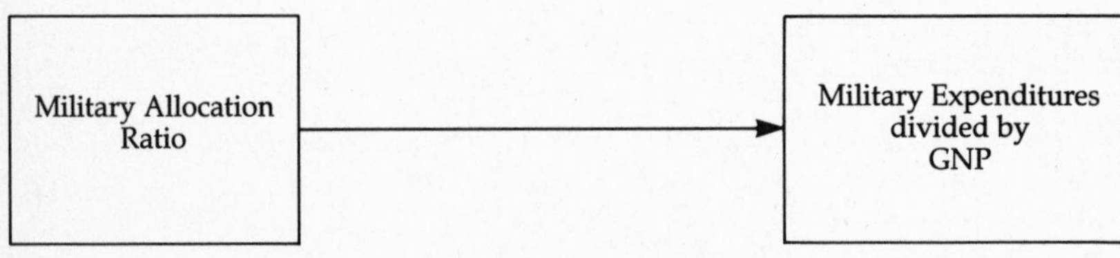

A non-contextual indicator

Figure 4.1 Measurement models of military allocation ratios

the World Bank (1983), US Bureau of the Census (1975), US Arms Control and Disarmament Agency (1983) and the International Monetary Fund (1982).[7] Missing data are a problem particularly for government expen-

[7] Banks (1971) supplied government expenditure data for all years except: 1966–70 (Mitchell 1978), 1971–80 (USACDA 1983), and 1929–33 for Germany and the Soviet Union (Mitchell 1978). Bairoch (1976) provided all data on GNP except for the US 1929–70 (US Bureau of the Census 1975), and for China 1950–80 (World Bank 1983) and 1971–80 (USACDA 1983). Other scattered missing data were filled in by data from the International Monetary Fund (1982). In all cases where data from different sources were used, I undertook a careful effort to make sure that the figures formed a consistent pattern. Where the data were inconsistent those years were coded as missing.

Table 4.3 *Correlations between the indicators*

Contextual	System %	1.00	−0.09	−0.19	−0.15	−0.05
	Epochs	−0.09	1.00	0.02	0.05	0.13
Non-contextual	Budget	−0.19	0.02	1.00	0.65	0.27
	GNP	−0.15	0.05	0.65	1.00	0.41
	Personnel	−0.05	0.13	0.27	0.41	1.00
		System %	Epochs	Budget	GNP	Personnel

Note: All coefficients are Pearson's r coefficients.

ditures of China, and to a lesser degree, Germany and the Soviet Union.[8] All monetary data are converted to a common currency (US dollars) according to Correlates of War exchange rates.

The simplest and most straightforward way to compare the measures is by correlating them; table 4.3 gives these correlations. For indicators purporting to measure the same thing, the low correlations are striking; only two coefficients are greater than 0.40. This is surprising since four of the five indicators use the same military expenditure data and differ only in the measure of economic resources and the technique of construction. The low correlation between the system percentage and the stratified epochs methods illustrates the importance of construction technique since both indicators use exactly the same data (military expenditures, iron and steel production, and energy consumption). The popular GNP method is not highly correlated with either of those two indicators, but is highly associated with government budget and military personnel measures. Indeed, the GNP method yields the highest average correlation with the other indicators, but that average is still quite low (0.24). (The average correlation for other indicators is system percentage (−0.12), stratified epochs (0.03), budget (0.19), and personnel (0.19).)

One possible explanation for the low correlations of the stratified epochs approach is that a different regression line for each epoch (1861–1913, 1919–38, 1946–80) determines the indicator. Using this hint I calculated correlations for the indicators by epoch. Table 4.4 reveals that the correlations are much higher for the epochs individually than for the whole 120-year period. A broad overview of the results for the three periods indicates that World War II is a watershed since correlations are significantly lower (except for military personnel) before 1939.

[8] Missing data for government expenditure included 1861–70 and 1934–8 for Germany, and 1934–8 for the Soviet Union. In addition, there are missing data for Chinese government expenditures and GNP for many years between 1950 and 1980.

Table 4.4 *Correlations between indicators by epochs*

	System %	Epochs	Budget	GNP	Personnel
			1861–1913		
System %	1.00	−0.22	−0.14	0.13	−0.03
Epochs	−0.22	1.00	0.27	0.36	0.21
Budget	−0.14	0.27	1.00	0.23	0.16
GNP	0.13	0.36	0.23	1.00	0.87
Personnel	−0.03	0.21	0.16	0.87	1.00
			1919–1938		
System %	1.00	0.00	0.45	0.39	0.33
Epochs	0.00	1.00	0.44	0.78	0.14
Budget	0.45	0.44	1.00	0.66	−0.04
GNP	0.39	0.78	0.66	1.00	0.40
Personnel	0.33	0.14	−0.04	0.40	1.00
			1946–1980		
System %	1.00	0.76	0.31	0.5	0.44
Epochs	0.76	1.00	0.37	0.52	0.09
Budget	0.31	0.37	1.00	0.17	0.32
GNP	0.75	0.52	0.17	1.00	0.65
Personnel	0.44	0.09	0.32	0.65	1.00

Note: All coefficients are Pearson's r coefficients.

If one examines the changes over time in the various correlation coefficients it becomes quite clear why the correlations in table 4.3 are so low. The evolution of the indicators over time with respect to one another is non-linear. For example, the correlation between the GNP and government budget indicators goes from 0.23 in 1861–1913, to 0.66 in 1919–38, to 0.18 in 1946–80. The correlation between the system percentage and stratified epochs approaches varies from −0.22 to 0.00 to 0.76 over the same periods.

One possible explanation for the low overall correlations comes from the dependency of certain indicators on the composition of the major power subsystem, and hence sensitivity to its changes. These indicators change when countries enter and depart the major power subsystem even if the raw data themselves remain the same. Epoch cutoff points include World Wars I and II when dramatic changes occurred in the composition of the major power subsystem. The non-contextual indicators use only country-specific data and thus are not influenced by system changes.

That the baseline changes for the stratified epochs indicator (Diehl and Goertz 1985) suggests that this kind of change may occur in non-contextual

Table 4.5 *Changes in non-contextual indicators over time*

Indicator	1861–1913	1919–38	1946–80
Budget	0.07	0.20	0.31
	(0.05)	(0.16)	(0.16)
GNP	0.01	0.04	0.11
	(0.003)	(0.05)	(0.08)
Personnel	0.009	0.007	0.01
	(0.006)	(0.005)	(0.006)

Note: Standard errors are in parentheses.

indicators. One way to test this hypothesis is to see if the average values of these ratios increase or decrease dramatically over time. To investigate this possibility I used an ANOVA[9] to test if the means of the three epochs are equal; these results are given in table 4.5.

The average value for each non-contextual indicator has increased over time (the F-statistic is significant at 0.0001 in each case, except for military personnel, and the follow-up tests between individual means are significant at 0.01), although the rates of increase differ in each case. What Diehl and Goertz found to be the case with their regression lines holds for two of the three non-contextual indicators. The consequence is that these indicators are quite period dependent, what is high in one period is not necessarily so in another. A high level of spending in the nineteenth century is low for the twentieth: the meaning of spending 5 percent of GNP varies from 1850 to 1950. If one wants to make cross-temporal comparisons this will not be possible with these indicators as they now stand. The stratified epochs indicator alone takes explicitly into account the possibility that average military spending may change over time and allows for that change.

This shows that even if the ME/GNP indicator used exactly comparable data for military expenditures and GNP there would still be a validity problem. The strategy of the same indicator/same concept cell can produce invalid indicators. Exactly the same number produced with data generated from strictly comparable methods can mean different things in different periods: below normal spending in one period may be aggressive spending in another. Most of the data gathering and indicator construction effort in inter-

[9] Technically significance figures would not be correct since time series data for each country are included; hence error terms are probably not independent.

Table 4.6 *Classification agreement among the indicators*

	System %	Epochs	Budget	GNP	Personnel
System %	1.00	0.23	−0.04	0.40	0.20
Epochs	0.23	1.00	0.32	0.46	0.10
Budget	−0.04	0.32	1.00	0.33	0.02*
GNP	0.40	0.46	0.33	1.00	0.38
Personnel	0.20	0.10	0.02*	0.38	1.00

Note: Correlations are τ_β coefficients. χ^2 values are not given but were calculated and were significant at 0.001 except where noted by an asterisk, and these are significant at 0.05.

national relations focuses on the same/same cell, but this example suggests that contextual factors can also play a crucial role. These factors perhaps help explain the widely varying correlations coefficients in tables 4.3 and 4.4.

When attempting to determine if various indicators measure the same concept the concern is central tendencies, and hence the use of correlational techniques is normal. The situation under investigation here differs somewhat since researchers have been particularly concerned with countries that are spending abnormally large amounts on the military; in statistical terms, they have been interested in outliers. The previous analyses focused on the degree to which these indicators have the same central tendencies. I now move to an analysis of the degree to which they agree on which states are "over-" or "underspenders."

In this analysis each state's military allocation according to each indicator was classified as either "high," "average," or "low." As I noted above, some indicators inherently define normal levels of allocation and some do not. For those that do not, the mean value for the epoch was classified as "normal" (as we have seen an overall mean would have been invalid). The definition of low or high allocation was being more than $\frac{1}{2}$ to 1 standard deviations away from the mean; this varied according to epoch and indicator because in some cases outlying values distorted the variance. (This procedure is quite similar to the "centering" technique used in contextual voting models.) Each pair of indicators was then compared in a contingency table analysis in order to test the similarity of their classifications of military allocations; the tau-beta (τ_β) values in table 4.6 give a summary of the test results.

The agreement between indicators on the outlying values is clearly higher than their agreement on central tendency (compare with table 4.3), particularly between indicators using military expenditure data. Again the GNP indicator has the highest average correlation, though even it is not very high. As in previous analyses the tests were repeated for the three historical periods separately; in contrast to the results reported above, I did not find a regular increase over time in the level of agreement between the different measures. This is probably due to the fact that I have "historicized" the non-contextual indicators to take into account changes in spending patterns over time.

By contextualizing the non-contextual indicators the widely varying correlations between them have been somewhat stabilized. All the indicators have some face validity (otherwise they would not have been used in the literature). While one would not expect them to covary exactly, the widely changing correlations in table 4.4 are surprising. Contextualizing these indicators has not raised tremendously the correlations between them but has significantly reduced the variation in their correlations over time. This in itself is a desirable result, stable correlations allow the researcher to combine and choose among the indicators in a way that widely varying correlations do not permit. Stable correlations also make it possible to successfully estimate multiple indicator models (like those estimated in LISREL, see chapter 12 for an example of this technique).

One clear conclusion from these analyses is that these indicators measure different things. A second conclusion is that using the non-contextual indicators in a longitudinal analysis is not valid since what is high in the nineteenth century is low in the twentieth. The only indicator that takes this systematic temporal change into account is the stratified epochs measure which recalculates the indicator for each epoch.

A structural test

The literature using military allocation ratios treats primarily the question of whether "high-allocating" nations are more war-prone than other countries. I shall test all indicators using the hypothesis: Are militarized disputes involving overallocating states more likely to escalate to war than disputes involving average allocating states? Although the indicators considered here do not have high correlations, it remains to be seen what results they produce in this common hypothesis.

Militarized disputes are "a set of interactions between or among states involving threats to use military force, displays of military force, or actual use of military force ... these acts must be explicit, overt, non-accidental, and government sanctioned" (Gochman and Maoz 1984, p. 587). All disputes that resulted in 1,000 or more battle-related fatalities are coded as a "war"

Table 4.7 *Indicator performance in predicting escalation to war*

	Initiator		Target		Ratio	
Indicator	χ^2	τ_β	χ^2	τ_β	χ^2	τ_β
System %	0.00	0.01	0.01	0.01	3.63	−0.20
Epochs	8.33**	0.31**	9.78**	0.33**	9.00**	0.32**
Budget	0.10	−0.04	0.08	0.03	0.43	0.09
GNP	0.79	0.13**	4.44**	0.23**	0.03	0.02
Personnel	0.28	0.06	0.33	0.06	4.33*	−0.22**

Note: * Significant at 0.05; ** significant at 0.01.

(Small and Singer 1982). All those not satisfying this criterion are labeled "no war." (This is the same data set and coding rules discussed in the previous chapter.) The Correlates of War Project provided a list of major power militarized disputes and wars.

In order to conduct this test each state in each year was categorized as an "average" (including "low") or "high" allocator in the manner described above. Two-by-two contingency tables were constructed with the allocation level as the predictor variable,[10] and the war/no war outcome of the militarized dispute as the dependent variable. The analyses were performed for:

1 the initiator of the dispute (the nation committing the first military act).
2 the target of the dispute (the victim of the first military act).
3 the ratio of the allocation levels of the initiator (I) and the target (T), where the two categories were "equal" ($0.67I < T < 1.5I$) and "inequality" ($T < 0.67I$ or $T > 1.5I$).

Considering the results in table 4.7 the stratified epochs approach is the only one that strongly and consistently associates high allocations with disputes that escalate to war; the χ^2 and τ_β values are significant at 0.01 under all three testing conditions. The τ_β's for the GNP method are significant in two instances but at lower levels.

The remaining three indicators turn in a poor performance in predicting the escalation of disputes to war. One reason why the system percentage

[10] Military allocation values in this analysis come from the year *before* the militarized dispute in order to insure that the resources allocated are actually available at the time of the dispute and to eliminate any distortions from allocations that were a reaction to the confrontation.

method fared poorly was its inability to reflect large concurrent increases in military allocations. This indicator remains unchanged if all or most nations in the major power system increase their allocations; in fact the indicator only reflects differences in the growth rates of allocations and not the growth itself. This crucial flaw did not permit the indicator to pick up the militarization of the major power system before world wars. In short, it was not sensitive to the historical dimension of comparison. At least in this regard some of the non-contextual indicators proved better in the short term. That military personnel performed poorly does not surprise since this indicator showed the least variation of all those considered, and one might suspect that drastic changes in troop levels occur after, rather than before, the war begins (Mullins 1975).

From this analysis, it is not surprising that past research has produced a diversity of findings on the effects of high military allocation on conflict. The differences between the indicators employed by various scholars explain a large part of the discrepancy. Only the stratified epochs performed well in the structural analysis. The GNP method shows some promise if the ad hoc procedure used to define "high allocation" were refined, but this means contextualizing the basic ratio indicator.

One obvious caveat to the structural analysis: if in reality there is no relationship between overallocation and dispute escalation then the stratified epochs indicator is the worst of them all. Although I believe otherwise, a greater knowledge of military allocations and conflict is necessary before offering a more definitive interpretation.

Conclusion

What does this all mean in terms of context? One important consideration is the theoretical perspective. The most popular question involving military allocation ratios concerns the effect of spending "more than normal" on the escalation of disputes to war. This question is fundamentally comparative. The standard approach lets the regression analysis define "more than normal." Although never stated or justified, this means that the reference group is all nations involved in militarized disputes. "Too much" thus refers to a very special set of nations in years just before disputes and wars. Once stated in this fashion it becomes quite clear that this procedure is really not appropriate. Some of the indicators, such as the regression or system percentage, move in the correct direction by explicitly defining more than normal *vis-à-vis* the spending of *all* nations in the system, not just the dispute-prone ones.

"More than normal" also refers to what is standard for the particular country. Thus an important part of the comparison is historical. As the empirical analyses showed the system percentage approach did not deal with the historical context of military spending and for this reason failed to capture the increasing militarization of the major power subsystem itself. Only the stratified epochs indicator took both the cross-sectional and the longitudinal aspects of the comparison into account. As the analysis of the simple non-contextual ratio indicators illustrated, "overallocation" means different things in different periods. The relationship between, say, ME/GNP and the concept of overallocation is not constant but varies over time. Conceptualizing indicators is theorizing about these changing relationships.

In the structural analysis the most context sensitive indicator – stratified epochs – was the only one to strongly confirm the hypothesis that disputes involving overallocating states escalate more frequently to war. This indicator was the only one to take into account two contexts that I emphasize throughout this volume:

- the importance of what other nations do in defining the international context;
- the relevance of the historical context for understanding behavior.

Postscript for baseball fans

The importance of contextual analysis can arise in the most unexpected fashions: in the discussion of "the oldest chestnut of the hotstove league – the extinction of the .400 hitter" (Gould 1985, p. 215). Ted Williams batted .406 in 1941 making him the last hitter of the .400 club. The suggested reasons for the extinction of this species include: more gruelling schedules, night games, and the invention of the slider; the most romantic is that there are no longer any giants of the same caliber. Gould examined some of the more plausible explanations, particularly the one that the average hitting level has declined. He showed that with a few ups and downs the batting averages of the two leagues have remained around .260, and that in any case the fluctuations in the averages do not coincide with the disappearance of .400 hitters. He then proceeded to show that while the averages have remained quite stable there has been a clear trend in the *variance*[11] around that average. In earlier times there were much higher averages *but also much lower ones.* Gould argued that as the game has progressed many of the rough edges have disappeared and the gaps that a truly excellent player could exploit in the early days have vanished. He concludes: "Giants have not ceded to mere mortals. I'll bet anything that Carew could match Keeler. Rather, the boundaries of baseball have been restricted and its edges smoothed. The game has achieved a grace and precision of execution that has, as one effect, eliminated the extreme achievements of early years" (p. 225).

A clear theme that runs through this discussion is whether the great hitters of yore like Ruth and Williams are the equivalent of today's Brett and Carew. As with military allocation indicators and much of social science, the issue is cross-temporal comparisons. Gould argued that in the context of a much more sophisticated game today's hitters are as good as those of the past. A hidden assumption is that raw batting averages are the best way to make this particular historical comparison. With contextual theory in hand I can propose another measure, one similar to the regression strategy. For these purposes we can replace the non-contextual raw batting average with the distance, expressed in standard deviations, of a player's batting average from the league batting average. This penalizes the earlier player because he was surrounded by weaker players. Though Gould did not give variances, I suspect that this new measure would make Ted Williams a clear contender for the best hitter in the history of baseball, since by the 1940s the extremes of the earlier era had dramatically shrunk. Thus his .406 performance in 1941 would put him well above the common .400 hitters of the pre-1930 era. This technique would also make more clear the astonishing performances of George Brett and Rod Carew who batted respectively .390 in 1980 and .388 in 1977.

This example illustrates the potential problem with the common assumption that the same numbers have the same meanings: batting .400 changes from being a sign of a good hitter to a sign of being one of baseball's all-time best. Although we are all under very practical data constraints, with a little creativity we can devise new ways to roast old chestnuts.

[11] Strictly speaking Gould does not give the variance but instead the extreme values (highest and lowest averages), however these do indicate a larger variance.

5 RATIONAL ACTOR AND DIFFUSION MODELS

> A new [disease] has spread itself over Europe; it has infected our princes and induces them to keep an exorbitant number of troops. It ... of necessity becomes contagious. For as soon as one prince augments what he calls his troops, the rest of course do the same; so that nothing is gained thereby but the public ruin.
>
> Charles-Louis de Secondat, baron de Montesquieu, 1748 (p. 237)

> History teaches perhaps very few lessons. But surely one such lesson learned by the world at great cost is that aggression unopposed is a contagious disease.
>
> Jimmy Carter, 4 January 1980 (cited in Nossal 1989, p. 318)

Introduction

Explanations which underline the relevance of context often stress the spatial and temporal connections of a phenomenon. But alternative explanations usually coexist that downplay such factors. In this chapter I introduce two such contrasting theoretical frameworks. Diffusion models focus on environmental factors; as the name diffusion implies, this theory suggests that outside factors determine behavior. Rational actor models, on the other hand, focus on the individual, her beliefs and preferences, in order to explain actions and downplay environmental factors. These two major theoretical approaches serve to orient the discussion of different aspects of contextual analysis, and as such they will be constant companions in the chapters to come.

Rather than just discuss these theories in general I shall focus on their application to the study of war – war expansion in particular – in order to motivate and illustrate the differences between the two theories. The rational actor approach to international war – associated with names like Bueno de Mesquita – argues that contexts, historical, normative, and structural, are of limited importance. Diffusion models represented by the work of Most, Siverson, and Starr (in alphabetical order) claim that the local environment and history are important in explaining war. Rational actor models represent a major research effort clearly visible to all who study world politics. Diffusion models do not occupy the central ground in any one social science that rational models do in economics, nonetheless a glance through the social science literature will confirm that diffusion models are present in all disciplines from economics to sociology to geography.

Instead of an abstract and purely theoretical discussion of these theories, which would be complicated by each of their many variants, I shall present the two in the context of their application to one specific, but important, problem of international conflict: the question of war expansion – or more alliteratively "why wider wars?" The problem of war expansion – the process by which additional states become involved in conflict once it has already begun – has exercised scholars already for several decades, and a significant literature on the subject exists. The various expressions used to describe the problem give an idea of the different approaches to the subject, for example, conflict epidemiology (Beer 1979), war contagion and diffusion (Siverson and Starr 1991), choosing sides in conflict (Altfeld and Bueno de Mesquita 1979) and alliance reliability (Sabrosky 1976). I propose that these approaches can be classified using the rational actor and diffusion archetypes. At the same time these paradigms represent two quite different views on contextual issues. Thus the problem of wide wars offers an excellent occasion to introduce theories and issues that occupy the following chapters.

The diffusion approach emphasizes the importance of the context – spatial and temporal – of a conflict in explaining conflict expansion. The alternative approach uses rational actor models and downplays the importance of the surrounding environment. States actively decide to intervene in ongoing conflicts. Though the two approaches are not necessarily incompatible, in their pure form their emphases, metaphors, and orientations offer two radically differing views on world politics. The diffusion approach sees wars as spreading like an infectious disease over space to other countries or like a disease spreading over time in the same country, i.e., conflict addiction. The diffusion approach also implies that involvement comes from the outside environment as indicated by language like "being drawn into a conflict" or "conflicts expanding or spreading." This kind of language implies a war expansion process where the actor is relatively passive *vis-à-vis* its environment which determines who gets involved in war. The alternative comes from the realist and rational actor traditions where states intervene in ongoing conflicts for specific security and other reasons. Conflicts from this point of view do not "spread," but rather states actively decide to become involved based on their beliefs and desires. These two paradigms are, in fact, approaches to the study of war and international politics in general. I shall discuss their application to the problem of wider wars but I think their theoretical extension to other problems will be clear.

Surprisingly, given the focus of this volume, a major contention of this chapter is that the diffusion framework – particularly in the war contagion form – poses many problems in understanding war expansion, and when pushed tends to transform itself into realism. Therefore these two approaches are not treated "equally." More space will be given to the diffusion approach – criticism tends to be longer than praise – than to the intervention approach. The rational actor framework is in the main stream of world politics, hence just representative studies are cited to establish its principal characteristics. Nevertheless, the rational actor approach does not escape criticism, since notably the strong points of the diffusion approach correspond to weaknesses of the other.

But the diffusion approach has much to teach about the importance of context. This chapter describes some of the pitfalls of an overemphasis on the environment as a factor, but the next chapter uses diffusion models to understand how system structure as a barrier influences states. The model of context as barrier draws heavily on the methodology of diffusion models, but modified theoretically and methodologically by goal-oriented facets of rational actor models. This chapter stresses the relative strength of the rational actor approach, but the chapters to come use diffusion models as a starting point to examine some of the underemphasized and weak points of rational actor models.

The various contextual analyses that are the heart of this book attempt to draw on the strengths of the two approaches, which are in many ways complementary. As a result rational actor and diffusion models will reappear throughout this volume; additional characteristics of the two will be introduced and emphasized in later chapters as they become relevant. I do not attempt to adjudicate between the two in general, but rather I use them as inspiration for thinking about how states interact with various contexts. In the theoretical chapters on norms, barriers, and historical contexts, diffusion and rational models will play important roles as I compare and contrast contextual notions with them.

Table 5.1 *Comparing diffusion and rational actor approaches to war expansion*

Criterion	Diffusion	Rational actor
Power	no	yes
Independent events	no	yes
Side as issue	no	yes
Focus	involvement	winning
Methodology	epidemiology	game theory
History	yes	no
Subject	passive	active
Affect	negative	positive
Source	anthropology	economics
Alliance joining	bandwagoning	balancing
Unit of analysis	state	war

Note: "No" – not theoretically emphasized, "Yes" – theoretically emphasized.

The differences between the diffusion and rational actor approaches on a variety of methodological and theoretical criteria are summarized in table 5.1. This table serves as a guide to the topics that I shall discuss in comparing the application of the two approaches to the war expansion problem. If diffusion models and rational actor models tend to take different positions on the role of power, on whether events are independent of each other over time and space, on the unit of analysis, affect, etc., then there is justification for qualifying them as different paradigms for the analysis of international politics.

Diffusion and rational actor models

War diffusion and war contagion are close theoretical companions. Rare are war diffusion studies that do not at some point adopt the disease metaphor. The disease metaphor has been around for a long time. Montesquieu, in the quote that begins this chapter, already captures its essence. More recently Jimmy Carter used similar terms in his reaction to the Soviet invasion of Afghanistan (my second introductory quote). The contagion metaphor provides in stark terms some of the characteristics of the diffusion approach. Disease – like war – is "bad" for human beings, though it may be an inevitable part of the human condition; perhaps scientific research can prevent war or mitigate its effects like scientific research has done for many diseases; war – like disease – is a process not completely under human control. The affect of the disease metaphor is negative; disease is not good, like war. A healthy body does not have disease, likewise healthy societies do not engage in war. The war contagion metaphor is at the other end of the spectrum from the Clausewitzian notion of war as politics by other means. War as disease is abnormal politics.

The diffusion approach, although having the basic characteristics of the contagion approach, makes fewer normative and affective evaluations of war. Its origins are also different since these models come from anthropology (originating in Galton's problem, Ross and Homer 1976) and the study of the acquisition of cultural traits. The concept of diffusion in sociology and anthropology is often more positive and less passive than the epidemiological metaphor because it involves theories of cultural and social learning or, more pejoratively, imitation. The movement of people, ideas, and the mass media play important roles as a means of knowledge diffusion, see for example the literature on the spread of domestic violence (e.g., Pitcher, Hamblin, and Miller 1978; Midlarsky 1970; 1978).

Most, Starr, and Siverson (1989) reviewed the literature on war diffusion as part of a larger survey of major approaches to the study of war. It is worth citing the beginning of their chapter at some length:

> In the late nineteenth century Galton pointed out that phenomena tend to diffuse from one locale to another ...
>
> In the empirical literature, the earliest suggestion that warfare might diffuse was made by Richardson. Richardson attempted to construct a mathematical model that would adequately account for the number of nations on each side of a war. The assumptions making up Richardson's best-fitting model were essentially that the number of nations on each side in a war was the outcome of a process heavily influenced by *geography* and modified by *infection* ...
>
> More recently, inquiry into the possibility of war diffusion has become a central focus of research, and the investigations have moved considerably beyond Richardson's data and methods. The use of other data sets on war has permitted the exploration of the extent to which the process of diffusion is general across different conceptions and measures of warfare. Moreover, better methodologies have allowed the more recent research to demonstrate that apparent "infection" can be produced by any one of several processes, and that some of these are non-infectious in character.
>
> The first question is this: Through what process does war appear to spread? As noted previously, there are several ways to conceptualize "diffusion." Different conceptualizations lead to, and derive from, different

> models of the diffusion process. We will begin, as did Richardson, with those models most closely associated with "infection" or the growth of an ongoing war. (pp. 112–13, citations removed, emphasis is the authors')

Bueno de Mesquita's (1989) contribution to the same survey of the war literature illustrates many of the features of the rational actor approach:

> A common theme runs throughout the classics of international relations. That theme is the self-interested pursuit of gain by national leaders on their own behalf and on behalf of their nations. This is also the theme of research concerned with exchanges in markets. Indeed, Adam Smith's description of the operation of markets as an invisible hand guiding production and investment decisions through self-interested choice is a widely used description of the interaction of nations. Here, I apply a version of that perspective – expected-utility theory – to the study of international conflict ...
>
> For instance, we know that great powers engage in warfare far more often than do lesser states, particularly as third-party participants to ongoing wars. It would be beneficial to have an explanation of this observation that is compatible with a broad array of other phenomena.
>
> The decision to enter an ongoing war is, as I demonstrate formally later in this essay, a function of the intensity of one's preferences for the goals of the combatants. It is also a function of one's perceived prospect of influencing the outcome. (pp. 143 and 147, citations removed)

One major difference between these frameworks is that in the rational actor framework the subject is active *vis-à-vis* its environment; it does not submit passively to surrounding events but actively seeks the war disease. States intervene, they are purposeful agents. This is clear in the language used; in the diffusion literature "war" spreads; in the rational actor perspective governments spread war by their decisions. Thus the semantics of the active versus passive voice are pregnant with theoretical implications. (The preference in social science prose for the passive voice has some subliminal effect here?)

Related to the active versus passive distinction and another major difference between the two is the positive affect of rational choice and the negative affect of catching a disease. Much of the diffusion literature in sociology and anthropology argues that actors "imitate" others, that they are subject to fashion, all of which produces a distinctly negative affect. The rational actor approach gives agency back to the state since decision-makers are confronting their environment and making the best possible choice under the circumstances.

Another significant difference between the two approaches is the importance attached to the concept of power. One of the consequences of the realist revolution after World War II was to make power the central concept in understanding international politics. An inspection of the diffusion literature reveals that the concept of power is notable by its absence (though not always, see below). In the realist school power is in some sense a means of achieving goals, how one state prevails over another when interests conflict. The emphasis of the diffusion approach on patterns of spreading conflict hides the adversarial nature of international conflict.

A corollary of the absence of power is the absence of an emphasis on winning or losing. According to the realist view nations act in order to promote national goals that conflict with goals of other states. Incompatible objectives such as the common desire to possess a piece of territory produce conflict. War is one way of deciding such zero-sum situations. Diffusion is in a peculiar way non-zero sum, war may spread or may not; there is no victory or defeat, just more or less conflict.

When countries face an ongoing conflict they are not indifferent to which side they prefer; for various reasons they will be much more likely to intervene for one side than the other. As Bueno de Mesquita suggests, states want to influence the outcome of a conflict in their favor. This preference for one side is on the contrary not central in the diffusion approach. States catch the disease from the war itself, it is not the participants that *individually* spread it. The conflict as a whole is the causal agent.

The diffusion approach starts with the fundamental question: "Are conflicts correlated over time and space?" If there is no pattern to the occurrence of war, if wars are a series of independent, scattered events, then a diffusion explanation is impossible. If, on the other hand, conflicts are correlated over time and space then this opens the door to diffusion explanations. Posing the question does not commit the researcher to the diffusion framework (e.g., Singer and Small 1974). But, nevertheless, this question is the starting point for diffusion analyses.

On the other hand, this is an irrelevant question from the rational actor point of view. Here, there is no central question, but rather a nexus of similar sorts of questions. Altfeld and Bueno de Mesquita (1979) ask about "choosing sides," Sabrosky (1976) about alliance reliability, and Yamamoto (1974) about intervention following the precepts of balance-of-power theory. Balance-of-power theory is a particularly apt example of reasons why a conflict might spread from a rational actor perspective. Instead of the generally negative connotation of diffusion theory, balance-of-power theory recommends intervention in unbalanced conflicts with the aim of preventing the rise of a system-wide hegemon. From the rational actor point of view conflicts may well be correlated over space and time, but these are *spurious correlations*, the result of, say, balance-of-power behavior of nations that when aggregated is correlated.

Diffusion models are very closely related to the concept of bandwagoning. The bandwagoning versus balancing hypothesis has generated a number of studies (Walt 1987; Synder 1991; Christensen and Synder 1990). Though one can develop self-interest, rational actor models of bandwagoning, the image of jumping on the bandwagon suggests spur-of-the-moment behavior. When does one jump on the bandwagon? When one sees others doing so, often without much reflection. This is precisely the imitative behavior that diffusion models often describe. On the other hand, balancing behavior implies a *calculation* of relative weights and a decision to go against the trend.

To test whether conflicts are related over time and space one needs a model of independent events. The classic discrete model of independent events is the Poisson distribution (the continuous analog is the exponential, Feller 1967). This model is used for counting the number of events occurring in a period when each event is independent. Thus if the number of conflicts occurring, for example, in the international system can be modeled by this distribution then the implication is that there is no conflict diffusion. Against this null hypothesis model is an alternative hypothesis of conflict diffusion where the parameter of the Poisson distribution is defined as changing depending on, for example, the number of conflicts in the region. Thus the likelihood of war depends on the amount of ongoing war. It is virtually always the case that the independence model does not fit well, and that the alternative diffusion model fits better (e.g., Davis, Duncan, and Siverson 1978; Yamamoto 1974). Poisson modeling techniques give methodological unity to the diffusion framework.

These models are not only used to study the diffusion of international conflicts, but they are also used to examine the diffusion of domestic conflict (Pitcher, Hamblin, and Miller 1978) and "coup contagion" (Li and Thompson 1975). Epidemiologists also use such techniques in modeling the spread of contagious disease. The importance of the diffusion framework thus goes beyond a simple choice of words, it often carries with it some methodological baggage. It is not surprising that where the diffusion metaphor is used the same kinds of models appear. It is not, of course, necessary to use these techniques, others such as simple correlation (Levy

1982), time-series methods (Davis, Duncan, and Siverson 1978), or contingency tables (Most and Starr 1980) have also been used.

The methodology of the intervention approach tends to come from game and decision theory. A game theoretic approach emphasizes the strategic and tactical issues facing a potential intervener. Should it intervene? For which side? What is the probability of success? A good example of this is given by Altfeld and Bueno de Mesquita (1979) who used an expected-utility model to predict which nations will intervene and for which side. The decision to intervene is based on power calculations, (i.e., the likelihood of prevailing in the conflict) and the relative preference of a potential intervener for one side *vis-à-vis* the other. Unlike the diffusion approach where conflicts are related to each other, expected-utility models consider each decision to intervene as theoretically and statistically independent of all past and current conflicts.

Turning from large overarching theoretical issues, it is interesting to compare what each approach defines as a "case" or the unit of analysis. This fundamental aspect of research design reveals the basic underlying orientations of these frameworks. Most and Starr (1980), for example, used as their basic unit of analysis war participations of individual states; the question of which war the state participates in does not arise, nor does the question of side. In a similar manner Davis, Duncan, and Siverson (1978) look at conflicting dyads. A "war" may be one conflicting dyad, or many conflicting dyads in the case of the world wars; for them this distinction is unimportant. Similarly, Levy (1982) looks at war contagion by aggregating individual conflicts at the system level and correlating aggregate conflict over time. From the rational actor perspective, a country intervenes for a specific side in a particular conflict; the unit of analysis is a nation's intervention decision in a given conflict.

Diffusion studies do make however an important point, one all too often ignored by those who do work in the rational actor perspective. Conflicts are *not* independent of each other; to focus only the current "conflict" and ignore its ties to earlier conflicts and to other conflicts in the region is certainly myopic, and a distortion of political relationships which are not quite so nicely broken up into bite-sized pieces. Conflicts are not atomistic events, but rather they are part of a web of spatio-temporal relations. Inspection of the major journals or work coming out of projects like the Correlates of War reveals that this essential point has often been ignored by quantitative work in international relations in general.

This brief survey of the differences (summarized in table 5.1) between rational actor and diffusion approaches to the problem of war expansion indicates the many important facets of theory, research design, and methodology about which these two paradigms take contrasting views. These differences illustrate many important issues of contextual analysis. For example, to argue that contexts matter is to argue that historical factors have an important role in understanding international war. The diffusion approach to war expansion systematically emphasizes those factors. We shall see in chapter 9 that close to 50 percent of all wars and militarized disputes occur within the context of enduring rivalries. This suggests that wars are connected to each other over time: a position that fits easily into the diffusion framework but less well into the rational actor approach.

One consequence of the emphasis on context is to move the explanatory focus away from individuals to environments. According to the rational actor view the cause of an event is located in the individual: beliefs plus desires are the *cause* of behavior (Elster 1986, p. 12). Beliefs in Bueno de Mesquita's expected utility model are represented by relative power relationships (i.e., the likelihood of prevailing in an eventual war). What if those beliefs (power relationships) change because of a dramatic power shock (e.g., regional war)? Then a country's expected utility may jump; hence it may become rational to intervene in an ongoing conflict (Most and Starr 1980). What is the "cause" of the intervention? The limited vision of the rational actor view says it is still beliefs and desires; but it would be legitimate to say that the regional war caused the intervention, which is the way the diffusion model would express it. With the understanding of cause given in chapter 2 this is completely justified since the regional war increased the likelihood of intervention. Thus there are ways in which diffusion models can be complementary and not contradictory to rational actor models. This helps explain the existence of mixed models.

Mixed models

Once it has been shown that conflicts are correlated over space, that conflict contagion or diffusion is a possible explanation, the question naturally arises about how conflict spreads or about the mechanisms of contagion. Like in epidemiology there needs to be an individual-level model of how conflict is spread across sample units. In medicine this was the great triumph of the germ theory of disease; interpersonal contact of various sorts transmits disease. Each disease has its own mechanism which must be discovered, the analogous problem must be resolved for the diffusion model of international conflict to be convincing. The reason for studies of a mixed sort is that if pushed a little the diffusion framework starts to transform itself into realism and loses its specific character. This comes out clearly once a study moves beyond the stage of correlation over space or time. When it comes to the *mechanisms of diffusion*, diffusion models start sounding like realism. Davis, Duncan, and Siverson (1978) consistently used probability models and the diffusion framework. Siverson and King (1979) in a follow-up article examined the "agents of contagion" or how the contagion mechanism works. The agent they investigated was alliances, which they saw as "deliberate choices in which nations make commitments to each other," a rather realist view of alliances; the paragraph ends with "One may reasonably investigate, then, the extent to which these commitments draw nations into wars" (p. 38), a more passive, diffusion image of alliances. Bueno de Mesquita (1981) used alliances and their configuration as a measure of current preferences. The diffusion perspective suggests that alliances may *draw* nations into war, implying that alliances may not be useful and, in fact, may be dysfunctional. Clearly alliances can take on active or passive interpretations.

One of the most notable characteristics of the diffusion approach is the absence of the concept of power. This absence inversely matches the importance that the concept of power holds in the realist perspective. Most and Starr (1980) used the concept of power as an important facet of a diffusion model of conflict expansion. They argued that changes in power due to recent wars may change the likelihood a state will become involved in future conflict. Conflicts are related to each other because virtually by definition they change the relative power of the countries involved: "For example, if a nation shifts from conditional to unconditional viability as a result of a war between other nations, it may join the conflict or initiate a war of its own in a process of positive spatial diffusion" (p. 936). Here changes in power levels incite nations to intervene; power shifts may make war involvement more likely. However, the opposite may also occur. One result of the Vietnamese victory in 1975 was to make it the most powerful country in Southeast Asia and perhaps inciting it to intervene in Cambodia, while the defeat of the US may have inhibited it from intervening in Angola. For Bueno de Mesquita power relationships are a given, for Starr and Most they are a *consequence* of war and hence condition future conflict. Most and Starr try to endogenize power relationships that Bueno de Mesquita takes as exogenous. Under this interpretation the war diffusion perspective complements and could strengthen the expected utility model. The important question then arises about the extent to which diffusion explanations differ from rational actor ones.[1] The rational actor model responds that the emphasis on diffusion is misleading because war diffusion is simply changing opportunity structures.

From a methodological point of view the use of probability models distinguishes the diffusion approach. These same models can be justified on realist grounds. For example, Yamamoto (1974) used Poisson techniques to model the expansion of major power war. As usual in the rational actor perspective, but unlike the diffusion methodology, each individual conflict was a separate case, it was not diffusion *across* wars but *within* a given one. He argued, based on balance-of-power theory, that the probability that another major power will intervene depends on the number of major powers that have already intervened. Given the limited number of major powers, the decision to intervene on the part of one increases the likelihood that others will intervene. Yet, like diffusion models he was not concerned about which side the nation intervenes for, thus he did not test whether major powers are actually intervening to balance power. This use of probability models as an interpretation of balance-of-power theories is not limited to conflict expansion, they have also been used to study alliance behavior (Yamamoto 1974; McGowan and Rood 1975).

There is a temptation to view context as a larger encompassing environment within which nations exist. However there is nothing in the concept(s) of context that obliges one to consider it only in this light. An important substantive context is domestic politics. Be it the form of government (e.g., democratic, communist, dictatorial) or the level of civil strife, there are a variety of different domestic factors that have been investigated as causes of external war. Related to this in the war expansion literature is the possibility of war diffusion from the internal to the international realm. There are numerous examples of civil wars that eventually become what Small and Singer (1982) call "internationalized civil wars," e.g., the Vietnamese, Laotian, and Cambodian wars. The diffusion,

[1] In their more recent work Most, Starr, and Siverson (1989) explicitly argue that their diffusion approach *is* compatible with an expected utility framework: "Nothing in this discussion of diffusion using the concepts of opportunity and willingness is inconsistent with the approach contained in expected utility" (p. 135). I would remark that "opportunity" corresponds to Bueno de Mesquita's "probability of success" and that "willingness" corresponds to his "preferences." But this again illustrates the point that the analysis of the mechanisms of diffusion leads to realism and that the distinctive character of the diffusion framework begins to fade.

however, does not run just in one direction, but in both. States involved in international wars are often weakened, thus providing the occasion for domestic conflict. For example, the Russian Revolution and civil war followed in the wake of Russian defeats in World War I (Skocpol 1979). The diffusion approach blurs the boundaries between conflicts, thus a plausible extension de-emphasizes the boundaries between "international" and "domestic" military conflicts.

It is interesting to note that some work in the war expansion literature implicitly ignores or minimizes the distinction between domestic and international conflicts. The studies by Tillema and Van Wingen (1982), Eckhardt and Azar (1978), and Pearson (1974) all treated in their universe of cases many incidents where outside powers intervened in domestic struggles. What distinguishes these studies is the definition of intervention. For example, Pearson (1974, p. 435) defined an intervention as "any organized border crossing"; or Tillema and Van Wingen (1982, p. 234) "we specify military intervention to be the beginning of military acts by the official armed forces of one state beyond its own borders and within the territory of another country." These definitions have the disadvantage of including all two-party international wars as "interventions." No longer does intervention mean a *third* party involvement in an ongoing war. But, if the conflict is a civil war then this definition corresponds to the internationalization of the conflict and is legitimately an intervention. War diffusion also means the spread of domestic war into the international realm and vice versa.

These few examples have indicated – and they could easily be multiplied – that many combinations of the theoretical and methodological characteristics of these two frameworks are possible, and in fact examples for a large number can be found. The movement toward realist and rational actor models indicates, I believe, that diffusion models are not very suited to the study of international conflict. If one looks at where these models originated – in anthropology and epidemiology – they tend to deal with effects propagated through the action of many individuals. In particular they seem appropriate for the social sciences in the context of learning or imitation. It makes sense to talk about the diffusion of cultural traits or the diffusion of technology but not the diffusion of conflict.

Contextual analysis

A wide range of studies support the spatial diffusion hypothesis. War does tend to appear in clusters. One merit of the diffusion approach has been to signal this important phenomenon, which requires explanation. Even if these are spurious correlations an explanation is necessary. A good theory of war will be able to account for the clustering of war. But war is not the only event that occurs in clusters. Diffusion models suggest that other potentially important international phenomena are spatially and temporally related (Starr has used the diffusion framework to study the process of democratization (1991)). Barrier models developed in the next chapter attempt to provide one solution to this puzzle. They emphasize that the behavior of other states in the system is crucial in understanding this important class of phenomena. These models borrow from diffusion theory since they emphasize how states interact with and learn from each other. For example, oil nationalizations (chapter 7) occurred in an avalanche because leaders learned that what had previously been difficult or impossible was now achievable at moderate cost. Diffusion of nationalization policies was the result of goal-oriented behavior, but that learning dynamic is quite foreign to most rational actor analyses which either assume perfect information or make assumptions about imperfect information approaching the correct on the average (Bayesian methods or rational expectations). Diffusion and contextual models both emphasize the importance of the spatial context in understanding international relations. Both argue against an atomistic view of events and for models that relate events to each other.

The diffusion approach's attentiveness to the impact of the external environment and history on states makes this perspective quite attractive. It is perhaps a widely accepted fact that the world constrains the nations that live in it, but little in most analyses reflects this belief. The rational actor approach on the contrary emphasizes the importance of the individual actor and her beliefs and preferences in explaining international behavior. For these theories the international system is a given, actors attempt to maximize their payoffs in a world with given preferences and structures. Symptomatic of this is Bueno de Mesquita's (1981) expected-utility model which is in fact a *game against nature* (Bueno de Mesquita and Lalman 1992 analyze an interaction model). Given a distribution of power and preferences, nations attempt to maximize their utilities. They do the best they can given the situation in which they find themselves. System structure in this sense is not a cause but rather a constraint in a maximization calculus. (Game theory of course adds a strategic dimension, but even there the structure of the game is exogenous.)

Rational actor models typically consider constraints and preferences as exogenous. War diffusion models suggest that constraints change and that understanding changing constraints is at least as important (or more) than the rational decision-making calculus. Starr, Most, and Siverson suggest that the "givenness" of the environment needs to be explained and that it has an important causal impact. In the discussion of barrier models I shall argue that the key factor in explaining dramatic change is the collapse of barriers to change: as long as barriers are firm states behave in one fashion but act in another when the barrier is crumbling. For example, once it became *possible* to nationalize oil many countries did so. This suggests that the "passive" character of the diffusion models is not completely inappropriate. If countries have no choice, if they are confronted with overwhelming power structures, then they are relatively passive, or at least they have little control. But I shall also argue that not all governments were "passive," some struggled against the system, even if their struggles were often in vain.

Rational models consider preferences as given, contextual models in various ways try to understand how preference structures are created and modified by the actions of the members of the system. For example, the normative environment discussed in later chapters is a creation of states – in particular large states – but at the same time that normative system acts upon all states in the system. As norms change so do preferences. The chapters on oil nationalization and decolonization emphasize the changing character of preferences over time.

One aspect of the contagion metaphor is "addiction" to conflict. Diffusion studies generally fail to show that conflicts are correlated over time within the same unit – be it individual, dyad, or global system. However, our historical knowledge indicates that wars are frequently related to each other, as illustrated by the continuing Arab–Israeli and India–Pakistan conflicts. Clearly certain countries or pairs of countries are repeatedly involved in conflict. Other countries or dyads, on the contrary, rarely conflict; they are immunized to conflict. By emphasizing the correlation of conflict over time war diffusion models seem to be pointing at an important problem, their merit is to suggest that we look at the temporal relations between conflicts and wars.

Again the diffusion framework points to a significant phenomenon. The diffusion model does not find correlations because its metaphors point the researcher in the wrong direction. With the sports metaphor of "rivalry" it becomes quite easy to show that conflicts are related over time. The analysis of "enduring rivalries" in chapter 10 shows that about half of the wars and militarized interstate disputes since 1816 have taken place within the context of a rivalry. Thus diffusion models while not providing the correct answer suggest avenues of research generally ignored by the rational actor framework.

The rational actor approach tends to be quite future oriented and does not emphasize how events are historically related (this is not necessarily or always the case, e.g., Morrow 1989). Rational calculators ignore sunk costs: past decisions should not influence current ones. The previous chapter showed that historical context was crucial in developing good indicators of military allocation ratios. Later the historical context plays an important role in the study of international norms. The temporal aspect of diffusion models points toward important contexts of state behavior excluded from the field of vision of many rational actor models.

Part of contextual analysis stresses the importance of factors taken as exogenous by rational actor models, such as beliefs about the world and preferences. A rational actor will often change her behavior when the environment changes. If environmental changes (e.g., regional war) cause a change in her beliefs about the world then those environmental changes are *a cause* of her changed behavior. Contextual analysis suggests a more balanced view of the factors that influence behavior; it completes and complements rational actor analysis. But contextual analysis also challenges some implicit assumptions of rational actor models. For example, barrier models borrow from diffusion models the idea that preferences are formed partially through group pressure and imitation. "Imitation" and "bandwagoning" do not fit well with the image of a rational actor with a coherent, stable, and consistent preference system, but suggest rather that desires are volatile and possibly contradictory.

Diffusion models have produced empirical findings and suggested hypotheses that must be addressed, and which rational actor models with their emphasis only on individual and dyadic decision-making (and other individual-level effects like imperfect information) have failed to attack directly. Symbolic of this is that Bueno de Mesquita (1981) uses system structure and its changes as a *measure* of belief uncertainty and not as a causal or contextual variable in its own right.

6 BARRIER MODELS OF CONTEXT

Paul Thibaud – Quelle liberté voulez-vous fabriquer?
Pierre Bourdieu – La réponse que je fais est d'une extrême banalité, peut-être simplement parce qu'elle est vraie: une des voies de liberté, c'est de savoir un peu mieux les constraintes auxquelles on est inévitablement soumis. A partir de cette liberté-là, on peut être un petit peu libérateur.

Pierre Bourdieu (1992, p. 6)

P.T. – What liberty would you like to create?
P.B. – My response is extremely banal, maybe because it is true: one of the ways to freedom is to know a little better the constraints under which we inevitably live. With this we can become a little bit liberators ourselves. (The translation is my own.)

Introduction

War diffusion research has shown that wars and military conflict do not occur "randomly" or "sporadically" but rather cluster in time and space. Many important events and changes in the international system have the same character:

conflicts and wars in Europe, 1907–18
nationalization of oil, 1971–76
"waves" of democratization, 1980s and 1990s
"coup contagion," military coups in Latin America and Africa, 1950s and 1960s
independence of African colonies, 1950s and 1960s
bank lending to South American governments, mid 1960s to mid 1970s.

All these events were rapid changes in the international system which occurred over a short period of time. The independence of most of the

English, French, and Belgian African colonies took place within a short period of about ten years. The world was fascinated by the rapidity with which Eastern European peoples overthrew their communist governments. Events that constitute dramatic change often occur in quick succession in many different countries. Considering these and other similar cases leads to the general question:

> What can explain explosive, rapid change in international politics?

The question I pose is whether there is some framework that permits us to better understand how change spreads rapidly throughout the system, change which usually happens unexpectedly and takes contemporary observers by surprise.

Yet dramatic change is a relatively rare event. Explaining this phenomenon also means explaining why dramatic change occurs infrequently. We live most of our lives in stable, slowly evolving environments. We tend to view change in an incremental "linear" fashion; as a practical rule we have little experience with exponential change. Why is it that revolutions of all sorts seldom arise? One way in which we intuitively think about the rareness of dramatic change is with the "barrier" family of metaphors. Be they "gates," "walls," 'iron curtains," or "dams", one often hears about barriers to change. I propose that it is valuable to take seriously the barrier metaphor.

What are the barriers to change in international affairs? To understand the process of explosive change one must move beyond the metaphor to ask about the builders of barriers. An obvious answer lies in the character of power relations. Powerful actors build obstacles to change because they benefit from the status quo. The cases that shall occupy the next two chapters involve relatively powerless groups, Eastern European peoples and Third World governments, faced with powerful adversaries who had created the status quo and strove to maintain it.

Individuals often face hostile environments. The environment provides a common context in which powerless groups live and in which they try to survive. They live in a hierarchical power relationship of dominance–subservience. Barrier metaphors have a "vertical" character; barriers are on "top" and individuals "below." In my terms they consist in relations between governments and the international context, a context consisting of structures that constrain the opportunity set of leaders. Understanding barriers means analyzing power relationships, how they prevent change most of the time, but also how when they break down the opportunity for change can emerge (see Knight 1992 for a similar conception of power).

Another common set of metaphors that journalists and analysts used to describe the revolutions in Eastern Europe were contagion and diffusion ones. One way change accelerates is from people jumping on the bandwagon. The basic psychological insight is that "everyone loves a winner" (like lovers). In elections once the outcome is clear some people vote for the winner who would have voted otherwise; the result is a "landslide" victory. As the bandwagon gets going its "momentum" increases (Adler 1981). We often use the momentum metaphor to describe social movements. Related images are explosions, chain reactions, and snowballing. Disease spreads through individual contact; at a certain point an epidemic breaks out. For example, one explanation of World War I is that since the pre-war period was one of increasing bipolarization, when war broke out it spread in a chain reaction along alliance lines (Sabrosky 1975). Also Siverson and Starr (1991) have studied in detail alliances as means of war diffusion. They quite explicitly see war being propagated along alliance ties. Common to all these metaphors is a process which begins with only a few, sporadic events, but that within a short period of time reaches a critical point, resulting in an explosion or a bandwagon/snowball out of control.

I propose a "barrier model" that takes elements of this individual-to-individual diffusion model and combines it with one focusing on the individual's interaction with a barrier whose character is changing (or not). In addition to the emphasis on individual-to-individual interactions characteristic of diffusion models, barrier models focus on the interaction between the individual and the power structures in which it acts. The barrier model argues for certain ways of viewing the structure of the international system and its importance in explaining state behavior. I suggest that much explosive change occurs as a response to a changing international context. When certain barriers weaken or disappear then nationalizing oil or removing communist governments suddenly become possible.

In the last chapter I suggested that war diffusion models could link up with expected utility models through endogenizing the relative power variable of the expected utility model. One part of barrier models emphasizes how changing opportunity structures can cause behavioral change. It was also in this sense that regional war could be a major cause of war expansion. In fact, regional war could become the major explanatory variable in a rational actor model:

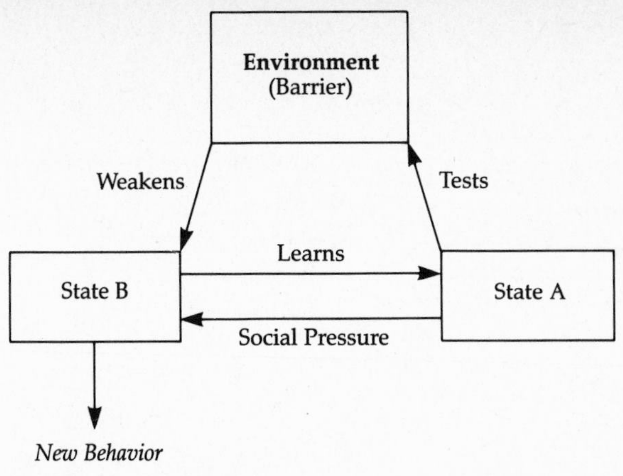

Figure 6.1 Barrier model

> Scholars disagree on the relative importance of preferences and opportunities in explaining behavior. Some economists argue that all people have essentially the same preferences and desires: only opportunities differ. Although usually staunch defenders of rational choice theory, they are led, paradoxically, to argue that choice almost doesn't matter because variation in behavior must be explained by variations in opportunity. (Elster 1989b, p. 15)

Barrier models stress the importance of changing opportunity structures in explaining explosive change; in this regard they draw on both war diffusion and rational actor models.

But barrier models stress two *processes* commonly left out of rational actor models. One is the dynamic of the learning process. If power relationships vary because of regional war then decision-makers must perceive, interpret, and learn about the new state of affairs before their behavior changes. States learn by watching what other states do as well as by their own actions: they learn from each other and their own past experience. This is the individual–individual dynamic that the diffusion framework emphasizes. Governments learn by watching what other governments do and by trying out new policies themselves that the constraints under which they operate are not constant but changing. In the oil nationalization case the oil-producing states were very interested observers of the Libyan and Algerian negotiations with the oil companies. When they later "imitated" them it was because they had learned that a desirable goal was achievable at modest cost.

The second process not included in the rational actor perspective is the changing preferences of the actors involved. To finish Elster's paragraph quoted above: "Most social scientists, however, believe that people differ in their desires as well as in their opportunities, and this view seems to me so obviously right as not to require further defense." In particular one essential aspect of the explosive character of these changes is that at a critical point in the process foreign policy goals change. For example, it is radical, nationalistic states that attempt, successfully or not, oil nationalization in the pre-1970 period, but at the point when the process takes off conservative states adopt this new behavior – often with some reluctance. Part of the revolution is that conservative states become convinced that they *should* control oil resources. Goals and preferences are also transformed by contact with the environment, it is not just rational calculation in a new situation.

Barrier models are doubly contextual, states react *both* to the barrier and to other states in the same situation *vis-à-vis* the barrier. As illustrated in figure 6.1 State B actively learns from State A's tests of the barrier, it learns not only facts about the likelihood and costs of success but eventually new goals. At the same time governments are subject to social pressure to conform: eventually even Saudi Arabia and Kuwait nationalize their oil. As the rational actor model argues, states actively interact with and test their environment as symbolized by the arrow from State A to the "environment" (see figure 6.1). At the same time, State B is constrained by the barrier which limits its options, here the arrow goes from the environment to State B. As in the diffusion framework, State B is more passive *vis-à-vis* the environment, the extreme case being, as Elster states, that it has no choice. Frequently the barrier and the "lessons learned" reinforce each other to maintain the status quo, but as the barrier weakens – either for exogenous reasons or endogenously as a result of pressure from states like A – State B is led to choose a new behavior.

This chapter describes in detail one specification of the third mode of contextual analysis: context as barrier. The model rests on a counterfactual proposition about what governments would do in an international system without certain constraints. Because barriers are counteracting forces they only make sense if there is a preexisting force to counteract. Barrier models make assumptions about government goals, but unlike most analyses I do not assume that goals are uniform across space and time. In fact spatial–temporal variation in goals is fundamental in the explanation of rapid change.

I suspect that one of the reasons why dramatic changes usually surprise observers is that we tend to think in linear and gradualistic terms. Certain methodologies seem to be more congenial to the context as barrier mode of analysis than others. Dynamic equation models (e.g., McGinnis 1990) quite naturally invite the inclusion of constraints, while this is much less the case with game theory. The methodological reflex to use linear equations is questionable since learning is dynamic and barriers often change at exponential rates.

This chapter also introduces the first substantive context that I shall treat: context as system structure. As the literature on system polarity illustrates (see Wayman 1984 for a good synthesis) both foreign policy decisions (e.g., alliances) and geographical/economic factors outside immediate government control (e.g., geographical contiguity) combine to create international structures. The barriers I shall consider involve a mix of structural components and foreign policies of leading powers. In the case of Eastern Europe, the immediate barrier is personified (or perhaps better, reified) in the USSR. Barrier change arises from changing foreign policy positions as well as from developments outside the effective control of governments, such as those in markets and technology.

Barrier models are one possible specific model of the Sprouts' general concept of environmental possibilism. The barrier determines what is possible and what is not. But "what is possible" changes, barriers evolve as do the individuals that confront them. Thus it is neither completely the exogenous effect of the barrier nor the endogenous interactions of states facing it that promotes rapid change. In level of analysis terms it is neither the state level nor the system level but rather their interaction which explains rapid change. The often-used language of "structure" is in many ways not the best one, in fact the barrier may be only one state as in the case of USSR–Eastern Europe.

Barrier models provide one possible answer to the question about dramatic change. The collapse of a barrier presents new opportunities that are quickly seized upon by interested parties – it is the rush of banks into new Latin American markets (Stallings 1987) or the various gold rushes of history. Since variations in the strength of the barrier are frequently not obvious, barrier collapse results in a rapid evolution of the situation. Behind stable situations often lies the potential for dramatic surprises.

This chapter discusses the theoretical and methodological aspects of barrier models. The frequent reference to oil nationalization and Soviet–East European relations alludes to the two following chapters where I apply the model to these – on the face of it – quite different cases. I argue that barrier models in fact provide a more coherent story, about periods of stability as well as about the character of the explosive changes when they do occur.

The barrier model

The nature of the barrier

References to dams and walls collapsing litter the literature on the East European revolutions of 1989; such images come instinctively to mind when describing these events. The barrier metaphor starts from the quite banal observation that various courses of action are not available, be it because the actor does not have the resources, because it is "unthinkable" behavior, because it is outside the world view of the actor, or because outside forces make the choice undesirable. I would like to examine barriers that *prevent* action.

The image of a barrier is a physical one, of dams, walls, and gates. When we move from physical barriers to ones that nations face it is necessary to pose the question about the nature of the barrier. Barriers may be geographical, technological, political, or economical, and are frequently quite stable and difficult to change by conscious governmental action. Barriers are *structures*. The international oil market was a structure of competition and collaboration between oil companies and governments of the major powers. No one actor could make fundamental changes, but many individual actions transformed the structure over time. In this manner barriers are rather impersonal, they are a conjunction of forces that act in relatively cohesive fashion to frustrate the desires of certain states.

But barriers are also *constructed*, they are the result of purposeful actions. Natural dams exist but the Corps of Engineers also builds dams. Important actors construct barriers because they have goals which conflict with those held by other less powerful groups.[1] Oil companies competed with each other for markets, but at the same time they had common concerns *vis-à-vis* producing countries, such as maximizing their control over oil and their profits from its production and sale. These goals ran systematically against the desire of local governments for more control and a larger share of the

[1] This contrasts with hegemonic regime theory (Gilpin 1987) where hegemons construct structures which *promote* the goals of other actors, such as free trade. The hegemon is often seen as paying for free-riders. In comparison, the barrier framework suggests that hegemons create structures that *prevent* other states from attaining their goals and which are profitable to the hegemon.

profits. Because of their goals, powerful actors such as the US, the UK, and the oil companies create obstacles to change. Similarly the installation of communist governments in Eastern Europe formed part of a clear Soviet policy to control them.

Thus the barrier can be quite specific as in the case of the USSR, or more complex and diffuse as in the case of oil, where market variations, changing technology, and political factors converge to make the barrier solid in 1950 but diverge to weaken it by 1970. The evolution of complex barriers is hard to chart. The implications of many small changes in the barrier and their cumulative impact do not become clear until nations test the barrier.

Barriers weaken because essential structural components change. In the case of oil, the rise of the independent oil companies who were willing to break the rules of the game, the rise of national oil companies in developed countries (e.g., Italy and Japan) looking for oil, the spread of oil technology to the producing countries themselves, all (and more) contributed to weakening the international oil-producing and marketing structure. Sometimes a government can work at cross purposes, such as when the US Justice Department initiated anti-trust suits against the oil companies while the State Department argued for a united front for the industry in order to strengthen its bargaining position with oil-producing countries.

Barriers are counteracting causes and as such they have the characteristics of necessary conditions. As structures they have components which are necessary to their well functioning. The weakening of any link in the chain results in the reduced effectiveness of the whole. If the reliabilities of the component parts of the barrier range from zero to one then the over-all reliability of the barrier is the product of the individual reliabilities of the parts (e.g., if each of four components has reliability 0.5 then the reliability of the whole is $0.5^4 = 0.0625$). Hence a small decrease in the strength of all parts or a dramatic decrease in one part can produce a large drop in the strength of the whole. Barriers differ significantly from context as cause where the environment is a sufficient reason for the outcome. Unlike the necessary components of the barrier, sufficient condition causes do not generally depend on other causes for their effect: necessary components interact multiplicatively and sufficient components interact additively.

In addition to the variability of barrier components, the barrier is not uniform across space. The colonial system is a good example of how when the barrier is composed of different parts it gives way unevenly. This will be important in my model of the decolonization norm whose strength varies from one colonial power to another. As Portugal and Spain illustrate, in spite of increasing pressure from all sides their isolation from the rest of the West meant that their decolonization was delayed.

Most frequently the word barrier activates images of physical obstacles, such as seas, mountains, and just plain distance, which play an important role in determining the military power of countries. But other important, if less tangible, barriers also play a role. One aspect of the history of the development of oil in Latin America, the Middle East, and Asia was the eventual diffusion of oil management and production technology. Local rulers and peoples did not know the value of what lay under their feet, they had no idea what was a fair price for this material, and they had little experience negotiating in a Western economic culture (see Munif (1984) for a fine fictional account of this in the Middle East). As these peoples learned about negotiation, oil technology, and financial accounting the barrier became weaker. Host governments were able to strike better deals with oil companies over time.

Even more intangible are normative barriers to action. One aspect of decolonization was that the British lost "the will to rule." What does this mean but in part that colonization was no longer legitimate. The rules of the game that regulated the rush to colonize Africa in the nineteenth century no longer applied. Or, more recently the collapse of military dictatorships in Latin America and communism in Eastern Europe signals that democracy is the only legitimate form of government. Widely held norms and values may constrain decision-makers who often have strong reasons (usually of a self-interested sort) to violate international norms.

At the same time powerful groups create systems of rules and norms, a point stressed by those who have found inspiration in Gramsci's thought (e.g., Cox 1983; see also Elias 1969). Rules can be an indirect expression of power. They usually do not have a neutral effect, they tend to benefit those that created them at the expense of other groups. (I shall treat these issues at some length in chapter 11 on international norms.)

For the rest of this discussion I will assume that the barrier is relatively homogenous. It is important to understand the mechanics of barrier models in the simplest case. Once the simple case is elucidated, it becomes possible to consider in detail complex barriers composed of many factors. Throughout this volume I consider simple, single-context models. The rationale is always the same, until we learn to model and explain these situations it is premature to explore multiple-context models. In the last section of this book I shall examine the concept of an international norm (singular) for the same reasons. I propose in the Postface the outlines of what a theory of complex contexts might look like, but this problem remains a subject for future contextual analysis.

Pressure on the barrier

Barrier models consist of two principal components: the barrier itself and the pressure upon it generated from below. There is no reason to put a dam in a valley unless a river flows through it. Likewise barrier models assume that there is desire for change to be blocked. As figure 6.2 indicates, barriers exist to prevent nature from running its course. Be it because of geography, markets, or other states, governments cannot attain many desirable goals. Barrier models suggest that even in periods of quiescence pressure for change exists latently. One essential part of the empirical validity of the model consists in establishing the existence of the desire for common goals in a significant number of countries. The desire to achieve these ends creates pressure for change.

The more countries that have common goals the more pressure on the system for change. To reduce this pressure barrier creators intervene in the domestic politics in states subject to the barrier in order to install governments with different sets of goals. For example, the US, the UK, the oil companies, and the USSR all intervened in the domestic politics of countries to install or maintain friendly governments. By putting friendly governments in power they reduce the forces for change in the world. At the same time the fact that they must vigorously intervene signifies that without their intervention other kinds of governments would have come into power.

Nevertheless, nationalist governments regularly come to power, setting the stage for a public test of the system. These probes constitute the best evidence about the solidity of the obstacles to change. These "revealed preferences" indicate a course of behavior that a number of actors would take if circumstances permitted. Figure 6.2 illustrates this graphically; from time t_0 to about t_{10} varied attempts are made to pierce the barrier, but they are rarely successful (the dotted arrows indicate failed tests around time t_6 to t_8). Tests are the tip of the iceberg, even though we only observe the tip we can use that evidence to infer the existence of a barely suppressed mass that can easily rise to the surface.

The countries that test the barrier are not chosen at random but select themselves because they have particular characteristics. First, they must be strong enough to even attempt a public test. Mexico nationalized its oil in

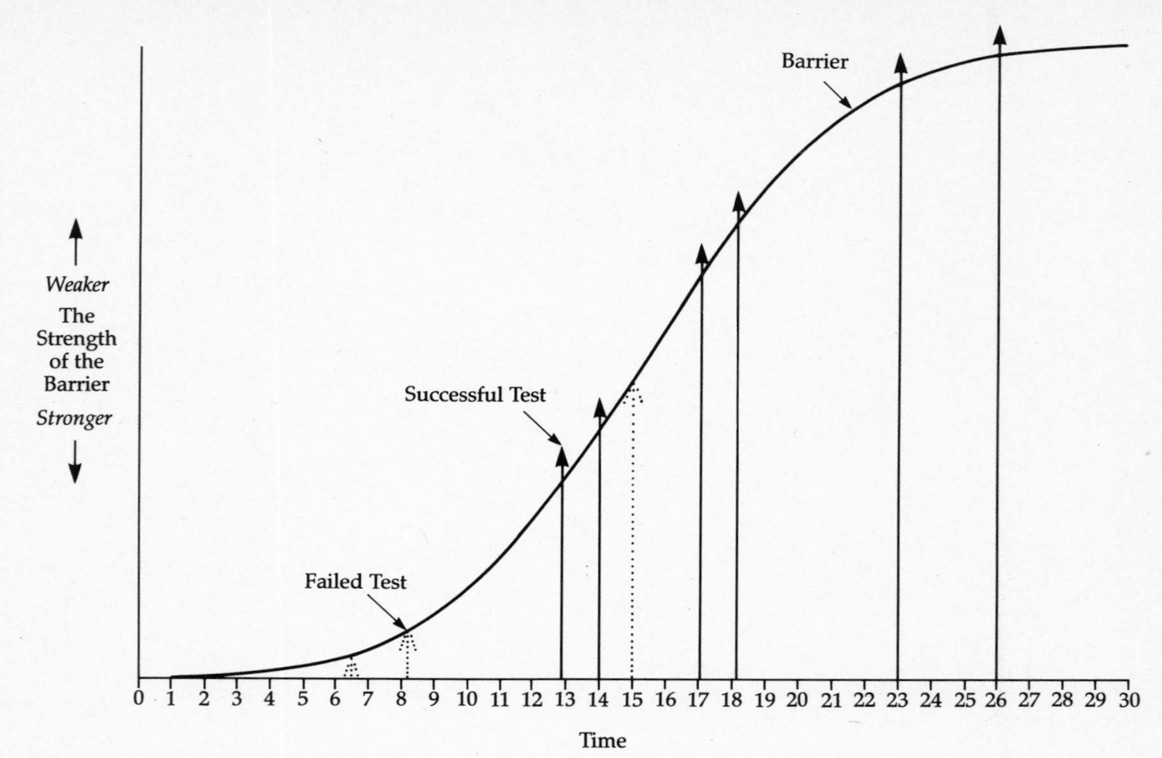

Figure 6.2 The barrier: Its evolution and tests upon it

the wake of a country-unifying revolution. The revolutionary government had the strength to withstand the immense pressures put on it to rescind its action; the same is true of the USSR in 1918. In Eastern Europe it is not surprising that the strongest and most constant opposition to Soviet control came from the Polish who had the most developed set of counter-institutions.

Secondly, the tests usually originate from the dynamics of domestic political change. Domestic events, like revolutions, compel governments to collide with the barrier. To assimilate these tests to information costs is unfortunate; the test often has little likelihood of success, it is not the result of conscious cost–benefit evaluation but a consequence of the dynamics and momentum of internal change.

Finally, these tests not only reveal the existence of a desire for a new state of affairs, but they also are a factor themselves in weakening the structures in place. If the barrier is attacked from too many different angles, internally and externally, momentum for change mounts. In figure 6.2 around time t_{13} there are more tests of the barrier indicating that the barrier is beginning to crumble; the probes themselves contribute to its decay. This dynamic explains in part the explosive character of the resulting revolution. Conversely, when the system works well governments believe change is impossible and hence exert less pressure for change. Also, it is easier during this period for those who construct barriers to manipulate domestic politics and keep conservative governments in power. The forces for stability or change often reinforce each other to maintain the status quo or to accelerate change.

The strong barrier period

The drama of explosive change really begins when the floodgates open, fundamentally altering the state of the world. However, a complete understanding of these revolutionary events requires equal analysis of the periods of little change. In particular the rare and usually unsuccessful attempts at change are important for gauging the strength of the barrier and revealing the desire for change. Many of the same dynamics that are obvious during barrier breakdown are also present during this calmer period. While the barrier is still strong there are scratches and dents in it which become visible once one begins to search for them. For example, one of the most interesting aspects of the history of Soviet bloc relations is the pattern of pressure and wear on Soviet policies. Similarly oil-producing countries were able to make significant gains in income from their oil resources from 1940 to 1970. As structures weaken these tests acquire new significance, but the underlying forces remain basically the same. Understanding periods of stability and change is all of one piece.

Critical mass and barrier breakdown

At some point – which may never arise if the barrier remains strong – the barrier begins to crumble and the process of change begins to accelerate. In figure 6.2 around time t_{13} the barrier begins to give way; more and more actors attempt to achieve a goal that now seems less than a pipe dream. It may not be obvious at first that the barrier is structurally unsound, because many of the changes are gradual and their implications not obvious. However, once the barrier is tested and found wanting, other actors with similar goals learn about their new environment and new options; they begin to reevaluate their previous estimates of the feasibility of a desired goal. The successful test at about time t_{13} leads in rapid succession to other successful probes shortly thereafter. After a period of time the situation stabilizes in a new status quo, and the number of cases drops dramatically (from time t_{22} to time t_{30}).

Tempting perhaps is to think of this model purely in terms of information processing, in other words, that all states do not perceive important changes taking place in their environment. The testing of the barrier is a search procedure where the sanctions that the testing parties undergo are the "costs" of the information. Particularly during the period of significant barrier strength these costs can be extremely high, but as the barrier weakens they drop dramatically. Since successful tests are usually very public, learning is quite rapid. The followers benefit from the cheap transfer of new knowledge via the mass media, personal contacts, etc.

But not only do nations learn about new possibilities, or that previous costs have been dramatically lowered, but what nations and peoples desire also changes. This can be seen in the following chapters by examining the countries that test the barrier when it is strong and those that adopt the behavior once critical mass has been achieved. In the case of Eastern Europe it is countries like Poland, Czechoslovakia, and Hungary that revolted first, then countries like Yugoslavia, Bulgaria, and Albania joined the parade, countries with firmly entrenched – and sometimes quite legitimate – communist parties. These latter countries had little or no experience with democracy and little experience with anti-communist movements.

In the case of oil nationalization governments of oil-producing countries had quite a clear nationalistic, if not economic, self-interest in controlling their oil. Part of the dynamics of the situation was nations beginning to believe in a new way that local control was desirable in itself. The conservative oil monarchies would have been content to leave ownership in the hands of foreign companies as long as the monarchies were kept in power and adequately remunerated, but part of the erosion of the barrier was the rise of economic nationalism which forced conservative governments to reevaluate their policies. The process of decolonization paints the same picture. World War II and the rise of the USA and the USSR weakened the colonial system created by powers such as the UK and France. But an important aspect of the equation was when the colonial peoples themselves began to desire independence with a new sense of their own value *vis-à-vis* the Europeans. This change of consciousness was not unrelated to the early successes of countries like Ghana which demonstrated that independence was possible.

Thus these two aspects of the model, changes in the barrier and changes in goals, reinforce each other. The exogenous weakening of the barrier alone does not bring about the rapid change, the pressure on the barrier also increases exponentially at the same time contributing to barrier breakdown. How each nation responds to the barrier, how it learns, and how it changes its behavior all depend on its own characteristics, but the strength of the barrier and actions of other states also have a strong impact on a state's behavior. Consideration of just system structure or just the state misses the mark, rather the interaction of the two must be considered.

Summary

It is perhaps useful to summarize the main characteristics of barrier models:

The *barrier* blocks *states.*
States *learn* from each other.
The barrier *changes* in strength over time.
States *test* the barrier.
Once knowledge about barrier changes becomes available *behavior* changes.
Pressure for change *accelerates* barrier breakdown.
Once the critical mass has been achieved states start to *change their goals.*

The model described here gives concrete expression to the context as barrier mode of analysis: barriers are counteracting causes, they prevent change from occurring. But for the concept of counteracting cause to make sense a preexisting cause must exist. Widespread goals and desires provide this force which drives governments against barriers. Dams lose their raison d'être if the river dries up. The "parasitic" quality of dams distinguishes the context as barrier mode from the context as cause mode: rivers can exist without dams but not vice versa.

This analysis reflects in many ways the emphasis that Starr (1978) has placed on "opportunity" and "willingness" as guiding concepts for the study of international relations. His use of the two concepts extends beyond the particular situation that concerns me here, but clearly "opportunity" corresponds to the barrier and "willingness" to the pressure for change. Opportunity is often a system-level property and willingness is a state-level one, just like the barrier and the pressure on it. In addition Starr has emphasized that it is the interaction of the two – their *joint* impact – that must be considered. Barrier models are thus a particular kind of an opportunity/willingness model.

Barrier models explain stability and rapid change. Focusing on the barrier itself may be sufficient for explaining periods of calm, but ignoring lower-level processes means that when the revolution occurs it will come as a surprise. The powerful countries and actors of the world tend to be the constructors of barriers, and hence it is natural to concentrate on their activities. In addition the characteristics of the barrier provide the key variables in the model. All this plus the tendency of many analysts to have a policy preference for "stability" means that the whole process is misperceived. The focus on contexts and governments' relation to them poses some important questions about stability and change. These problems will arise again in the discussion of the contexts of history and international norms.

Learning about barriers

A perennial question in international affairs is whether states and statesmen "learn." The aphorism that generals are always "fighting the last war" means that they have learned something about the world by their experience; the expression, of course, also means that the world is changing and their knowledge is no longer relevant. There exist few attempts to develop explicit models of state learning. Leng (1983) has constructed one of the most interesting. He argued that leaders view the world through realpolitik lenses; because of these glasses leaders draw certain conclusions from their successes and failures in crisis bargaining. Notably, they learn that a crisis bargaining failure results from a lack of resolve and the failure to demonstrate sufficient strength. Hence in future crises the state will employ more coercive bargaining tactics. The winning side learns that its success is due to a strategy of strength and will repeat that strategy in future conflicts. Thus states learn to bargain more coercively in future crises resulting finally in a war; and Leng's empirical data support his conclusion. The "learning" is less about "facts" than ideologically driven inferences. Leng's archetypal leader is not really acquiring information about the world but using his experiences to confirm already held opinions. I do not suggest that Leng's portrayal of the process is not correct, but rather that to call this learning is to use the concept in a special sense. In contrast, barrier models emphasize that actions supporting the barrier and those testing it are frequently the result of quite lucid understandings of the workings of the system. Leng's learning is dysfunctional while barrier learning is quite adaptive.

More frequently, learning is *historically* specific learning (e.g., Jervis 1976; Neustadt and May 1986; Breslauer and Tetlock 1991). While Jervis, and Neustadt and May use the word learning, its scope remains limited to historically specific lessons that are often of limited value, both in their truth value as well as in their range of application. When these authors refer to "learning" they appear to mean inferences that decision-makers draw from other conflicts. These discussions rarely draw upon the extensive literature on learning from cognitive science, psychology, or education. It is perhaps more accurate to call it argument by analogy than learning. The example of the Gulf War reveals the ambiguousness of the standard usage. There were frequent references made by members of the Bush administration and the military to Vietnam and Munich 1938 throughout the crisis and war. To what extent was the strategy used the result of learning from those particular experiences? (See Gilovich (1981) for an experimental study of the use of the Vietnam and Munich analogies and Khong (1992) for a more traditional foreign policy analysis of learning by analogy.) To what extent were these references part of the political justification for a policy decided upon for other reasons? Public discourse about conflict is full of references to supposedly similar cases, either to be avoided or emulated. Does this rhetorical device show learning? The historically specific narrative is the modal methodology in discussions of state learning. These stories are often quite convincing, but they provide little useful theoretical material for the construction of a general learning model.

Many learning theories, particularly those from the cognitive science tradition (e.g., Newell and Simon 1972; Staddon 1983; Holland *et al.* 1986; see Lave and March 1975 for an introduction to learning models) assume that individuals have goals that are relatively constant, and learn ways to achieve these goals via rewards and punishments. In barrier models it is the same sort of learning (the exception being the acquisition of new goals), governments learn about the barrier through tests which are sometimes "punished" and hence not repeated, while others are successful and hence rewarded and imitated. Tests represent knowledge about what is possible and realistic as a foreign policy goal. Through experiences like Mexico's (1938) and Iran's (1951) successful, but very painful, oil nationalizations (Iran's was technically successful but practically it was not), nations knew that this strategy, however desirable, had high costs. Through Libya and Algeria's relatively painless nationalizations in 1971 nations learned that this policy was now a real option.

The small but growing work in international relations on cognitive, adaptive models provides a methodology for specifying the learning process implicit in barrier models (Sylvan and Chan 1984; Hudson 1991). I have assumed a simple adaptive learning response. Except during the barrier breakdown period, governments have simple goals and their behavior changes according to whether tests are rewarded or punished. Clearly learning is more complex than I have assumed; much needs to be done to explicate how goals change and how learning does or does not take place.

A formal model

Now that the essential aspects of the barrier framework have been outlined it is time to become more concrete and create a formal barrier model. It is important that its various facets receive appropriate formal expression. Once formalized I can test it with real data.

One important aspect of many diffusion models is that they usually contain *no* exogenous variables: they are more "models" than "explanations" (Midlarsky 1970). Kobrin's model of oil nationalization (1985) did not include the explanatory factors that he emphasized in his discussion. The cumulative number of successful oil nationalizations does fit an S-curve typical of diffusion processes, but the leap to a diffusion explanation remains a significant one. We have already seen the same problems with diffusion models of conflict where the explanation of the diffusion mechanism moves toward realpolitik modes of analysis. Kobrin employed the language of barrier models: "Once Libya had broken the ice" (p. 25), or "the beginning of a landslide" (p. 25), or "pressures building over a period of time" (p. 24). He noted goal changes as barriers fell: "Yamani of Saudi Arabia observed after the Algerian take-over that participation had become a national demand" (p. 25). His *explanation* is close to the one proposed here, but his "model" is not. Diffusion models themselves rarely indicate *why* the explosion occurs and *when* it does. Since these models generally consist in only endogenous variables (like the war diffusion studies where war causes subsequent war) they cannot explain either why the process gets started in the first place or the differing rates of spread. It is not sufficient to show that the distribution of the outcome variable fits an S-curve, it must be shown that the dynamics are those of a barrier model and not another: explanatory variables must be included.

Pressure for change is one major component of barrier models. The pressure from below depends on the number of recent successful tests ($Y(t)$) and the number of potential future tests ($\bar{Y} - Y(t)$), the parameter π measures the rate of pressure increase on the barrier:

$$P_t = [\pi Y(t)][\bar{Y} - Y(t)] \quad (6.1)$$

P_t is the pressure on the barrier at time t
$Y(t)$ is the number of recent changes
$\bar{Y}$ is the maximum number of possible changes
$\bar{Y} - Y(t)$ is the number of potential changes in the current period
π is the rate of pressure increase

We can split the group of states facing the barrier into two groups, one including those states that have achieved their goals ($Y(t)$) and the other consisting of those that have not ($\bar{Y} - Y(t)$): the two groups divide those that are on the bandwagon and those that have yet to jump on. P_t reaches a maximum when the barrier is breaking down but when there are still many states yet to adopt the change. P_t is small either when the number of testers is few or when almost everyone has done so. That the pressure is greatest in the middle of the process can be seen in the simple numeric example where $[Y(t)][\bar{Y} - Y(t)]$ is $(1)(9) = 9$, $(2)(8) = 16, \ldots, (5)(5) = 25, \ldots, (9)(1) = 9$. This basic logic underlies most diffusion models: disease contagion is a model of the interaction between those with the disease and those without it.

Since we are dealing usually with relatively small populations eventually the number of cases will be exhausted. Be it democratization, decolonization, or nationalization, the size of the population ranges from about 10 to 100. We need to take into account that the universe is limited, symbolized by $\bar{Y}$ which is the maximum number of possible break-throughs.

Equation 6.1 is a standard diffusion model (Mahajan and Peterson 1985) where *all* testers ($Y(t)$) interact with *all* potential testers ($\bar{Y} - Y(t)$). While this assumption is implausible in diffusion across individuals it is much more believable in international relations where tests of the barrier are extremely public. While there are regional differences, the assumption of "perfect information" is quite reasonable for the class of problems treated by barrier models.

Instead of considering all tests from time zero to the present I include only tests conducted in the recent past. Unlike most diffusion of innovation models where it is assumed that the innovation is always useful and the adopter continues to spread the word, I consider only recent information about the barrier to be relevant. Infrequent success signals barrier strength and does not incite others to test the barrier. In international affairs only recent tests – or their absence – provide useful information. Only the recent values of $Y(t)$ provide relevant information to potential nationalizers.

The amount of pressure depends on how quickly nations learn from their experiences and the experiences of others, symbolized by λ (for learning). The rate of pressure (π) increase varies according to local conditions, one important aspect of which is the character and policy preferences of the government. Clearly the desire to challenge international barriers depends on the values of the groups in power. In general the more nationalistic the country the more likely it is to challenge the barrier and to learn rapidly from the experience of others. So π varies according to the number of potential adopters who have favorable learning characteristics:

$$\pi = \iota_0 + \lambda_1 L \qquad (6.2)$$

L is the number of favorably disposed learners

The variable L is the first exogenous explanatory variable in the model. The standard model cannot predict or explain why the process starts or the rate of change, but by looking inside the actors – instead of assuming they are all the same – we can explain why or why not the process gets going and in part its speed.

The second factor that determines the pressure for change is the bandwagon effect. The bandwagon effect suggests that the social pressure to conform is proportional to the number of individuals that are pushing for change ($Y(t)$). By substituting for π in equation 6.1 we get the term $\iota Y(t)$. Hence ι represents the imitation or bandwagon effect. The rate of pressure increase π in equation 6.2 consists of two parts: one represents the force of countries that have some goal whose attainment is frustrated by the barrier (λ), the second is the force of social pressure on those who do not have that goal to adopt it (ι).

Barrier models contain two processes: one is the effect individuals have on each other. In figure 6.1 State A interacts with State B; loosely, State A becomes group $Y(t)$ in equation 6.1 and State B becomes $\bar{Y} - Y(t)$. The two arrows linking them are the two parts of the pressure increase parameter in equation 6.2, λ for learning and ι for social pressure and imitation. Equations 6.1 and 6.2 thus capture the bottom half of the barrier model in figure 6.1.

The process described in equation 6.1 once started – say by a successful nationalization – does not stop until all have nationalized: what must be explained is why dramatic change is *rare*. What keeps the process from getting underway in the first place? This force of course consists in barriers to change. Thus to equation 6.1 I add a negative force $-B(t)$ which keeps the process from getting started or slows down its progress. $B(t)$ forms the second explanatory variable in the model, determining if and when the process gets going and in part its rate of spread.

$$B(t) = X_1(t) * X_2(t)$$

where the X_i are barrier strength factors

Equation 6.1 assumes that once the process gets underway there is nothing to stop it until all countries have changed their behavior. While in some applications this makes sense, such as the diffusion of technological innovations (e.g., Griliches 1957), in world politics this assumption is very unrealistic. Those that profit from the existence of the barrier will not stand by and let the situation get out of control, they will attempt to strengthen the barrier. It is possible for the barrier strength variable ($B(t)$) to vary in many ways. It may temporarily drop and then increase rapidly, thus stopping the bandwagon before it gets underway. The case of oil in the 1980s (which I do not cover in my analysis) shows how powerful actors can regain control of the situation.

In the oil nationalization case X_1 will be the percentage of the world oil market not controlled by the major oil companies, and X_2 the world excess production capacity (which indicates the availability of alternative sources of supply). Reflecting that the reliability of the whole barrier depends on the well-functioning of *all* its parts, the functional form is multiplicative not additive.

Putting this all together we get a barrier model:

$$\frac{dY(t)}{dt} = [-\beta B(t) + \pi Y(t)][\bar{Y} - Y(t)] \tag{6.3}$$

$$\text{where } \frac{dY(t)}{dt} \text{ is the success rate at time } t$$

Barrier strength and pressure upon the barrier are joint sufficient conditions, which can be seen by their presence in the first set of brackets, $[\pi Y(t)]$ reflects the pressure on the barrier and $\beta B(t)$ indicates the firmness of the barrier. Or by rearranging terms, $-\beta B(t)[\bar{Y} - Y(t)]$ is the force preventing change, and $\pi Y(t)[\bar{Y} - Y(t)]$ represents the force for change due to imitation and learning. The sum of the two would need to be above a certain level for successful change. This implies that the combination of the two is a sufficient cause for a leak, either very strong pressure (like in the Mexican oil nationalization) or a weak barrier (like in the 1970s) can provide the occasion for a successful test.

The second major component of the barrier model consists in the hierarchical, state–barrier effect. In figure 6.1 the barrier prevents State B from achieving its goals. In equation 6.3 the influence of the barrier on State B becomes the negative influence of $B(t)$ on $\bar{Y} - Y(t)$. The final model includes the two contexts – horizontal and vertical, or state–state and state–barrier – that form the core of barrier models.

Equation 6.3 is a differential equation model. The term $\frac{dY(t)}{dt}$ is the rate of break-throughs per unit time (dt). One cannot understand revolutions in international affairs without considering the *dynamics* of the phenomenon, thus it is appropriate that the final model takes this explicitly into account.

Conclusion

At the beginning of this chapter I asked how one might explain dramatic change in international politics. The heart of my response to that question is that shifts in the international context allow new behavior to emerge and spread. Barrier models resemble biological theories of "punctuated equilibrium" (Eldredge and Gould 1972; Eldredge 1985) which argue that species are generally quite stable except during periods of dramatic environmental change. But environmental change does not suffice, there must also be genetic variation and species available to take advantage of new situations. Similarly in barrier models, shifts in system structure do not force change, they permit change if states exist that want to take advantage of new possibilities.

A central component of this book concerns how states interact with their environments. The Sprouts coined the term "environmental possibilism" and that is what barrier models are all about. And for this reason barrier models are closely related to theoretical concepts like opportunity and willingness. Opportunity and barrier breakdown are not sufficient, willingness and appropriate goals must be present as well. Without these state-level factors pushing in the right direction, barrier breakdown or environmental opportunities will have no impact on governmental behavior.

Although the environment plays a large role in determining behavior, the rate of learning depends on domestic politics as well. Domestic political developments can vary drastically the pressure put on the barrier. The result is an interaction between the domestic evolution – in the case of oil, the coming to power of nationalistic governments – and the world in which these countries must operate. Theories like Waltz's (1979) which emphasize the importance of system structure tend to downplay domestic factors; contextual models emphasize the interaction between the domestic and the international: the joint condition of domestic policy and environmental changes characterizes the system.

Throughout this chapter I have talked about "states learning." What this means is not clear: Do organizations learn or is it just leaders learning? Leng's work suggests there are rules that guide learning. This seems a fruitful avenue of research since many cognitive models (e.g., Holland *et al.* 1986) of human learning use rule-based approaches. Barrier models emphasize – rather assume – that certain learning rules are operative. The cognitive literature on learning also suggests that it is very goal oriented: pragmatic considerations determine the rules learned. Barrier models incorporate a simple dynamic of relatively constant goals, simple testing of the environment, and belief revision. But much remains to be done at a finer level to explicate the learning dynamics of states and the extent to which this differs from individual learning processes.

Barriers may be physical but they can also be normative. Characteristic of norms is that they can on occasion change quite rapidly. The rapid change in the status of colonies is typical of barrier dynamics. Starting in the mid 1950s the pressure for independence grew as the colonial system collapsed. As the *legitimacy* of colonial rule disintegrated one of the barriers to change did as well, and the always desirable goal of national self-determination became a realizable one. Not only power and self-interest create barriers, but also values and norms are hurdles to be overcome. As norms evolve barriers are created and destroyed. Since these non-material hindrances are in the hearts and minds of people they can change in an explosive manner unchecked by the material requirements of military and economic power.

One characteristic of contextual models is that basic parameters (e.g., the β's in regression models) are no longer fixed but vary: the context as changing meaning mode. The standard diffusion model is a non-contextual one with a constant rate of learning (λ) reflecting the assumption of uniformity across space and time. This results in part from the fact that there are no explanatory variables in the model, hence no reason why individuals or epochs differ. I contextualize the basic diffusion model by making the learning rate a function of domestic factors, represented in the next two chapters by the degree of nationalism of governments or opposition groups.

Barrier models have other close ties with simple context as changing meaning models. Although the literature on "contextual models" and that on diffusion are isolated from each other with few cross-references, in fact they are closely related. The missing link is the habit of considering context only as an independent variable, and in ignoring the feedback loops whereby contexts are created by individual action. If we include feedback loops that endogenize context in context as changing meaning models they become diffusion ones like equation 6.1 (Przeworski 1974). As we see throughout this volume contextual models form a family; system structure, history, and norms are related to each other as are the contextual modes of cause, changing meaning, and barrier.

The two case studies that follow in the next two chapters are quite different. They are symmetric in that the barrier in one case is the USSR and in the other the USA, the UK, and the large oil companies (the majors). They differ significantly since one involves the actions of the "masses" in Eastern Europe and the other the elites in the Third World. Also, they are dissimilar in that one is eminently political while the other is also economic. In the case of oil nationalization the barrier is more diffuse, the US played a central role but the British were also involved. The oil companies urged the US government to protect their interests, but it never automatically protected US firms. In the Eastern European case the barrier was quite clearly the USSR, a much more homogeneous obstacle to change. The existence of quantitative data on the oil industry allows me to estimate the formal model developed in this chapter, while the East European chapter is a descriptive case study. These differences and contrasts reinforce each other suggesting that barrier models provide a powerful analytic tool for the study of international relations.

States cannot do everything they desire, in large part because of power relations. Barriers are one way to discuss how power is exercised in world politics. This can be quite direct as in the case of Eastern Europe, but it is sometimes much more diffuse as in the case of oil. "Diffuse power" does not have the usual sense of "obliging" a country to do something, but it is rather the power to prevent certain things (analogous to the difference between compellence and deterrence). One of the facets of power illuminated by barrier models is that power relationships are not necessarily a dyadic, eyeball-to-eyeball affair, but can be much more indirect. "Market forces" are constraints that cannot be localized in one point; they are a structure, an invisible hand that slaps deviants (Hirschman 1970). We shall see that the weakening cohesion of the world oil market was in part responsible for the rush to nationalize oil.

The power to set the parameters becomes crucial in rational actor models. Because preferences are given, the opportunity set determines behavior. Control the opportunity set and you control behavior. Power does not have to be directly expressed through the mouth of a gun, but perhaps is more effective if used indirectly. The mechanisms are hidden and thus appear more impersonal, "natural," and easy to accept. Private banks agree not to lend more money to debt-ridden countries unless they implement IMF agreements, that *norm* is a sophisticated power relationship between the *system* of private banks and indebted countries. That norm restricts the possible sources of new non-IMF approved loans to approximately zero. But, as the following two chapters indicate, barriers are neither monolithic nor immutable.

7 OIL NATIONALIZATION, 1918–1980

There is a worldwide trend toward nationalization and Saudis cannot stand against it alone.[1]

Ahmed Zaki Yamani, Saudi Oil Minister (cited in Yergin 1991, p. 584)

Introduction

Oil is a keystone of a modern economy, but historical and geological accident determine where it is to be found. For a number of nations in the Third World oil provides the main source of wealth, and hence is a central concern of government. At the same time, the security and stability of oil supply pose a constant problem for the industrialized countries of the North. The Gulf War was just another in the series of dramatic events in oil history revolving around these two basic facts. Using the barrier model I focus on the part of oil history involving Third World states struggling to gain control over their petroleum industries. This struggle shifts from an emphasis on increasing revenues – royalties and taxes – to the additional demand for ownership and control. Pitted against these countries were the major oil companies and their allied governments, who in the beginning completely controlled and dominated the international oil system, but whose control by 1960 had seriously eroded.

[1] Frank (1985, p. 18) reports on a 1970 film where that "veteran student of human nature Allen Funt ... placed his telephone number in a help-wanted advertisement, then arranged personal interviews with those who responded. We are shown an interviewee as he is directed to a small office in which several other persons are already seated, apparently waiting. To the experimental subject, the others appear to be fellow interviewees, but we know they are really confederates of Mr. Funt. Responding to no apparent signal, the others abruptly rise from their seats and begin taking off their clothing. We are shown a close-up of the experimental subject, his face a mask of apprehension as he surveys what is happening. A few moments pass, then he, too, rises from his chair and proceeds to disrobe. At no point in the process does he ask any of the others why they are removing their clothing. As the scene ends, we see him standing there, naked alongside the others, apparently waiting for some clue as to what happens next."

The 1970s saw a dramatic change in the character of the oil industry. Oil-producing countries successfully challenged the system whereby the major oil companies controlled all aspects of the process which took oil from well-head to gas station. The restructuring of the international oil economy took place over a very short period of time: in 1970 the major oil companies owned 69 percent of non-communist oil supplies, by 1979 this had declined to 24 percent. Undoubtedly oil nationalization was a revolutionary change in international political economy and hence provides a good test case of the usefulness of barrier models.

States have different oil-related goals which depend on the local government, on relations with oil companies, and on security relationships with the major powers. The Saudis clearly had quite a different attitude toward nationalization than did Libya. Differences across space and time toward oil nationalization illustrate how national goals can vary. Rational actor models assume constant goals and preferences, barrier models propose that changing goals play a crucial role in the explanation of explosive change.

Just as the Third World countries had differences between themselves so did cohesion and unity vary on the opposing side. Oil companies competed among themselves and had conflicts with their home governments. The US Department of Justice attempted to break up oil cartels while the State Department would press for exceptions to give the US industry greater power abroad. Sometimes the US government went against the interests of the oil companies for strategic and security reasons (Krasner 1978). Neither camp achieved complete coordination of goals and action, which was a source of weakness for both sides. Nevertheless, the interests of the two were basically opposed, which justifies the Manichean division of the system into the "barrier" and "pressure upon it."

I propose that the barrier framework integrates many intuitions that are common in the immense literature on oil nationalization. I shall provide no new facts about the process of oil nationalization but rather a conceptual framework that seems to fit the facts well. One measure of progress in science is when disparate phenomena are shown to be driven by the same underlying process. This chapter and the next are modest attempts to suggest that barrier models capture one important international phenomenon.

The principal elements of barrier models organize the telling of the story that follows. Since the barrier plays the central role in determining the rate of change its characteristics are discussed first, followed by a discussion of the pressure for change from below. Then I examine how the barrier changes over time and how it finally collapses. The period of explosive change is analyzed particularly from the point of view of the spread of information about the changes in the international system and the changing character of national goals. I end this chapter with a statistical estimation of a model of oil nationalization.

The barrier

The actors that constructed the international oil system are the UK, the US, and the major oil companies. The US government after World War II had several interlocking goals all of which meant US domination over the production and marketing of oil, as put by a Senate committee:

> US foreign policy objectives were threefold. First, the US desired to provide a steady supply of oil to Europe and Japan at reasonable prices ... Second, the US desired to maintain stable governments in the non-Communist pro-Western, oil exporting countries. Third, the US desired that American-based firms be a dominant force in world oil trade. These three ... goals were generally attained during the 1950s and 1960s. (Cited in Roncaglia 1985, p. 102)

The major oil companies – for short, "the majors" – completely dominated the international production and trade of oil until the 1960s. These firms were vertically integrated and controlled the oil industry from production to retail sale. They possessed the technology, tankers, pipelines, and essential chemicals such as tetraethyl lead, all necessary components in a production process starting from oil discovery and ending with its marketing. Oil-producing countries are at the beginning of a chain which usually ends at a consumer in an industrialized country. While oil-producing countries might have some influence at the beginning of the process they need to be able to bring the final product to the consumer, either themselves or in collaboration with other companies. If the majors present a united front then the bargaining power of the producers is dramatically reduced. The principal hope for producers was to play one company against another, a possibility reduced by the fact that many oil companies were involved in joint ventures, particularly in the Middle East. For example, ARAMCO in Saudi Arabia involved Socony (Mobil), Standard of New Jersey, Socal (Standard of California), and Texaco.

Conflict often erupted between the US, UK, and France over oil in the

Middle East. By the end of World War I it had become clear that oil was a strategic resource – a lesson reinforced by World War II (Yergin 1991). Already in the 1920s the Middle East was the scene of great power rivalry over oil, but local powers had very little to say in the final agreements, e.g., Red Line, "As is," and the Achnacarry Agreement. Great power conflicts did not provide much leverage for the oil-producing states. Many of these conflicts occurred when the oil-producing states were weak and inexperienced in the oil business. By the time they had developed enough experience to profit from great power conflict the US had become the dominant power in the region. Had the USSR been an oil importer like the rest of Europe, rather than an oil exporter, the same sort of situation might not have arisen. But as it was even radical regimes had little choice but to sell to capitalist-imperialist countries.

With the Soviet Union supplying itself and Eastern Europe the other remaining possibility for producers was to sell for local consumption. This was a viable option for larger countries. The net effect of the Mexican nationalization was to divert oil from the world market – where Mexico had been a leading exporter – to local use. This was basically the state of affairs in large Latin American countries such as Mexico, Brazil, and Argentina. State oil companies in these countries tended to be less efficient or at least unable to compete in international markets. Countries only producing for local consumption were much less vulnerable than those producing for export to the pressure the majors could exert on them.

A central thesis of Krasner's account of the oil industry (1978) is that the US government did not support the oil industry down the line, at least in the industry's short-term interests. Strategic and Cold War concerns could and did take precedence over strictly defined oil company interests. Since US foreign policy goals included friendly relations with conservative Arab governments and a desire that they remain in power the US did not always support the companies' position. For example, the US supported the spread of the 50–50 agreement (which increased producing countries' share to 50 percent) through the Middle East as a way to keep friendly governments satisfied, but intervened in the Iranian nationalization attempt when it perceived Mossadegh as going too far left. The rule was if *either* security goals coincided with industry objectives *or* security issues were not relevant then the oil companies could count upon the support of the US government. This can be seen in cases like World Bank loans which were consistently denied to national oil companies in the Third World, usually on the grounds that private firms were more efficient.

This rule did not just apply to the Middle East but was already in application in Latin America during the late 1930s. With prospects of war in Europe the Roosevelt administration wanted good relations with Latin American governments. This meant that the administration did not always strongly support oil company claims on the eve of World War II. For example, Bolivia was able to retain oil that it nationalized in 1937 (Klein 1964). The prospect of war in Europe also helped improve US–Mexican relations after the Mexican nationalization in 1938.

Even without government support the oil companies themselves had many effective sanctioning tools. In the Mexican case the oil companies themselves organized the response. They orchestrated an embargo on Mexican crude, tankers, and exports of tetraethyl lead, and even travel agencies owned by oil companies discouraged tourism to Mexico. Oil companies could also exert pressure through Congress as illustrated by the Hickenlooper Amendment, which required the administration to cut off aid to countries nationalizing US enterprises.

A continual problem of the oil industry was overproduction. This occurred regularly when major new sources of oil were discovered, e.g., East Texas. Huge new discoveries normally led to price-cutting, hardship, and bankruptcy for many small oil companies. This almost chronic overproduction had two negative affects on Third World producers. One was that these crises eventually led to the concentration of the industry and cartelization. Even the independent Texans finally accepted a rationing system under the Texas Railroad Commission. Similarly, the majors managed production in the Middle East in order to keep prices at a profitable level.

The second major advantage of a system that tended to overproduce was that virtually no Third World nation's supply was crucial, other sources could usually replace lost supplies. In addition, protectionist measures insured that US domestic oil was produced thus maintaining other alternatives. It is not surprising that the wave of oil nationalizations occurred when world surplus capacity had dropped to very low levels. A nation whose oil became crucial to the system, such as Iran and Saudi Arabia, was constantly courted by the US and the UK. The two big oil shocks of 1974 and 1979 were associated with these two countries' production being removed from the market; while excess world capacity explains the relatively little panic associated with the Gulf War. As long as crucial countries' production was assured the system had a margin to work on. Oil producers created OPEC as a natural response to this situation. Only if a critical number of producers could work out a joint policy would their bargaining position improve.

One way to maintain the system was to reduce the pressure for change from below. This meant installing and maintaining in power conservative, dependent governments. Great Britain had used traditional elites to control its colonies, and these elites usually assumed power when independence arrived. Small countries like the oil monarchies and Saudi Arabia depended on the Americans and the British for defense against more powerful countries, and frequently for defense against domestic opposition groups as well. Even though conservative governments did press for better deals from the oil companies, this pressure always remained within well-defined limits.

Not only were the great powers involved in local politics but the oil companies themselves certainly intervened in the domestic affairs of producing countries. Unlike governments who eventually declassify documents, little is known about the actions of the majors. In Latin America there is evidence they contributed large amounts of money in elections where one party was nationalistic (Klein 1964). Also, the history of Louisiana – an underdeveloped oil-dependent state – shows that when "nationalists" like Huey Long became a threat Standard Oil did not hesitate to use its power to defend its interests (Williams 1969).

The end result was a system that strongly discouraged nationalization. Kobrin states that "[t]he cry 'remember what happened to Mossadeq' was an effective deterrent to nationalization by a major producing country for over two decades" (1985 p. 23).

Pressure from below

For barriers to fulfill their functions they must block desirable ends. In the case of oil this translates into a claim that as a rule host governments were not happy with their arrangements with the major oil companies and that they were constantly trying to improve their position *vis-à-vis* them. Turner's overview of the early history of the industry argues that this desire for change was not just the product of the politics of the 1960s:

> The first point worth stressing is that from the moment the companies were awarded concessions they were on the defensive. As early as 1900 the original Standard Oil ran into bitter political resistance in Romania, then a major oil producing power. During the 1910s the oil industry's assets in the major oil province in Russia were expropriated and they were legally challenged in Mexico. In the same decade the Peruvians began a

> feud with Jersey's [Standard Oil] IPC which was to drag on for the next fifty years. The 1920s brought the first Latin American state company in the form of Argentina's YPF, while in the Middle East the Persians under Reza Shah demanded that Anglo-Persian [British Petroleum] increase its tax payments and agree to a revision of the terms of its concession. The 1930s saw expropriations and the creation of state company competitors in Uruguay, Peru, Bolivia and, most importantly, Mexico; the death of Venezuela's President Gomez, who had been very generous to the industry; and the revision of Anglo-Persian's concession at the request of what was now the Iranian government. The 1940s saw the start of significant interaction between Venezuela and Middle Eastern oil countries and the spread of the fifty-fifty tax principle ... In addition, this decade [1950s] saw the creation of a further three state [oil] companies in Latin America, the Iranian expropriation of Anglo-Iranian and the growth of pressures against the companies in Iran after the overthrow of the pro-British regime. (1978 p. 69)

Though Turner exaggerates a bit when saying that the companies were "on the defensive" from the start, host governments clearly made continual efforts to improve the bargain with the oil companies.

Nationalization was the extreme demand in the struggle for more control and profit from local resources. Most frequently governments negotiated for higher taxes and royalties. Slowly oil producers were able to extract more money from the oil companies. While the oil companies staunchly fought such demands, the US government sometimes supported the oil producers as part of a larger policy of maintaining friendly relations. For example, the Shah, by no means a radical, was in the forefront demanding a larger share of the oil pie for Iran.

One of the results of decolonization and the rise of nationalism in the Third World was that governments began to desire a new kind of relationship with oil companies. In addition to more revenues they began to demand control over resources, prices, and production levels. Barrier models imply *both* changes from beneath and changes from above. The changes from below brought about by the growth in Arab nationalism are well illustrated by Nasser who increased the pressure for dramatic change that could not be accommodated by purely financial renegotiation of previous contracts.

The evolution in the Middle East symbolized by Nasser was occurring elsewhere in the Third World. A large number of producing states were former colonies and were going through a period of nation-building. They wanted more than just a bigger piece of the pie, they demanded strategic

Table 7.1 *Successful nationalizations, pre-1965*

Nation	Year	Type of government*
USSR	1918	nationalist
Chile	1927	nationalist
Bolivia	1937	nationalist
Mexico	1938	nationalist
Iran	1951	nationalist
Cuba	1960	nationalist
Indonesia	1960	nationalist
Iraq	1961	nationalist
Egypt	1961	nationalist
Algeria	1962	nationalist
Burma	1962	conservative
Sri Lanka	1962	nationalist
Egypt	1962	nationalist
Argentina	1963	nationalist
Ghana	1963	nationalist
Egypt	1964	nationalist
Brazil	1964	conservative

Note: * The "type of government" was coded depending on policy preferences of groups before they came to power. The group coming to power must have proposed either nationalization, the formation of state enterprises, or greatly increased government control over foreign enterprises to be coded "nationalistic"; otherwise, it was coded conservative. Regime type was coded based on the economic policy preferences of groups *before* they came to power in order to exclude nationalizations that were opportunistic.

control over national resources. As decolonization proceeded it became possible for nationalist groups to implement their policies *vis-à-vis* multinational raw material companies. Pressure increased as the governments left – or installed – in power by the colonizer were replaced by nationalist groups. In the Middle East nationalist military officers frequently replaced pro-Western monarchs in countries such as Egypt, Iraq, and Libya. These nations and others formed a bloc in the UN which passed the resolution Sovereignty Over National Resources. At the same time they formed producer organizations like OPEC.

An early sign of pressure from below was the formation of national oil companies (NOCs). They symbolized the desire to acquire the technology and management skills necessary to be effective in international markets. An unnoticed fact is that the formation of NOCs occurred in a similar fashion to the nationalization of oil. The first wave of NOC formation was in the late 1920s and 1930s throughout Latin America. Latin American states had been independent for decades and usually had policies promoting local industrialization. The second wave of NOC creation broke in the late 1950s and 1960s, and significantly most of the major producers in the Middle East, Asia, and Latin America that did not already have a NOC formed one. The expertise and experience provided by these companies made nationalization a more serious threat since oil exporters were acquiring a clearer understanding of costs, prices, and taxes as well as oil technology itself. The creation of a NOC expressed the desire for control and set the scene for nationalization.

The first country to nationalize oil was the Soviet Union in 1918. This first case illustrates several important aspects of early barrier tests. Nationalization often came after a revolutionary transfer of power when the government had established control domestically with few effective rivals for power. This explains the occurrence *and* the success of the Soviet and Mexican nationalizations, and the *de facto* failure of the Iranian (the 1951 nationalization was a *de jure* success). For an early nationalization to be successful a state had to be able to withstand exclusion from world energy markets in particular, and often world markets in general. A large domestic market was useful though not absolutely necessary. For example, the Soviet Union was able to market some of its oil to Europe in the 1920s, just as later the Italian state oil company ENI would break ranks and buy Soviet oil in the early 1960s. The pre-1965 *successful* attempts to nationalize oil production listed in table 7.1 illustrate this pattern.[2] The Egyptian nationalizations were part of Nasser's general policy which also nationalized the Suez Canal. In the Bolivian case a nationalist party was elected, and the revelation of underhanded practices (tax evasion, illegal actions, and fraudulent reports to the government) on the part of Standard Oil led to nationalization. Probably the more important the country the stronger and more radical the revolution or transition to independence needed to be in order to successfully nationalize oil.

Decolonization increased dramatically the pressure for change in all raw material areas. If nationalist and revolutionary regimes were relatively rare before World War II they became increasingly numerous as colonies gained their independence. Figure 7.1 shows the steady increase in the number of nationalist and revolutionary regimes from 1950 to 1980.[3] In addition

[2] Steven Kobrin kindly furnished the data on oil nationalization, see Kobrin (1984) for a description.

[3] The group coming to power must have proposed either nationalization, the formation of state enterprises, or greatly increased government control over foreign enterprises to be coded "nationalistic"; otherwise, it was coded conservative. Regime type was coded

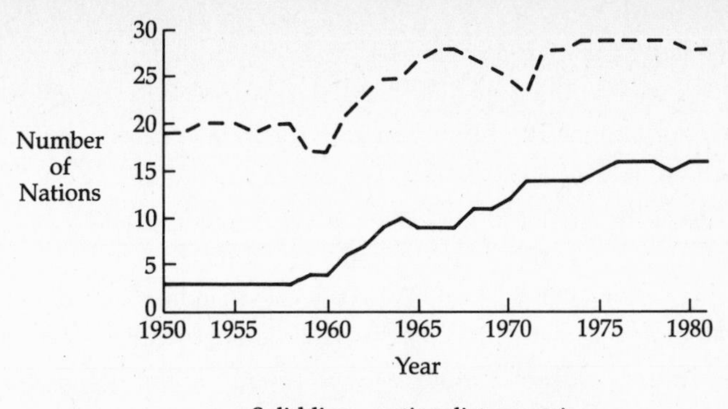

Figure 7.1 Pressure for nationalization: growth of nationalist regimes

nationalist groups – often from the military in the Middle East – frequently replaced soon after independence conservative governments left in power by the colonizer.

The barrier crumbles

New players and changing markets

Within the oil industry there were a number of developments that decreased the strength of the majors and their ability to control world oil markets. One was the rise of the independent oil companies which began to account for a larger and larger share of the US market. Since the independents were not members of the old boys' club of the majors they felt no need to follow their cartel agreements. Turner (1978) estimates, for example, that the number of companies involved in exploration in the Middle East increased from nine in 1940 to 126 in 1976. Jacoby (1974) estimates that between 1953 and 1972 more than 300 private firms and fifty state-owned firms entered the industry. Unlike the majors who had production in a variety of countries, the independents concentrated heavily their non-US production in one country

based on the economic policy preferences of groups *before* they came to power. In this fashion I attempt to exclude nationalizations that were opportunistic. I did not code changes of policy once a government was established: regime type changed only with a change in government, and only attitudes toward nationalization and general economic policies were considered. Standard historical sources provided the necessary information about the policy preferences. I coded all countries as either "conservative" or "nationalistic," the latter including revolutionary governments.

and were thus extremely vulnerable to demands of producing governments. As a consequence they were willing to pay more for oil, and to buy it with fewer conditions than the majors. Qadaffi, when faced with the solid wall of the majors, found a crack in the system with the independents, and was able to gain significant concessions from Occidental Petroleum.

The cracks in the barrier did not just come from independents in the US, but also from NOCs of industrialized countries in Europe and Japan. NOCs were not only formed in the Third World but also in industrialized countries, and for analogous reasons. The Japanese government forced the majors with local refineries to purchase a certain amount of oil from the Japanese-owned Arab Oil Company. Particularly in France and Italy, but also in Germany and in Scandinavia, governments subsidized and supported the creation of local oil companies that increased the number of "independents" competing for oil in areas like the Middle East. As the new boys on the block they were in a weaker bargaining position than the majors, hence they were often more willing to give the oil-producing nations a better deal. Thus not only in the United States, but also in Europe and Japan, the amount of oil retailed and refined by non-major companies grew dramatically in the 1950s. These developments are illustrated in table 7.2 which shows that the independents held only 7 percent of the world oil market in 1950, tripling to over 20 percent by 1966.

The extent to which the situation in Europe and Japan had changed the whole international oil market was revealed in the 1971 negotiations with Libya. When the London Policy Group was formed to negotiate with Tripoli and Teheran its membership indicated how the industry had changed. The group was an oil company organization, but one that included US independents and non-Anglo-Saxon national companies from countries like Spain, Belgium, Japan, and Germany. In fact, representatives from companies, such as the German Gelsenberg and the US independent Bunker-Hunt, played a central role in the negotiations: the Anglo-Saxon major oil companies no longer ruled the oil world. Later, Jim Akins, an American diplomat involved in the negotiations, said:

> The main reason for not following this course [daring the Libyans to nationalize] was the fact that the loss of all oil from Libya alone would have meant the drawing down of more than half of the European oil reserves within a year. It seemed unlikely, indeed inconceivable, that France, Germany, Spain or Italy would have allowed that to happen; especially as the goal would apparently have been only to protect the Anglo-Saxon oil monopoly, which they had long sought to break ... We

Table 7.2 *Changing barriers: international oil marketing (percent)*

Year	Majors	Independents	NOCs
1950	92.8	7.2	*
1957	82.4	17.6	*
1966	80.0	22.5	*
1973	69.6	22.5	7.9
1976	59.1	16.3	24.6
1979	46.6	11.2	42.2

Note: * negligible.
Source: Levy 1982, p. 121.

in the State Department had no doubt whatever at that time, and for those particular reasons, that the Europeans would have made their own deals with the Libyans; that they would have paid the higher taxes Libya demanded and that the Anglo-Saxon oil companies' sojourn in Libya would have ended. (1973, p. 471)

The shift from a buyer's to a seller's market

The standard state of affairs in the oil industry was one of oversupply. This buyer's market weakened the bargaining power of oil-producing states, but in the crucial period of the late 1960s and 1970s demand began to outstrip supply. Table 7.3 shows the dramatic drop in world excess capacity from 1969 to 1974, the period when the US ran out of surplus capacity. US production reached its peak in 1970; imports went from two million barrels a day in 1967 to six million barrels a day by 1973. The US which had been the supplier of last resort in two World Wars became dependent like the rest of the industrialized world on imported oil. These data underestimate the real impact because even though excess capacity did not change much in absolute terms throughout the 1950s and 1960s in relative terms it went down dramatically as demand doubled between 1960 and 1970. The Middle East supplied most of this increase in demand. There was potentially oil in Alaska and the North Sea, but it was an expensive and long-term alternative to Middle East oil.

Oil companies like Occidental Petroleum and regions like Europe were extremely dependent on just a few countries for their oil. An accident which could take out a pipeline could mean almost an instant shortage. The Libyans were the first to show in 1970 how vulnerable oil companies and oil consumers were when such an accident occurred and the Libyans obtained

Table 7.3 *Changing barriers: excess capacity*

Year	Excess capacity
1959	17
1960	16
1961	17
1962	17
1963	17
1964	15
1965	15
1966	17
1967	19
1968	17
1969	8
1970	8
1971	9
1972	10
1973	7
1974	8
1975	17
1976	11
1977	10
1978	16
1979	14

Source: Stevens 1985, p. 43.

a 20 percent increase in royalties. This success might be enough for a conservative regime, but a more radical regime would certainly seize the occasion to press for more concessions.

The international oil system was a complex one, not without contradictions and conflict, but one key to the control of the majors was their stranglehold on distribution and marketing. With the rise of US independents, and European and Japanese oil companies, this grip was dramatically loosened. Oil-producing countries had many more potential buyers for their oil than did the Mexicans when they nationalized. Thus one barrier strength factor is the percentage of international oil marketed by the majors (table 7.2). The bargaining power of the producers also depends on the possibility of substituting oil from other sources; the barrier is stronger when much excess capacity exists (table 7.3). The barrier will hold if all these factors are strong, but if one is weak the whole structure is threatened. The strength of the barrier is thus the *product* of the barrier strength factors (each is standardized to lie between zero and one, one being strong and zero being

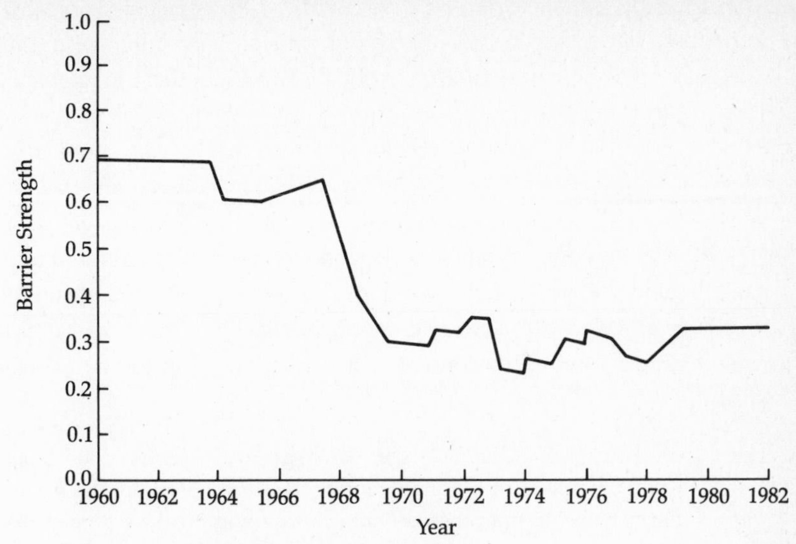

Figure 7.2 Changing barriers to nationalization

weak),[4] i.e., the percentage of world markets controlled by the majors times the excess capacity of the system.

Figure 7.2 shows the evolution of the barrier to oil nationalization over time. There is a dramatic drop in the strength of the barrier around 1968 which coincides with the beginning of the wave of nationalizations. Though most (e.g., Kobrin 1985) consider that the full force of oil nationalization hit in the early to mid 1970s it is clear that the situation became favorable in the late 1960s.

Old technology

Another development that weakened the barrier was the diffusion of oil technology from a few Anglo-Saxon companies to many all over the world. The rise of the independents illustrates this diffusion in the North. The endogenous process of development in the producing countries themselves helps explain the diffusion in the South.

The dissemination of oil knowledge goes beyond the scientific and engineering aspects of finding and producing oil; it extends to the

[4] The excess capacity was standardized by assuming that anything above twenty million barrels/day excess capacity did not strengthen the bargaining position of the majors; this is slightly more than the excess capacity throughout the 1950s. The standardized value of excess capacity is then actual excess capacity as a percentage of maximum excess capacity (twenty million barrels). This is a conservative procedure since total demand was rising very rapidly during this period.

economics and management of the oil industry. One constant problem faced by national oil companies was marketing their oil once they had produced it. It was relatively easy to reserve national markets for local companies, and this was frequently done. But venturing into international markets was another story altogether. As the Shah of Iran, one of the more militant figures in OPEC, remarked in describing the early 1960s: "I must admit we were just walking in the mist; not in the dark, but it was a little misty. There was still that complex of big powers, and the mystical power and all that magic behind the name of all these big countries" (cited in Sampson 1975, p. 160). Even relatively advanced producers like Venezuela had difficulty coming to grips with the economics of marketing oil in the industrialized North:

> Before 1959, Venezuela[n] experts were generally well informed about the technical aspects of oil production within the country, in the sense that they knew the principles of conservation and the best procedures for bringing oil to the surface; but they had very little idea of what went on in the industry as a whole. (Tugwell 1975, p. 56)

Part of the knowledge and technology diffusion process was the increased sophistication of the organizations and negotiators of the producing states. The earlier generation of leaders in the Middle East had no education in Western market economies. But the negotiators of the 1960s had been educated in the best US universities. For example, the OPEC Gulf Committee consisted of Iranian Amouzegar (educated at Cornell and the University of Washington), Saudi Yamani (educated at NYU and Harvard Law School), and Iraqi Hammadi (Ph.D. in agricultural economics from the University of Wisconsin). Another example is the scheme whereby royalties were to be counted as tax credits (hence transferring the costs to the US taxpayer) which was devised by Saudi tax experts. No longer could oil companies claim like D'Arcy Thompson (founder of Anglo-Persian, later BP) that it would take sixty years for oil fields to become profitable.

The nationalization of oil

By the late 1960s the international oil system was under great stress. The increased number of nationalist regimes in the Middle East and the shift from a buyer's to a seller's market meant that changes of some sort were quite likely. Nationalization was still seen, particularly by conservative governments, as an extreme measure that would upset the stability of the oil

Table 7.4 *Oil nationalization: crude oil ownership (percent)*

Year	Seven majors	Other companies	National oil companies
1950	98.2	1.8	*
1957	89.0	11.0	*
1966	78.2	21.8	*
1970	68.9	22.7	8.4
1979	23.9	7.4	68.7

Note: * negligible.
Source: Levy 1982, p. 117.

market. But something had to be done, by 1970 the era of concessions was over:

> But now [late 1960s], as far as the oil exporters were concerned, concessions were already a thing of the past, holdovers from the defunct age of colonialism and imperialism, wholly inappropriate to the new age of decolonization, self-determination, and nationalism. Those countries did not want to be mere tax collectors. It was not only a question of garnering more of the rents. For the exporters, the greater question was sovereignty over their own natural resources. Everything else would be measured against that objective. (Yergin 1991, p. 583)

"Participation" was the conservative governments', particularly the Saudi, response to this situation. Participation was a middle ground between the old concession system and the "too radical" step of nationalization. It was in large part the pressure from radical states that forced Saudi Oil Minister Yamani to devise this less extreme measure. Oil companies half-heartedly agreed to these proposals from fear of even more extreme ones. Such half-way measures, neither fish nor fowl, did not survive once the wave of nationalizations got underway.

Once the surge of nationalization was underway in the 1970s there was little left to stop it. As shown in table 7.4, even in the mid 1960s Third World producers owned very little of their oil; this was still the period of concessions. When nationalization took off in 1970 producers owned 8 percent of crude, but by the end of the decade this had reached the previously unimaginable level of 69 percent. International oil had always been a very politicized system, and the oil embargo of 1973 was part and parcel of that history. The embargo provided even more impetus for nationalization as the tight market became a shortage. By the end of the decade most Third World oil was the property of the producing country. The spot market had become the world market as oil marketers and refiners met oil producers to buy oil. Buyers now met sellers on relatively equal footing. The future would favor one then the other depending on global supply and demand, but one remnant of the colonial system had been removed.

Jumping on the bandwagon

I have emphasized the importance played by nationalist regimes in testing the system and pressuring for change. But one very distinctive aspect of the barrier decay process is the impact of "group pressure" on regimes that otherwise would not consider nationalization. Once the system begins to crumble "dominoes begin to fall" and governments "jump on the bandwagon." If we consider 1971 the turning point in the process this bandwagoning can be seen from the data in table 7.5. Conservative governments performed only six out of forty-two (14 percent) of all nationalizations by conservative governments before the explosion of 1971, while a much higher percentage (37 percent) of the nationalizations by radical regimes took place before the bandwagon got underway ($\chi^2 = 5.85$, 1 DF, significant at 0.01). This effect illustrates the importance of contexts in understanding behavior. A myopic focus on domestic or bilateral factors misses how social pressure influences behavior: in other circumstances conservative governments would not have nationalized oil. One distinguishing characteristic of really dramatic change is when the new behavior is "forced" upon recalcitrant states. If this does not occur then the process aborts early.

Much has been written about bandwagoning in the area of international security (Walt 1987; Jervis and Snyder 1991; Snyder 1991), particularly in contrast with "balancing"; the question being whether countries bandwagon (join the stronger side) or balance (join the weaker). The bandwagoning I discuss is of a qualitatively different sort. In the security literature the goals of governments remain constant, differences revolve around how to achieve those goals (which is more efficient, balancing or bandwagoning?). In contrast, barrier models suggest that goals change, that nations are under pressure to change their foreign policies. As Saudi Oil Minister Yamani said: "There is a worldwide trend toward nationalization and Saudis cannot stand against it alone" (cited in Yergin 1991, p. 584). This kind of bandwagon effect also stands in stark contrast to the assumption of

Table 7.5 *Changing national goals*

		Period	
		pre-1971	post-1970
Regime	Nationalist	17	29
	Conservative	6	36

Note: $\chi^2 = 5.85$, significant at 0.01.

stable preferences common in rational actor models. Barrier models challenge this assumption, but also suggest that preferences can be endogenized, since they are in part a function of the preferences and actions of other nations in the system.

A model of oil nationalization

In this section I describe a barrier model of oil nationalization. The rationale behind it was given in the previous chapter hence I focus on the particular realization of its components for the nationalization of oil.

The endogenous variable (Y) of the barrier model is the act of nationalizing oil. In particular I have used data on oil industry nationalizations which include refining and other aspects of the petroleum industry (Kobrin 1984). This nationalization may be partial or complete, but since the most frequent case is partial nationalization the possibility arises that a state can nationalize oil several times. In fact, this occurred on a number of occasions, Algeria leading the way with seven separate nationalizations. If more complete data were available I could make Y not just the act of nationalizing some part of the petroleum industry (the data I have) but what percentage of the industry is nationalized. This means that the total number of possible nationalizations is ambiguous. One reasonable, but *ad hoc*, assumption is that each country can nationalize on the average three times, making $\bar{Y}(t)$ equal to three times the number of Third World states with petroleum industries (this *ad hoc* assumption seems quite robust, I tried values of two and four in the empirical analysis with little change in the results).

Unlike most diffusion models that study a large number of individuals, I deal with a limited number of well-known actors. I shall consider as a possible nationalizer all Third World independent states (not colonies or dependent territories) that have petroleum industries. I thus exclude the USSR, East Europe as well as industrialized countries (by the OECD definition) of the West. The definition of "independent state" is a member of the international system as defined by the COW project (Small and Singer 1982).

The speed and extent to which nationalization spreads depend on the characteristics of the individuals in the population. Some are more favorably disposed to learning the lessons from nationalization attempts and in testing the barrier than others. The rate of pressure increase parameter π depends in part on the number (L) of countries likely to nationalize as soon as this is feasible. Operationally this is determined by whether the government in power is conservative or nationalist. This coding is based on the policy positions of the group *before* they come into power. The group coming to power must have proposed either nationalization, the formation of state enterprises, or greatly increased government control over foreign enterprises to be coded "nationalistic"; otherwise, it was coded conservative. The coding remains in effect as long as that government is in power. The number of nationalist and revolutionary oil-producing states indicates the pressure for change and the likelihood that change will spread rapidly.

The crucial component of the model is the barrier whose deterioration allows the process to get underway. I measure the strength of the barrier as described above (as illustrated in figure 7.2), as a function of decreasing control of the major oil companies over international markets and the decrease in world surplus capacity.

In summary the barrier model for oil nationalization consists of:

$$\frac{dY(t)}{dt} = [-\beta B(t) + \iota Y(t) + \lambda L(t) Y(t)]\,[\bar{Y}(t) - Y(t)]$$

$$\frac{dY(t)}{dt} = \text{the nationalization rate}$$

$$Y(t) = \text{cumulative number of nationalizations}$$

$$\bar{Y}(t) = \text{total number of possible nationalizations}$$

$$L(t) = \text{the number of nationalist or revolutionary regimes}$$

$$X_1(t) = \text{international market share of majors}$$

$$X_2(t) = \text{world excess capacity}$$

$$B(t) = X_1(t) * X_2(t), \text{ barrier strength}$$

For purposes of estimation I consider the discrete version of equation 7.1 where $Y(t+1) - Y(t) = \frac{dY(t)}{dt}$. As opposed to most diffusion models I consider that only recent nationalizations are relevant to the current process, hence $Y(t)$ instead of being cumulative nationalizations is the number of nationalizations in the previous two years. Since the barrier acts against nationalization it is appropriate to make the sign of β negative so that when the barrier is strong, i.e., $B(t)$ is large, it brakes the nationalization process, but as the barrier weakens, i.e., approaches zero, the braking pressure gradually reduces.

In summary, β represents the "barrier effect" and reduces the rate of nationalization. ι is the "imitation" effect, as $Y(t)$ (the number of recent nationalizations) increases so does the social pressure to nationalize. λ adds the effect of the number of nationalist regimes likely to push for nationalization.

Results

Table 7.6 presents the results of the OLS estimation of the barrier model given in equation 7.1. It should be recalled that the equation explains the number of *new* nationalizations, not the cumulative number of nationalizations over time. The results indicate that the barrier model fits quite well the data on nationalizations. The overall model is significant at 0.0001 with an R^2 of 0.83. All the parameter estimates are significant at the 0.005 level or better.

The "intercept" represents the base rate of nationalization, what one might expect in the absence of barriers or diffusion. If no external factors come into play we would expect a certain number of governments to come into power with nationalization as part of their agenda. The intercept suggests a rather high rate of three nationalizations per year as a base rate, the implication being that international barriers do play a significant role in preventing nationalization.[5]

The "barrier" parameter (β) is negative as hypothesized (since the barrier variable always remains positive the product is negative), and it is

[5] The continuous version of the model (equation 7.1) has no intercept term. If I force the intercept term to zero then in effect I am suppressing the number of nationalizations predicted in any given year. Statistically the result is that the model fits a little less well (since there is one less parameter estimated it must fit less well by definition) with $R^2 = 0.77$ and with the barrier coefficient significant only at the 0.10 level. This is not surprising since forcing the intercept to zero has a repressing effect. I think it makes more sense to assume some natural rate of nationalization independent of learning, social pressure, and barrier effects; this is naturally the intercept in a regression model, but the concept fits less well in a continuous dynamic equation model. The problem does suggest that refinements in the model would be useful.

Table 7.6 *Empirical estimation of a barrier model of oil nationalization*

Source	DF	Sum of squares	Mean square	F value
Model	3	363	121	43.8
Error	26	72	3	
Total	29	434		

Note: $R^2 = 0.83$. F-statistic is significant at 0.0001.

Parameter estimates

Variable	Parameter estimate	Standard error	*t*-stat	Prob > |*T*|
Intercept	2.81	0.90	3.11	0.005
Barrier (β)	−0.06	0.018	−3.46	0.002
Imitators (ι)	0.009	0.009	6.24	0.001
Nat. Regime (λ)	−0.0004	0.00006	−5.76	0.001

statistically significant at the 0.002 level. The barrier acts as a brake on the speed of the nationalization process. If the barrier is strong (i.e., equals one) the parameter estimate of −0.06 means that the barrier dramatically reduces the number of nationalizations. Thus both the significance and the magnitude of the effect show the importance of barrier strength in the nationalization process.

The variables "Imitators" (ι) and "Nat. Regime" (λ) describe the diffusion of nationalization to new countries (or repeated nationalization by the same country). The "imitator" parameter describes the interaction between the number of recent nationalizations and the number of potential nationalizers: it measures the combination of the social pressure to conform and the tendency of governments to imitate the behavior of others. The "Nat. Regime" variable adds (multiplicatively) the pressure of nationalist regimes to the diffusion rate. It acts as a "quadratic" term, being negative (typical of polynomial approximations of diffusion models) means it slows the diffusion process and eventually helps bring the number of nationalizers back down from its peak. Both variables are significant at the 0.001 level.

Figure 7.3 plots the actual number of nationalizations per year (solid line) versus the estimated number of nationalizations based on the model (dashed line) in table 7.6. In general, the predicted curve follows quite well the actual process of nationalization. The major "misses" of the model are two. The first is that the model "predicts" the little wave of nationalizations in the

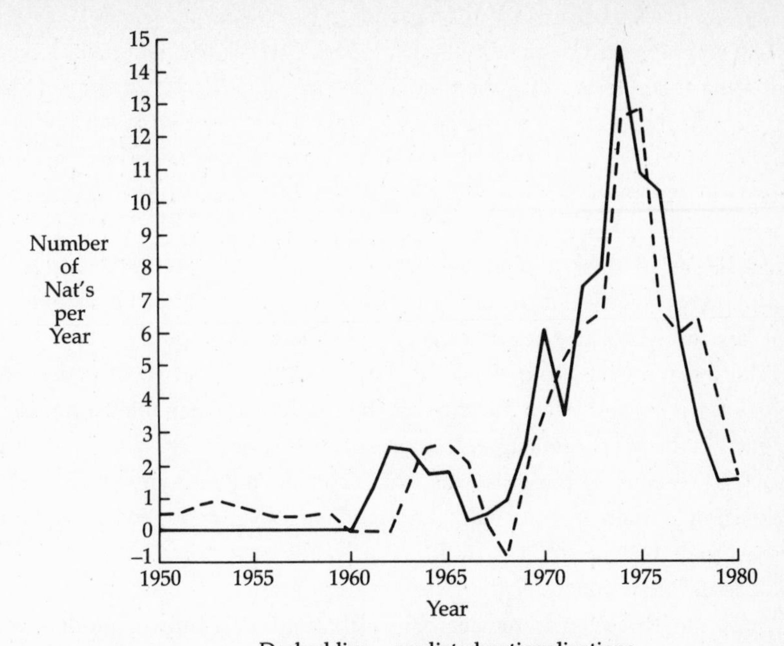

Figure 7.3 Predicted versus actual nationalizations

early 1960s a couple of years too late. This is not surprising given the coarse grain, yearly data I use: the process of oil nationalization is much more continuous than the yearly data I have show. The second miss is that the model underestimates the peak of nationalizations in 1974–5 and then overestimates their decline. The underestimation of the peak results from the dip in nationalization in 1971 which takes the steam out of the estimated process. The model does not capture the fact that the process "caught up" and proceeded at a rapid rate through the mid 1970s.

Conclusion

Midlarsky (1970) emphasized that his diffusion models were *models* but not *explanations*: barrier models are explanations. While there are numerous assumptions and data problems, barrier models appear to capture one process by which change spreads through the international system. The existence of exogenous variables in the model allows one to explain dramatic, systemic shifts in international politics.

In one sense barrier models tell us nothing new about oil nationalization, all its components are prominent in the literature on the nationalization of oil. What I suggest is that the model does integrate many elements of the oil nationalization story in a coherent explanatory framework. Also, barrier models provide a theoretical framework for exploring other cases of dramatic change in world politics. I suggest that the same process underlies many similar phenomena. The framework may serve in a quantitative analysis, as in this chapter, or may provide the theoretical tools for a descriptive, historical analysis, such as in the next chapter where I explore the breakdown of the barrier to change in Eastern Europe.

But much remains to be done. The dynamics of barrier construction and breakdown require much more research than I have been able to furnish. I argued in the previous chapter that pressure for change, i.e., $Y(t)$, accelerates barrier breakdown, but this was not incorporated into my model. One extension would be to add another equation endogenizing barrier breakdown: instead of $B(t) = f(X_1(t), X_2(t))$ another separate equation would be added $B(t) = f(X_1(t), X_2(t), Y(t))$.

Also on the agenda remains the elaboration of *learning* models that explain the dynamics of goal change and bandwagoning. We saw that as the process takes off there is a qualitative change as conservative governments begin to nationalize. This bandwagon effect is not explicitly included in the model (the imitation parameter partially captures this phenomenon). What is required is a theory of preference change; preferences clearly depend on the values and actions of other actors in the international system. Similar issues arose in the study of indicators of military allocation ratios, whose validity depended on the extent to which they incorporated the behavior of other states in the system. Some of the techniques I found useful there could be applied in barrier models: one possible indicator of the pressure to conform is the "distance" a country lies from system or regional norms. As nationalization becomes the expected behavior for Third World countries the pressure on conservative governments to do likewise increases.

The spatial and normative context is thus crucial in the explanation of explosive change. We see here the interaction of two modes of context: the barrier which prevents nationalization while the social pressure to conform is a good example of context as cause. Both are necessary for explaining dramatic change in international affairs.

8 EASTERN EUROPE, 1945–1989

> Evils which are patiently endured when they seem inevitable become intolerable once the idea of escape from them is suggested.
>
> Alex de Tocqueville (1856, p. 214)

Introduction

The world was shocked and fascinated by the speed with which Eastern European peoples threw off the yoke of Soviet-imposed governments. Throughout the post-World War II period there were attempts to change the Soviet-imposed system. The USSR resisted such attempts and showed itself willing to intervene militarily. Barrier models emphasize that it is not just the barrier but the interaction of the barrier and the pressures on it that set the scene for rapid change. Because most Soviet and East European experts focused on politics in a "top down" fashion they tended to ignore the popular support for change when change seemed possible (see Kuran 1991 for a model of change focusing on popular attitudes).

One question is why this structure collapsed in 1989: why not in 1968 or 1956? Indeed, taking other outbreaks of popular revolt at random, "why not 1953 or 1970?" One part of the answer clearly lies in Moscow. A change at the center altered the external constraints on popular movements in 1989. Barrier models are necessary condition explanations. Once Moscow had changed, then the *possibility* of reform could be posed in Eastern Europe. The other part of the answer lies in what opposition movements learned between 1968 and 1989. Gorbachev's reforms did not force reform on East European governments – many of them did not approve of what he was doing in the USSR. Revolution occurred when people took advantage of a new situation.

In chapter 6 I presented the theory of barrier models along with a formal model that could be estimated if data were available. In the previous chapter

I estimated this model using data on oil markets and oil nationalization. In this chapter I use a narrative approach to emphasize the learning and perceptions of individual actors in Eastern Europe. I will be quite interested in the perceptions of the various actors of what was going on around them, how those perceptions evolved from 1947–89, and how they changed in response to success and failure. In the oil nationalization study, the focus was on large-scale movements of technology, oil markets, and so forth. This chapter complements that one since it centers on another aspect of the overall process. It emphasizes individual perceptions and not the impersonal march of history – a false impression that the use of coarse-grain data and formal models can often give.

It is quite clear that the policy changes in the Soviet Union allowed the changes in Eastern Europe in 1989; the cause of the revolution was the action of East European peoples (as in the last chapter context as barrier and context as cause form a pair). I argue that the revolutions of 1989, dramatic as they were, represent a continuation of a basic process underway for several decades; just as the oil nationalizations of the 1970s were a culmination of a process underway since the 1920s. Like with oil nationalization, to understand the breakdown of the system it is important to understand the system when it is functioning well.

It is helpful to first clarify the nature and the origin of the system that began to give way in 1985. For the American observer Soviet military presence in Eastern and Central Europe posed a serious security threat to Western Europe. For those on the other side of the wall Soviet presence imposed constraints on the "host" country. From the perspective of local communist leaders, the problem was how to govern without legitimacy, for the very actions that would legitimate their rule were prevented by Moscow. As a bloc they depended on the USSR to support their one-party rule, but as individuals each sought to increase his independence from the center.

A key element of the system, created by force and maintained by varying degrees of terror, was the capacity of the local regimes in Eastern and Central Europe to govern according to policy set in Moscow. Because ruling leaders never dependably established their legitimacy, it all came down to their capacity to maintain order. Forced to wield their authority over their domestic societies using what were referred to euphemistically as "administrative measures," these states experienced constant pressure from below. Soviet armed force upheld the outer limits, but it was only employed when local developments threatened the central tenets of the system itself.

The principle at the heart of this system was the leading role of the communist party itself. Political pluralism was anathema to the one-party state in both Eastern Europe and the Soviet Union. If one of the local regimes lost its monopoly on state power as a result of societal pressure, it would serve as an example for neighboring societies within the bloc. (The oil companies had the same fears with regard to changes in the status quo in the international oil industry as a result of events like the Iranian nationalization of 1951.) As the character of Soviet–East European relations changed over time, from maximum repression under Stalin to liberalization under Khrushchev and back again under Brezhnev, the one-party state remained the inviolable limit beyond which no reformer could go. If local regimes could no longer maintain order by local means, as happened in 1956 and 1968, it fell to Moscow to maintain or reimpose the status quo by force.

The amount of opposition to this system in East European countries varied according to the relative strengths of the domestic societies. Local communist party elites in countries like Hungary and Czechoslovakia maintained a higher overall level of domestic legitimacy than their counterparts in the GDR. Their interest was to moderate Soviet policies and attempt to loosen their constraints, particularly where relations with the West were concerned. The Polish regime faced perhaps the worst of both worlds: it lacked domestic legitimacy precisely because of its association with Moscow; this gave the communist government little room to achieve relative independence from Moscow.

If we take the essential nature of the system constructed and maintained by the Soviet Union to be one of interlocking one-party states, and note that this chain was only as strong as its weakest link, the actions of Soviet leaders from Stalin up until Gorbachev take on some consistency. In the initial stages of "socialist construction," rival models of development would undermine faith in Moscow's leadership. Thus the USSR sealed the newly established regimes within the Soviet orbit from any high-level contact with the West and nationalist communist leaders were overthrown. Under Khrushchev policies shifted away from ideological hegemony toward unity within the socialist camp. Different roads to socialism were acceptable so long as they did not become divergent ones. Thus Gomułka's 1956 return to power in Poland was acceptable, while Nagy's attempt to withdraw from the Soviet bloc in the same year was not.

I will first look at the circumstances surrounding the construction of the Soviet system in Eastern Europe and then chart some of the initial attempts to test its permeability. Next I will examine each wave of the reform movement from 1948 to 1968 that increased both the autonomy and the vulnerability of local elites at each stage of the process. Then I examine in detail the final days of the system as each state goes through the process of testing its environment, learning about new possibilities, seizing new opportunities; finally I show the rapid spread of movements contesting Soviet policies to states with strong local communist parties, as other peoples jump on the reform bandwagon.

Building the Iron Curtain

The post-1945 period preceding the final bringing down of the Curtain saw both the US and the USSR maneuver for incremental advantage in Germany and shore up vulnerable allies on their side of the divide. Within Eastern Europe the Soviets had the more difficult time. For example, in Hungarian elections Zoltán Tildy's Smallholders' Party formed the government while the communist party polled only 17 percent of the popular vote. The consistent failure of Soviet-backed alternatives in electoral politics, with the notable exception of Czechoslovakia, meant that Stalin could not rely solely on elections to secure his East European position. Under the auspices of Soviet occupation local communist party officials secured the crucial government positions within the Ministry of the Interior before turning security and investigatory organs loose on their political opponents. By removing political opposition before legitimating elections were held Stalin followed his 1936 United Front policy to its logical conclusion. For example, in February 1947 communist-controlled security forces arrested the leadership of Hungary's independent Smallholder's Party and ended its reign. That same month a peace settlement was reached with Hungary on Soviet terms. This example illustrates that Soviet goals in this period went beyond favorable post-war territorial settlements. Stalin sought to entrench political parties subservient to Moscow.

Soviet policy in this period defined acceptable political independence within a particularly narrow range. Local governments would observe the following limits on their independence. First, they would not tolerate any independent opposition within their societies. Competing political parties were either coopted into coalitions under Soviet direction – as in Romania where social democrats and communists merged to form the Romanian Workers' Party – or were arrested and executed by the state. Rival national leaders were imprisoned like the Hungarian Smallholders' Party General

Secretary Béla Kovács, pushed into exile like Prime Minister Ferenc Nagy, or compelled to defect to Moscow as did the majority of the Smallholders' leadership cadre.

Second, the local communist parties were not to become centers of opposition to the USSR themselves. Moscow expected the newly founded People's Democracies to follow its foreign policy direction. Any deviation from Soviet foreign policy brought reprisals. This policy was designed to block a European rapprochement, particularly initiatives that might draw central and East European states back across to the West. Some years later Brezhnev delivered a candid assessment of Soviet interests in maintaining the system: "Your country is in the region occupied by Soviet soldiers in World War II. We paid for this sacrifice and we will never leave. Your borders are our borders" (Abel 1990, p. 193).

The rules were institutionalized in the Cominform and given theoretical substance by Andrei Zhdanov's "two camps" speech. Foreign policies of the People's Democracies were run from the center and direct military occupation assured conformity. Once the limits had been firmly established Soviet forces were partially withdrawn and the policing of the bloc fell to each local state apparatus under guidance and supervision of its counterpart in the Soviet Union.

The Iron Curtain did not merely encircle and seal off the two camps; it also descended vertically into the domestic societies of the nations themselves. The depth and character of this barrier can best be seen in the circumstances surrounding the *coup d'état* in Czechoslovakia in 1948. Unlike Poland, there lingered in Czechoslovakia sufficient ambivalence regarding the West that the veto of participation in the Marshall Plan and the cutting of ties to the West did not become the primary issue leading to the communist coup. Rather the issue was the extent to which the Soviet Union would permit socialism in Eastern Europe to diverge from a specifically stalinist model.

It is worthwhile to note the special position accorded the Soviet Union in Czechoslovakian history. Ethnic divisions and a weakened state, combined with the failure of pre-war leadership and betrayal by the West in 1938, created genuine sympathy for the Soviet Union. When the Red Army entered Prague it was greeted as an army of liberation. These factors, in stark contrast to the historical experience of the Poles, made the Czechoslovakian communist party the most successful electoral performer in the bloc. In May 1946 the CPCz polled 38 percent of the popular vote. Real support for the CPCz would remain a significant factor in Czechoslovakian politics right up until 1968 – a reserve of sympathy within the society itself impossible in Poland.

The first test: nationalist deviation

Divergence from the stalinist model brought Soviet pressure on local leaders to conform. Those suspected of harboring independent inclinations were charged with "Nationalist Deviation" and often tried for treason. In March 1948, the same month Soviet agents murdered the last remaining non-communist leader in the Czechoslovakian cabinet, a dispute erupted between the Soviet Union and Yugoslavia over the issue of the applicability of Stalin's model. Because of its historical independence from Soviet support, and thus from its control, Yugoslavian communists thought of the Soviet communist party as a brother rather than as a father.

Tito became the leader of the first significant challenge to the Soviet system in Eastern and Central Europe. Not only was Tito unwilling to impose the stalinist model of socialist development on Yugoslavia, but he also recognized Stalin's willingness to sacrifice Yugoslavian international interests. At this time Stalin had ordered Tito to cease aiding the communist rebellion in Greece in order to prevent further instability in the Balkans and to avoid provoking a Western response.

The Soviet Union descended with all its force at the Cominform conference in Budapest. Tito himself was denounced for nationalist deviation and ordered to recant. Stalin warned listeners that he had but to raise his finger and Tito would fall. By the end of the conference his finger had proved ineffectual. Tito's successful challenge constituted the first breach in the barrier. What factors made the Yugoslavian breakaway possible, and why was it successful when similar efforts on the part of nationalist communists in Poland and Czechoslovakia failed conclusively? From Khrushchev's memoirs it is clear that Tito presented stalinist policies with a number of obstacles. First and foremost the Soviet Union lacked a common border with Yugoslavia:

> I'm absolutely convinced that if the Soviet Union had [had] a common border with Yugoslavia, Stalin would have intervened militarily. As it was, though, he would have had to go through Bulgaria, and Stalin knew we weren't strong enough to get away with that. He was afraid the American imperialists would have actively supported the Yugoslavs. (Khrushchev 1970, p. 181)

A second factor was his status as a genuine and successful anti-Nazi leader. Like Enver Hoxha, and unlike Czechoslovakian and Polish leaders, Tito did not need Soviet help to remain in power. His control over his own party was complete. And the proven capacity of Yugoslavian Partisans to turn their country into a military and strategic porcupine may have given Stalin second thoughts.

Here we see some of the elements that permitted Yugoslavia to breach the rules of the stalinist system: (1) national political mobilization around an independent leader, (2) a complete erosion of confidence in any Soviet-backed alternative and the undivided opposition of virtually all sectors of society to the imposition of Soviet hegemony, (3) a sense within the Soviet leadership that the repercussions of the break could be limited with regard to its vital strategic interests, and (4) the high cost of an attempt to enforce Soviet policies by military force.

Tito's experience taught the East European leaders three important lessons. He demonstrated first that a break with Moscow was possible; second, that in the absence of the preconditions mentioned above it was political suicide to try; and, third, that testing the barrier was very costly.

The latter lesson was reinforced by what happened to the other leaders after Tito's break. East European leaders like Prime Minister Georgii Dimitrov of Bulgaria fell over one another to demonstrate their loyalty as the system closed tightly behind the exiting Yugoslavs. In September 1948 a massive purge was conducted in Poland. Those who wittingly or unwittingly appeared sympathetic to Tito in Stalin's eyes were purged throughout the People's Democracies. Vice-Premier Kostov was removed from the Bulgarian Politburo and executed a year later along with nine other officials. The reaction reached Hungary ten months later with the arrest in June 1949 of Foreign Minister László Rajk, followed by his execution. In November of 1949, over a year after the denunciation of Tito at Budapest, Gomułka was pushed out of the Central Committee of the PUWP. In Romania over 192,000 members were purged from 1948–50. More ominous for the other Republics was the appointment of Soviet Marshal Rokossovski as a Polish Politburo member and Polish Minister of Defense. (This same Soviet commander had halted Soviet forces on the east banks of the Vistula river during the Warsaw uprising while the Polish resistance was massacred.)

For the East European leaders the message could not have been made more clear, the wages of "nationalist deviation" were death, or, at the very least, political exile. It also brought another characteristic of the system to the foreground: a successful breach of the barrier by one party brought punishment down upon them all.

The Yugoslav case illustrates how those that create barriers intervene to limit damages caused by successful tests like Tito's. The punishment exacted on other East European countries assured the maintenance of the system, at least in the short term. Analogously in the case of oil, the US and the majors were able to limit damage caused by the Mexican nationalization and reverse that occasioned by the Iranian. The factors that permitted the Yugoslavs to be successful (except for the threat of military intervention) were identical to those that permitted the Mexican oil nationalization to succeed.

Destalinization: 1953–1956

Soviet leadership changes tended to act as the catalyst for tests of the barrier. The uncertainty surrounding a new Soviet leader inevitably moved local elites to reevaluate their connections to the center. It was, in short, a time for experimentation on all fronts. The death of Stalin in March of 1953 brought a particularly unstable transition. It was unclear who would succeed Stalin, or even whether an uncontested succession was possible. The second leadership crisis in Soviet history, it could potentially have degenerated into a contest between rival factions along the lines of the Stalin–Trotsky split from 1924 to 1928. Who wielded power and in what amounts was uncertain, as was the extent to which East European communist leaders could depend upon Moscow for support in the event of a crisis.

Two months after Stalin's death the Soviet presence in Germany ceased to operate under the auspices of the post-war Control Commission. A Soviet party member was appointed High Commissioner and assumed direct control. Within a month East German workers were rioting in the streets of Berlin. As revolt spread to other cities elements of the Soviet army present in Berlin moved on the strikers. The heavy use of Red Army military units, up to and including T34 tank divisions, helped reestablish order.

The suppression of the German riots brought several developments to a head. First, in July 1953 Stalin's likely successor, Lavrenti Beria, was executed, and the government declared a new course in bloc politics. Destalinization changed the rules of the game: the Soviet leadership would no longer administer the internal affairs of the East European states directly. In keeping with the end of the harsher stalinist policies, Beria's Soviet secret police organizations were dismantled in Eastern Europe, local political prisoners were released, and purged communist leaders were rehabilitated. With the removal of the Red Army and Beria's secret police the Soviet leadership ceded some independence to local parties.

As in other periods when the Soviet policies weakened local leaders took steps to increase their level of support with the people and to undercut potential opposition. As Soviet control decreased local leaders adopted more popular economic policies. Most were quick to abandon the stalinist model of socialist development, which had already brought domestic unrest to Berlin and food rationing to Czechoslovakia. Immediately after Beria's execution Hungary ended forced collectivization. Six months after Stalin's death the Czechoslovakian government announced that its economic policy would focus on consumer goods. In practice "national deviation" was no longer an executable offense, a major change which led up to the events of 1956.

Ruling elites in the East European states were also given some independence in shaping their own communist party organizations. Most attempted to moderate the unitary character of party structures left over from Stalin. The 6th Bulgarian Communist Party Communist Congress took steps to limit the power held within the party by any one man by separating party secretary and governmental leadership into two offices. One year after Stalin's death, Poland's PUWP went so far as to formalize the principle of collective leadership at its 2nd Party Congress. In July 1954 the Albanian Workers' party was reorganized to reflect the new orthodoxy. At the least this seemed to promise an end to the direction from Moscow of the East European parties. For example, Moscow's attempt to install Hungarian leader Imre Nagy in July 1953 was overturned two years later by the stalinists led by Rákosi, who purged Nagy for "Rightist Deviations."

If the character and composition of local party leadership was no longer strictly Moscow's affair, even more remarkable was the level of foreign policy independence shown during this period: at the same time as purged party members were leaving prison Yugoslavian diplomatic representatives were returning to East European capitals. Considering that it was precisely this issue which caused the 1948 crackdown, Khrushchev's June 1955 agreements with Tito marked a turning point in Soviet–East European relations.

It is crucial to remember, moreover, that all this occurred in the years before Khrushchev made his 20th Party Congress speech. The Soviet position had gone from the direct, coercive management of East European politics to that of a hegemonic veto. Moscow's new course weakened the ideological strictures on local parties, and the dissolution of direct military control made Soviet intervention less likely. Thus in a crisis the Kremlin would be faced with an array of increasingly costly alternatives. In exchange for devolving the per diem costs of maintaining the system to local parties Moscow had to accept a measure of autonomy on their part.

This new-found independence was not always entirely welcomed by local parties. Lacking the repressive resources of the Stalin years these communist leaders faced their ongoing legitimacy crisis with reduced power. The dilemma was to maintain Soviet structures while gaining a workable level of popular support in their own societies. Into this narrow and thoroughly unstable political equation was injected an added measure of uncertainty as to what Moscow really wanted.

Indeed, most crises begin with a misperception of an initiative taken by the Soviets. A message delivered from Moscow for one purpose was often read to entirely different effect by the East European societies. In his speech to the 20th Party Congress in February 1956 Khrushchev stressed Stalin's culpability for the horrors of the post-war years visited upon the parties in both the Soviet Union and Eastern Europe. By calling stalinism into question he tacitly exonerated the men who had been its first victims. It was clear that in future there would be "different paths to socialism." So long as the communist party retained its leading role and governments enforced limits on the expression of "anti-Soviet slander," local leaders would enjoy some independence in their domestic policies.

Quickly East European societies began to test the limits of Soviet policy. Within five months of Khrushchev's speech strikes broke out in Poland and free debating societies were formed in Hungary. According to Khrushchev's recounting of the 1956 crisis the Soviets were less concerned with the ideology of potential replacements than their reliability: Would these men cooperate with the Soviet Union? If reform-minded party members, intellectuals, and striking workers were powerful enough to topple one party leader then every bloc leader was in jeopardy. Control from the center was crucial during changes in East European communist parties. Moscow was to be consulted, not merely informed.

Another criterion imposed by Moscow was acceptance that equality of rights between socialist countries ended at the border with the West. The newly formed WTO alliance made coordination of policy more important than ever. Managing East–West contact was the sole province of Soviet diplomats.

The Soviets were willing to accept a local leader who could deliver on two points: respect for the principle of democratic centralism, and adherence to Soviet leadership in dealings with the West. In October 1956 the Polish leadership crisis brought a top-level Soviet delegation to Warsaw, but Khrushchev's personal intervention came too late. Władasław Gomułka had already resumed his post as General Secretary of the Polish communist party. Khrushchev's account noted that Soviet antipathy to Gomułka was balanced by the reality that only he could restore order and preserve the leading role of the party. Furthermore, military and security forces remained loyal to the Polish leader during the crisis. Gomułka's appointment would stand.

The contrast in Hungary is striking. What followed neatly illustrates the limits beyond which societal pressure could not go. There were, in fact, two Soviet invasions. The initial invasion ended when Prime Minister Imre Nagy took power and ousted General Secretary Ernő Gerő, who had lost the support of key Soviet Politburo members.

Nagy, however, went farther than anyone had expected. Public demonstrations went from anti-stalinist to anti-communist. In response Nagy declared a series of democratic reforms. This premature experiment in *glasnost* brought the inevitable corollary. On the last day of October 1956 with the leading role of the communist party now an open question, Imre Nagy announced that Hungary would withdraw from the Warsaw Treaty Organization. On 6 November 1956 Soviet troops returned and restored communist control with unprecedented violence.

Once again the limits had been enforced. The return of Soviet troops and the creation of a 62,000-man party army solidified communist party control. Soviet troops remained on Hungarian soil. Henceforth Soviet troops in barracks would play a role in local leaders' calculation of political possibilities. The Kádár government clamped down on dissent and shock waves traveled throughout the bloc: students at Sofia University in Bulgaria who had sympathized with the Hungarian revolt were expelled. In June 1958 Imre Nagy was executed.

After 1956

In the ebbing of the second wave of reform it is easy to miss what had been accomplished. Beneath the repression of 1956 there were undercurrents of change. Soviet troops left Romanian soil in July 1958, demonstrating the rewards that a faithful ally could expect. East European leaders who had supported the Soviet invasion, including Gomułka in Poland, learned from

Hungary's mistakes. One lesson was that de-stalinization would not be permitted to threaten the leading role of the party. Another was that an unpopular leader who could not control his own people was useless to Moscow.

The period leading up to the third wave of reform in 1968 is replete with examples of East European leaders attempting to compromise with domestic societies. For example, in April 1960 reports reached the West that rioting had broken out in Nowa Huta, Poland over the removal of a cross from a church. Earlier that same year Gomułka had reportedly held a secret meeting with church officials to bring them into an accord with the government.

The years before 1968 also demonstrated the limits of Soviet control. With the Sino-Soviet split in 1960 countries like Albania and Romania found an alternative to the Soviet model. Both China and Albania were distinct from the other East European states in that their party organizations were self-reliant. In February 1961 Albania followed suit and supported China in the dispute. Albania also had the advantages which made a break with the Soviets possible. Unlike the Central East European states Albania was both geographically isolated and irrelevant as far as Soviet military policy was concerned. The cost occasioned by the Albanian exit was primarily an example of defiance. Even here, however, the recalcitrant stalinism of Albanian leader Enver Hoxha allowed Moscow to turn the Albanian defection in its favor. East European states were unable to emulate China's example, and unlikely to follow Albania's lead in anything.

A clear lesson was that independence in foreign policy began with control over the local party organization. Within the WTO only Romanian leaders Georghe Georghiiu-Dej and Nicolae Ceauşescu could follow this path. Here the fundamental issue became economic independence. Romania opposed the "socialist division of labor" proposed at a Comecon meeting in March 1962. In 1964 Romania secured a trade agreement with the United States. In July 1965 the Romanian Communist Party Conference adopted a five-year plan designed to secure greater economic independence by increasing ties with the West.

A further consequence of the Sino–Soviet split was the ouster of Khrushchev in a 1964 palace revolt. As always, leadership changes brought opportunities and uncertainties. East European states attempted to discern precisely which of Khrushchev's policies had been repudiated. The foreign policy line remained unchanged as Brezhnev and Kosygin maneuvered to solidify their control, but uncertainty increased in the years after Khrushchev's fall. Also, the quasi-collective leadership of the pre-1968 period had the effect of multiplying the voices East European reformers could hear at any one time. This would prove increasingly important as the reformers of 1968 would come to rely increasingly on the personal assurances of Brezhnev and Kosygin who were not always in agreement with each another.

Prelude to 1968

The manner in which Romania secured incremental gains from 1961 to 1967 demonstrated that there was room to maneuver in Eastern Europe. Romania moved first to consolidate domestic control before moving to foreign policy. The Romanian leader's reading of the Soviet position allowed him to present small steps toward independence as a *fait accompli* which did not threaten the integrity of the system as a whole. After a purge of the officer corps Romania joined Albania and Yugoslavia in adopting a military posture consistent with total territorial defense.

Following this Romania made an unprecedented test of Soviet politics. In January 1967 Romania became the first East European state to establish relations with West Germany (FRG). The "German" question lay at the heart of Soviet security policy in the post-war period. Any diplomatic advance by the West Germans constituted a direct military, strategic, and political threat to the Soviet Union. On the other side of the Wall, no East European state's diplomacy was as tightly monitored by the center as East Germany's. It was over the diplomatic and legal status of the GDR (East Germany) that the Kremlin could least afford a foreign policy reversal. Rapprochement between the FRG and East European states could undermine the Soviet position in Eastern Europe. In a furious display of damage limitation the Soviets moved to reaffirm all the relevant bilateral treaties in force. For its part Romania refused to accept new agreements but did allow the previous Friendship Treaty to remain in force.

The Karlovy Vary Conference in April 1967 reaffirmed Soviet primacy in managing East–West relations, particularly when it came to Germany. It also drew a clear line separating East European states from West Germany. Trade contacts with the United States and even revisionist domestic policies were permitted so long as they strengthened the leading role of the party, but recognition of Germany threatened bloc cohesion. No East European state would be permitted to undermine East German and, by extension, Soviet security. East German insecurity was the tripwire that would undo the third wave of reform.

At this point the rules of the game centered on two main injunctions: do not compromise bloc unity and do not threaten the position of fellow socialist leaders by counter-revolutionary domestic policy. In practical terms bloc unity meant relations with West Germany and open criticism of bloc allies, while counter-revolutionary domestic policy comprised any popular movements that threatened the leading role of the party.

The Prague Spring

Throughout 1967 Czechoslovakia moved toward greater domestic independence from Moscow. Criticism of the party and government by the public increased. Party leader Novotný took a hard line and announced there would be "no compromise" with the bourgeoisie. In December 1967 Novotný condemned the 4th Writers' Congress in Prague for trying to form "a third force." In January 1968 Novotný was forced out of the Presidium by the reformers. Brezhnev declined to intercede on Novotný's behalf, actually saying at the time "It's your affair" (Mlynář 1980, p. 71).

The role public criticism had played in Novotný's ouster left the deceptive impression that popular pressure alone could produce political change. This revolutionary idea, combined with Soviet acquiescence to Novotný's ouster, suggested further reforms were possible. The belief that popular support would strengthen the party and bring gains for socialism was predicated on the false assumption that the popular movements would not lead Novotný's replacement Alexander Dubček to challenge the system. However, according to Mlynář's account:

> Dubček was unaware that ... a mechanism had been introduced capable of forcing change on the system ... a kind of public lobby backed by a free press. (Mlynář 1980, pp. 102–3)

In fact the Prague Spring soon brought both the leading role of the party and its subservience to Moscow into question. As Dubček's popularity increased it became less necessary to adhere to Soviet foreign policy strictures, and less useful. Once the CPCz sought to govern on the basis of genuine popular support, it could only do so by distancing itself from Moscow's example. By the end of the crisis Dubček's approval rating with the Czechoslovakian people reached 98 percent according to Radio Free Europe's "Popular Support of Dubček and the Action Program Czechoslovakia" (August 1968).

At the same time the opening of society invariably put pressure on the other bloc states to do likewise. They faced the same contradiction closing in on Dubček: the necessity of popular support to govern while this support demanded the surrender of the very instruments that maintained communist rule throughout the bloc.

Dubček compounded these contradictions with a complete lack of clarity regarding Soviet motivations and goals. Brezhnev's attempts to correct preliminary drafts of Dubček's speeches were rebuffed. Ideology was not primarily at issue: the CPCz very capably defended its actions in terms of marxist–leninist theory and practice. There is little evidence that Dubček sought to reverse "socialism" per se. Nevertheless, the Czechoslovakian experiment was beginning to become a direct challenge to the integrity of the Soviet system itself.

Although the CPCz never lost control of the reform movement as Nagy had in 1956, it could not contain the effects on surrounding East European states. The Prague Spring reintroduced popular movements as a force in bloc politics for the first time since 1948. The spread of reform was anathema to the Soviet Union and its Eastern Bloc allies. Extra-party opposition undermined democratic centralism and threatened the leading role of the party itself.

As in 1956 there was a push to test the barrier. In 1968, however, divergent tendencies at the center were more pronounced (Dawisha 1984, p. 15). This led Czechoslovakia's leaders to misinterpret personal assurances and friendly gestures from leaders such as Prime Minister Kosygin. The initial intervention in 1956 had ousted an unpopular leader unable to secure order. Brezhnev's decision not to support Novotný in 1968 was a clear warning that leaders unable to keep their domestic house in order could expect no assistance from Moscow. But the Soviets dropped Novotný quickly precisely to avoid a repeat of 1956. Although Dubček learned from Nagy's mistake and offered consistent support for the WTO – even to the point of authorizing the WTO exercises on Czechoslovakian territory that facilitated the invasion – the Soviet leadership had also learned from 1956: a local communist party in the sway of popular pressure was a threat to Soviet interests.

Some members within the CPCz understood the nature of the barrier they confronted. In April 1968 Zdeněk Mlynář drafted the so-called Action Program which provided for the democratization of the CPCz. This blueprint was written with the understanding that there were two threats to the Prague Spring, the "major problem" of how to avoid a demand for "opposition parties ... in the early phases of the reforms" and the "international factors – that is to say, the possible interference of Moscow." In Mlynář's view, a "rapid and orderly change of functionaries in the party and state organs would ... give the politics of reform all the trumps" (Mlynář 1980, p. 9).

Reform communism recognized the dangers posed by popular movements. A key aspect of the plan was the need to channel popular discontent into the party elections leading up to the 14th Party Congress. These would still be one-party elections, but delegates could be selected on the basis of support for the Action Program. Thus hardline opponents could be dropped from power in a legitimate fashion without threatening the leading role of the party itself. In turning democratic centralism against itself the reformers thought they could gradually reduce Soviet influence within the CPCz. The unspoken purpose was to forestall increasing pressure from below that might trigger a Soviet response.

Throughout the crisis one of the constant issues raised by the Soviet leadership was violations of "cadre policy"; Dubček failed to consult with the Soviet leadership on appointments and removals within the CPCz and the state. Brezhnev's post-invasion summary of events emphasized this point: he had been willing to support Dubček against his rivals in the CPCz and even backed him within the Soviet Politburo – so long as Soviet interests were respected. Brezhnev's disavowal of Novotný in January and his offer to replace Novotný sympathizers lends credibility to his statement.

Dubček further misunderstood the impact of domestic reform on other states – particularly the GDR and Poland. The threat liberalization posed to Ulbricht and Gomułka, both of whom were vulnerable, is clear from their reactions in bloc conferences. Gomułka's position in Poland was similar to the one that had led to the fall of Novotný at the end of 1967. On 8 March 1968 large-scale riots broke out in Poland calling for a "Polish Dubček." Poland's Prime Minister stressed that bloc cohesion was not just an ideological issue: "It is also a dictate of the instinct of self-preservation, in order that we may not be grabbed by the throat one by one, in order that the weakest links shall not be picked out from our camp, and so that those links shall not be thrown at others" (Dawisha 1984, pp. 112–3).

The danger to Ulbricht went beyond even the issue of his personal power. He consistently warned Moscow that failing to take action against Dubček would undermine the cohesion of the bloc. The GDR began banning Czech newspapers and canceling travel visas. Visiting Czech students were prevented from participating in student debates in East Berlin.

In a closed meeting with Pact leaders he said "if the January line is continued in Czechoslovakia ... [w]e may all find ourselves kicked out" (Dawisha 1984, p. 45).

From the Soviet vantage point the openness of the Prague Spring would inevitably call the leading role of the party into question closer to home. Where reform communists in Prague believed that a dialogue with civil society could only strengthen socialism, there was no question but that anywhere else it would undermine it. A participant noted that the Soviets were less concerned with the huge displays of support for Dubček than with the activities of opposition groups. Thus international issues inevitably became domestic issues for the Soviet Union's polyglot empire. Ukrainian nationalism linked up with the Prague Spring leading to an exhibition of Ukrainian art on 17 June 1968. This seemingly unremarkable event assumes its true weight because it was the first such exhibition since 1945. Later a seminar on "Ukrainian National Consciousness" was planned and unrest also spread to Latvia and Lithuania.

Tito, having broken with Moscow in 1948, showed every sign of actively opposing Moscow over the Prague Spring. In the last hours of the crisis he rushed an interview into print stating: "I do not believe that there exist in the USSR people so shortsighted as to resort to a policy of force to resolve Czechoslovakia's internal questions ... Moreover, I do not believe that there is anything about the present situation in Czechoslovakia which constitutes a threat to socialism" (Dawisha 1984, p. 198). Having already achieved virtual domestic independence, Romania also opposed Soviet intervention from within the WTO itself. In the last days before the invasion, Ceauşescu and Tito both refused to cancel visits to Prague, where they were treated as allies against a hostile power (Dawisha 1984, p. 277).

The Hungarians faced a dilemma. Kádár supported the Czech Action Program as an example of reform communism, but he was also aware of the risks. A Party editorial referred to the Prague Spring as a "renaissance, full of political hopes and socialist in content," and went on to note "for us, the renaissance ... cost a high sum" (Dawisha 1984, p. 33). The Hungarian communist party had also launched its own economic reform program the same month Dubček came to power. Support for the Prague Spring risked the Hungarian New Economic Mechanism.

From the first-hand accounts it is clear that Dubček sincerely did not believe the bloc countries would take military action against his country. The CPCz continued to rely on formal agreements and ideological arguments to support its position in a context that was increasingly shaped by Soviet hegemonic interests. Kádár made the point plainly when he took Dubček aside at a meeting on their border on 17 August: "Do you REALLY not know the kind of people you're dealing with here?" (Mlynář 1980, p. 157).

The Bratislava Conference produced an agreement that recognized the duty and responsibility of the bloc to protect and defend the gains of socialism in each member state. When the CPCz delegation tried to delimit this by adding a clause stating "while respecting the sovereignty" of the individual states, Brezhnev replied that such a grammatical insertion would "go against the spirit of the Russian language" (Mlynář 1980, p. 154). Soviet and WTO troops invaded. Brezhnev made his understanding of Soviet policies clear to his Czech captives: "For us, the results of the Second World War are inviolable, and we will defend them even at the cost of risking a new war" (Dawisha 1988, p. 7; Mlynář, 1980, p. 241).

The social pressure, imitation process stressed by barrier models was clearly already present in 1968. Popular protest spread rapidly in 1968 just as it did twenty-one years later, but the necessary condition for its success was missing: the Soviets had the means and the desire to maintain the system in place. But in one important way the events of 1989 and 1968 were driven by the same basic forces. The lessons of 1968 did not change the basic conjunction of forces, but it did mean that tests would be infrequent and people more hesitant to jump on the reform bandwagon – something which comes out clearly in the events in Poland in 1980 and 1989. Just as most Middle East governments would remember what happened to the Iranians so would most people remember what happened to the Czechs. Barrier models emphasize that the forces for change often lie hidden, and sometimes become invisible, but nevertheless are present waiting to erupt.

Results of 1968: The Prague Resistance

Unlike Stalin, Brezhnev and the Politburo had no desire to use the military to flatten the Czech landscape into a mirror image of Soviet communism. Their objective was to restore party discipline and bring the population to order. The initial plan was to install a "revolutionary government" of "honest communists" and then use enough force to support this new regime as it complied with the terms of the Warsaw Letter. Instead, control of the situation slipped rapidly from Moscow's grasp.

Post-invasion events tell us more about the viability of the barrier than the Prague Spring itself. Many of the strategies that were to be used successfully in 1989 make their appearance here. The first was non-violent popular mobilization. The country began what amounted to a "white mutiny" against the Soviet occupation forces – orders were given, there was no violent resistance, yet nothing was done. In the Novotný years, reform CPCz members like Zdeněk Mlynář had used this tactic to limit the authoritarian tendencies of the regime: "I tried to formulate a line of approach that, although it did not radically disturb anything, obliged them to strictly observe the legal norms in force" (Mlynář 1980, p. 39). Now this same strategy was turned against the Soviet occupiers.

Immediately after the invasion Czech and Slovak workers began a series of *ad hoc* strikes that paralyzed the country. Intellectuals of the Prague Spring worked alongside the strikers and continued an underground campaign of anti-Soviet agitation. Reform communists, meanwhile, called the 14th Party Congress into session and demanded a Soviet withdrawal. This alliance between workers, intellectuals, and reform communists made the Soviet "Revolutionary Government" a dead letter. Mlynář was taken from house arrest to meet with the Soviet Ambassador and saw post-invasion Prague for the first time: "It was the picture of a city whose inhabitants were absolutely united in unarmed, passive resistance against alien interlopers" (Mlynář 1980, p. 163).

The reform communists resorted to a tactic that would reappear in the revolutions of 1989: they took refuge in what might be called "socialist due process." Soviet occupation lacked a legal instrument through which to work. It became clear that while overwhelming force could repress individuals, it could not govern a society effectively. The Soviets were forced to choose between massive repression and restoring Dubček to power.

The resolution of the crisis gradually gave control over to the Soviets, but it also showed the system's vulnerability to popular mobilization. The majority of Czechoslovakian people had supported Dubček and opposed the invasion. The Soviets were forced to return Dubček to power until a suitable quisling government could be set up. Anti-occupation demonstrations continued into 1969. In March 1969 the Soviet Defense Minister publicly threatened the use of Soviet troops to put down violent anti-Soviet protests.

Within the CPCz Husák replaced Dubček and began the long process of restoring control. From the beginning in September 1969 it is estimated that over 1.5 million CPCz members were purged. In the revolving door of the post-1968 purges, Dubček and the other reformers were expelled from the party and Novotný was rehabilitated. Out of a population of fifteen million, up to one million at a time were assigned to manual labor by the party. The suppression after 1968 cost Husák the loyalty of his people and pushed reform communists into opposition with liberal intellectuals and students. Polish dissident Adam Michnik noted that this was not "socialism with a human face" but "communism with a few teeth knocked out." Thus the government reconstructed after 1968 was in many respects weaker than its predecessor. Domestically, the purging of reform communists weakened the party immeasurably. Mlynář writes that the reformer's creed had always been "for power to serve our needs, we in turn had to serve it" (Mlynář 1980, p. 57). After 1968 this was no longer true. Internationally, the Brezhnev Doctrine was a frank recognition that the system was in the final analysis dependent upon Soviet military power. The misuse of WTO in 1968 stripped it of the facade of a defensive alliance; it was understood that Soviet and WTO existed as much to uphold the system from within as to protect it from without.

After 1968: normalization

In the period leading up to the final phase of reform beginning in 1980 several factors worked to undermine the system. The first was constant threat of popular revolt. "Normalization" was a frank recognition that the CPCz could no longer govern without Soviet support. Related to this was the legitimacy crisis experienced by all the Soviet satellites in the wake of the Prague Spring. In December 1970 strikes and riots led to the overthrow of Gomułka by Edward Gierek. In the GDR Eric Honecker succeeded Ulbricht six months later. In 1972 the first student demonstrations since 1956 took place in Hungary commemorating the revolt of 1848.

After 1968 the leaders of East European states made an implicit bargain with their own people to strengthen their position: they would provide material prosperity in exchange for outward loyalty. For example, the Comecon created an investment bank in 1970 as Poland began accumulating its hard currency debt. At the 6th Party Congress of the PUWP Gierek declared that the "supreme goal" of the party was the improvement of living standards. As with Czechoslovakian "normalization," the government's legitimacy depended increasingly on the living standards of their workers.

Throughout the 1970s and 1980s the raw materials for domestic "normalization" – economic prosperity – depended on normalization of relations with the West. This inevitably meant closer ties with West Germany. In 1972 the GDR and the FRG concluded a series of agreements normalizing their relationship. In June 1973 Ceauşescu became the first East European head of state to visit West Germany. The next month the Conference on Security and Cooperation in Europe opened. The "Helsinki Conference" recognized the post-war borders in Europe and cleared the way for East–West cooperation in Europe.

The Helsinki Process also included a pro forma section on human rights. Western negotiators underestimated the impact this document would have in Eastern Europe. Czechoslovakian dissident groups, drawing an arrow from the quiver of 1968, banded together to monitor compliance with this declaration. Like K 231 during the Prague Spring, which was a human rights club open to anyone imprisoned under the 1948 Law 231, Charter 77 was effective because it claimed to uphold the letter of the law. It was not a political party or an anti-socialist group, it "merely" publicized violations of an international agreement freely signed by the government. In taking a clear ethical and legal stand the Chartists became a focal point for dissidents in other states.

While the intellectuals were being imprisoned in Czechoslovakia, sporadic popular revolts continued to pressure the East European regimes. There were price riots in Poland in 1976, and miners organized a wildcat strike in Romania's major coal fields in 1977. What was missing was a force that could merge protesting workers and dissident intellectuals into a political force as the Soviet invasion of 1968 had done.

Prelude to 1989: Solidarity

In 1980 price increases once again brought strikes from the Polish workers; this time they spread into the heart of the country bringing production to a virtual halt. The strikes continued into August after which General Secretary Gierek resigned. The Soviet reaction was consistent with the current WTO line which stressed the need to protect détente. As in the early phases of 1968 the Soviets treated the matter as an internal Polish affair.

The PUWP Central Committee led by General Secretary Stanisław Kania proceeded to purge party members opposed to a compromise with Solidarity and subsequently gave it legal status in exchange for recognizing the leading role of the party. When this failed to end the crisis, however, bloc defense ministers began a series of hurried meetings and troops concentrated along the Polish border. Solidarity, cognizant of the 1968 precedent, canceled a strike planned for December. The war of nerves continued into 1981 as food shortages compounded the labor movement's grievances. Warsaw Pact forces held maneuvers around Poland under the command of a Soviet marshal. US and European pressure on the Soviets to refrain from intervention, in marked contrast to the free hand given in 1956 and 1968, complicated matters for the Soviet leadership.

In November 1981 Lech Wałęsa met with Jaruzelski, who had taken over the leadership of the Polish government, to stabilize the situation, but he subsequently issued demands that pointed at the heart of communist control of the state: these included open elections, media access, and power-sharing between the union and the PUWP (identical in substance to the demands acceded to by the PUWP in the 1989 round table discussion). The Soviet press announced that the crisis now posed a direct threat to Soviet security and Jaruzelski declared martial law. It was clear that the primary obstacle preventing the Polish leadership from settling with Solidarity was the threat of Soviet intervention. Public protest against martial law undermined the authority of the Polish government and led to a series of clashes throughout the period. The Polish government's attempt to dismantle Solidarity led the US to suspend Poland's Most Favored Nation status. Nationwide demonstrations in support of the banned trade union continued throughout the period while the government-sponsored unions languished.

During the ongoing Soviet leadership crises up to 1985 the East European states came under increasing pressure from grassroots organizations. The deployment of INF missiles in Europe produced an independent East German peace movement. In Hungary the leadership faced the wrath of environmental groups capable of mobilizing 10,000 people in a public demonstration. All these groups had one thing in common: they were not overtly political in intent. Throughout East European states, the rebirth of civic society filled the gap between people and party with an independent agenda for reform. They avoided threatening the party directly, but focused their energies on popular issues that the government did not address. They did not rely on illegal actions to achieve their goals and so made it more difficult for the party to attack them. Rather they used variations on the strategy of "socialist due process" used by Charter 77 in Czechoslovakia, calling on the government to abide by its own laws and treaties.

All of this – the radicalism of Solidarity, the moral authority of Charter 77, and the popular pressure of the grassroots movements – constituted the civic society that was the focus of dissidents like Adam Michnik and Václav

Havel. This network of people and ideas became a kind of internal government in exile. Leaders like Havel and Wałęsa were able to assemble dissident intellectuals into a shadow cabinet awaiting its historical moment; it was in the words of one dissident "a conspiracy of caution" (Abel 1990, p. 44).

The learning that led to the revolutions of 1989 was grounded in previous failures. After each failed attempt at revolution the societies enclosed within the system evaluated their situations and learned the lessons of the previous tests. Similar obstacles recurred with dismaying frequency, foremost among these was the obstructionist role played by the Soviet Union. In 1956 and 1968 popular movements had been broken by direct Soviet intervention, while the reality of Soviet forces had brought on martial law in Poland in 1981. As long as governments retained the trump of Soviet intervention real reform was unlikely. A second obstacle was the weakness of the societies themselves; denied freedom of expression and forbidden to organize political opposition to the communist party, opponents of the regimes lacked a political base to give force to their demands.

These two factors, ironically, persuaded dissidents like Václav Havel and Adam Michnik of the effectiveness of renouncing force. By avoiding direct confrontation with the regime they were able to impose strains on the ruling parties without provoking a crackdown. Reaching back to successful examples of resistance under martial law after 1968 and 1981, the dissident leaders adopted passive resistance and focused their efforts on the strengthening of civil society. Accepting constraints where the regime was strong, but working within these to build up pressure for change, Havel and Michnik became artists of the possible.

The key to converting dissent into political power was the alliance forged in 1980 between workers and intellectuals. As that summer demonstrated, wildcat strikes could bring temporary concessions from government negotiators, but meaningful change required an overall program. Labor unrest had been a constant feature of life in East European states since their formation, but it only brought political results when allied with broader social forces. Intellectuals gave strategic purpose to tactical strikes: "They always tried to find a deal acceptable to the communist government, one which it in turn could sell to Moscow" (Echikson 1990, pp. 128–9).

Adam Michnik, "spiritual father of social self-organization," had formed Workers' Defense Committees in 1976 to assist striking workers who had lost their jobs. This kind of "social work" was instrumental in building the informal network that bound the opposition together. From his early work came the basic strategy used after the crackdown in 1981. Michnik recognized the constraints that had turned back previous reform movements and sought to avoid precipitating a crisis within the system. Instead the reformers adopted an evolutionary approach to social change; rather than challenge the state directly they concentrated on incremental gains.

Nevertheless, before *glasnost* the prospects for change in Eastern Europe were bleak. Most of the familiar limits remained in place. In 1981 the Soviet Union formally protested a memorial to the murdered Polish officer corps and criticized the "so-called renewal" of the Polish Catholic Church. Under pressure from Moscow Honecker suspended his historic visit to West Germany in 1984. On 26 April 1985 treaty members formally extended the Warsaw Pact for another twenty years.

The beginning of the end

From 1986 onwards the barrier imposed upon Eastern Europe began to disintegrate from within. Gorbachev seemed to suggest a change in fundamental doctrine in a speech to the 27th Party Congress in February 1986. He spoke of a need "to understand the processes of protecting democracy, management methods, and personnel policy on the basis of several countries rather than of one country" and promised "a considerate and respectful attitude to each other's experience and the employment of this experience in practice."[1] One year later he affirmed the independence of each state's communist party and stressed "its responsibility to its people, and the right to decide in a sovereign manner how each country should develop" (Dawisha 1988, p. 170). The culmination was Gorbachev's speech to the Council of Europe in July 1989 in the midst of the revolutions in Eastern Europe: "Any interference in domestic affairs and any attempts to restrict the sovereignty of states, both friend and allies or any others, are inadmissible ..." (Rathwald 1989, p. 379).

By the time Gorbachev came to power in 1985 it was clear that the Polish communist party could not govern without coming to terms with the society it ruled. In June 1986 the PUWP Party Congress formed a Consultative Social Council of non-party intellectuals to advise Jaruzelski. He met with the Pope and Gorbachev in turn and came away a convert for

[1] Foreign Broadcast Information Service (FBIS) III, 25 February 1986 G 27th Congress speech: 01–42; 59–60.

reform. On 21 October 1987 Jaruzelski promulgated a communist code for democracy in socialism. It stated that "both ignoring contradictions and exaggerating and badly resolving them result in social tensions, hinder development, and may become sources of conflict and even crises that enable counter-revolutionary forces and trends to take action" (Dawisha 1988, p. 181). It was clear that one such force was the Solidarity movement. The government made concessions to settle individual labor disputes and allowed a grassroots peace group to substitute alternate service for military service in 1988, but it refused to recognize the necessity of negotiations with Wałęsa. One government spokesman stated "the Solidarity movement ... belongs to the past for good" (Garton Ash 1989, p. 16).

According to an official government release Gorbachev's July 1988 visit to Poland was crucial and "in particular, influenced the change of political line among a considerable section of the opposition [within the PUWP]" (Staar 1989, p. 407). In August 1988 the Minister of the Interior offered to legalize Solidarity if Wałęsa would persuade the striking workers to return to their jobs. Wałęsa rejected the compromise gesture and called for full negotiations pertaining to the future of the country. The PUWP lacked the foresight of its counterpart in Hungary, which was already engaged in a rearguard action, the party continued to oppose any concessions to Wałęsa. Through the winter of 1988 Jaruzelski apparently fought the PUWP leadership to a standstill over the Solidarity issue. In January 1989 he secured approval for negotiations with Wałęsa only by threatening to resign and take the military with him.

Roundtable negotiations opened on 6 February 1989 with a photo session that produced shockwaves throughout the bloc. Each party came to the table thinking it understood the limits the other faced. The government knew that Solidarity had lost its numerical strength, and that only Wałęsa's personal integrity had convinced workers to return to work. Solidarity negotiators, on the other hand, expected the central issue to be the international and ideological implications of legalizing an opposition group. As a dissident made clear at the time "we don't have to be warned that post-communist democracy is best when cooked on a low flame" (Abel 1990, p. 44).

Once the talks began, however, it became clear that the external constraints no longer existed. The absence of external constraints substantially increased Solidarity's power. Jacek Kuroń, later Solidarity candidate for Minister of Labor, compared the situation with 1981: "Everybody knows that the decision to bring Solidarity back depended on our own government, and not on the tanks over the border" (Echikson 1990, p. 6). For the first time since 1945 Poland's communist leadership could negotiate independently of Moscow. According to one mediator at the talks "Moscow's message was 'don't be so careful. Do whatever is necessary to get your house in order'" (Echikson 1990, p. 20).

The April agreement was largely a product of Geremek's prudence. It set a schedule for comprehensive democratization and permitted Solidarity to run opposition candidates in elections held on 4 June 1989. These would be the first contested elections in forty-four years – a breakthrough that was less remarkable in the final analysis only because events moved faster elsewhere. During the negotiations the government suggested that the final agreement include a statement that identified "parliamentary" with "socialist" democracy. The Solidarity side suggested that they could only add a sentence about the agreement's role as "the beginning of the building of a sovereign, independent Poland" (Garton Ash 1989, p. 18). The alliance of workers and intellectuals formed in 1980 had won a crucial victory.

The agreement as negotiated gave Solidarity candidates access to 35 percent of the electoral seats and control of the Senate. The purpose was to make certain that Jaruzelski, who would retain substantial influence through his military connections, would be ensured the Presidency. But Solidarity's carefully designed face-saving exit was closed by the voters themselves. With the ominous images of the massacre in Tiananmen Square beaming around the world, the Polish elections produced a minority communist government. This occurred because voters took the trouble to scratch off every PUWP candidate on the ballot thus leaving them with less than the necessary 50 percent of the votes in many districts.

Solidarity then contrived Jaruzelski's successful election to the presidency. Wałęsa explained the need for circumspection during the vote for Jaruzelski:

> Everything has to be calculated very well on the computer. We want to stay on the reform course and not provide arguments against us by those who are just waiting for them. (Abel 1990, p. 90)

In the end some Solidarity members simply called in sick.

Events in Hungary, meanwhile, proceeded along a somewhat different track. Having long maintained an independent economic policy, and distanced itself from repressive Soviet policies, the HWSP was less threatened by a withdrawal of Soviet support than leaders in Poland and Czechoslovakia. Party members responsible for interbloc relations had long called for Soviet recognition of the principle of non-interference. The party moved quickly to increase support from within Hungarian society and disavow its past. The HSWP strategy appears to have been to coopt the same movements that were threatening the party in its bloc partners.

In November 1986 "populist" leader Imre Pozsgay used his support among intellectuals to push out several Kádár loyalists. Soon Pozsgay was saying that "communism had reached the end of its usefulness" (Abel 1990, pp. 20–1). Hungarian nationalism soon reappeared in party policy as well. In March 1987 the Hungarian regime permitted a demonstration of 1,500 to march in Budapest commemorating the national uprising of 1848, despite some demonstrators' calls for a monument to Imre Nagy. One year later the Hungarian communist party, as part of an ongoing battle with Romania over its minority Hungarian population, supported a anti-Romanian demonstration in Budapest. One party member commented on the scene:

> It's all very well to have thousands of people out in the streets shouting anti-Romanian slogans. But what was to prevent their shouting "down with socialism?" (Abel 1990, p. 39)

At the same time pressure against the communist parties of all the East European states continued to mount as individuals and societal organizations tested their new-found freedom. One of the best examples is the story of Augustin Navrátil, a Moravian peasant who learned about the Helsinki Agreements from BBC radio and began circulating petitions for religious freedom. His first petition garnered 500,000 signatures and led to his arrest. Upon his release he began a letter-writing campaign asking whether or not his right to petition was covered under Article 29 of the Czechoslovakian constitution. He suffered harassment and beatings, but finally organized enough mass support for the government to accede to the appointment of new bishops for the first time since 1973. In explaining his success Navrátil placed great emphasis on the crumbling of the external barrier: "The atmosphere is different now with *perestroika* and *glasnost*. Everything depends on how the situation develops in the Soviet Union" (Echikson 1990, p. 182).

Larger groups also prepared for the coming confrontation. Hungary's first Independent Union of Scientific Workers demonstrates the interconnection between the changed external environment and evolutionary learning. Pál Forgács first got the idea for an independent union of scientists in December 1987: "The changes that led to our forming the union started with the example of Solidarity in Poland and of Gorbachev in the Soviet Union." Forgács utilized a provision of Hungary's constitution that provided for free entry in mass organization in order to avoid the hurdle of gaining governmental permission. When the government tried to halt the union on the grounds that mass organizations had to have party approval, a team of volunteer lawyers discovered that Hungary was party to an International Labor Organization agreement that contained the right of workers to unionize. Imre Pozsgay accepted the new union in May 1988 and it soon had over 10,000 members. And true to the tactics of Michnik and Havel, Forgács disavowed comparisons with Poland's banned trade union: "we have no political line and we are determined not to become one more anti-communist organization" (Abel 1990, p. 35).

Civic groups like these were, in the words of one of its members, "a laboratory for mobilizing opposition" (Echikson 1990, p. 233). Rendered ineffective in the face of such national protest, the instruments of one-party rule fell by the wayside. In January 1989 as Poland was entering the first stages of its revolution the HSWP gave guarantees of freedom of assembly and association. One month later the party promised a gradual transition to a multiparty system. In April 1989 the party proclaimed the end of "democratic centralism."

More than any other East European state Hungary's transition to democracy was managed by the party. In the face of popular protest the HSWP adopted "Reform Circles" to renew its contacts with the people. By staying ahead of the wave the party was able to maintain enough support to elect a former Social Democrat as its head in June 1989. It made one final momentous decision before dissolving itself on the 33rd anniversary of the 1956 uprising: on 13 September 1989 Hungary suspended its bilateral consular agreement with East Germany.

The impact of this decision on East Germany was enormous: of all the East European states, the GDR was most threatened by the dissolution of the Soviet system, and consequently remained the bellwether by which the other states gauged their own chances for successful reform. The unspoken wisdom was that if it could happen in East Germany, it could happen anywhere. This was in part due to the special role the GDR played in Soviet security policy. It also had one of the hardest line party organizations. Unlike Hungary and Poland, the opening to the West did not just threaten the legitimacy of the communist party, it also threatened the dissolution of the East German state itself.

The real question surrounding revolution in the GDR was not whether society could peacefully bring reform to a communist system, but rather whether the state would preside over its own destruction without resorting to force. As Egon Krenz put it "without the Communist Party there is no German Democratic Republic" (Abel 1990, p. 113). Honecker had resisted Gorbachev's reforms as a matter of survival, claiming that the GDR would not join a "march to anarchy." When the Soviet Union published articles suggesting that Stalin was responsible for the Nazis coming to power, Honecker began banning Soviet newspapers; East German papers carried the story of Gromyko's ouster on pages 11 and 12. During the crisis period the GDR party line showed a discomfiting admiration for the conduct of the Chinese government at Tiananmen Square.

International pressure increased in March 1989 when Hungary signed the United Nations "Convention Relating to the Status of Refugees" in order to protect the Hungarian refugees from Romania. By accepting the principle of non-refoulement the Hungarian government set in motion an exodus from East Germany. Two months later the HSWP dismantled the barriers along its border with Austria. Gorbachev's visit to celebrate the 40th anniversary of the GDR left no doubt that Honecker was completely isolated. The Soviet side leaked reports that Gorbachev had ruled out any use of Soviet forces and that the General Secretary had warned the German leadership publicly that "life itself punishes those who delay" (Garton Ash 1989, p. 66).

Public demonstrations centered on Leipzig where a local church's Monday peace service became the jumping off point for progressively larger protest marches. These soon became the largest demonstrations seen in East Germany since the repression of 1953. On 9 October combat groups were deployed in Karl-Marx-Platz and a local commander stated he was ready to defend socialism "with weapon in hand" (Garton Ash 1989, p. 67). One insider later confirmed that "there was a written order from Honecker for a Chinese solution" (Abel 1990, p. 115). Only a last-minute meeting of the concerned parties at the home of Conductor Kurt Masur avoided bloodshed. Nine days later Honecker was deposed and the order to fire was published by his successor Egon Krenz who moved quickly to establish himself as a reformer.

The GDR retained an effective and potentially vicious repressive apparatus, but the use of force carried with it certain isolation from the world community. It soon became clear that Moscow's decision to cut off its most prominent ally left the East German government without a counterweight to the pull of the West. This appears to have been a conscious decision on Gorbachev's part. When asked what the Soviets called their departure from the Brezhnev Doctrine, Soviet spokesman Gennady Gerasimov deadpanned that this was the beginning of the "Sinatra Doctrine," in which each state could say "I had it my way" (Garton Ash 1989, p. 141).

Soviet unwillingness to intervene to preserve the East German leadership formalized Gorbachev's policy of non-intervention and demonstrated to the world that hardline regimes were living on borrowed time. This worked to accelerate the pace of change elsewhere, particularly in Czechoslovakia: "Everyone knew, from their neighbors' experience, that it could be done" (Garton Ash 1989, p. 127). Czech students had helped East Germans to escape, watched events in Hungary and Poland, and listened to Radio Free Europe and the BBC throughout. A Slovak dissident writer noted that communication played a major role in the spread of revolution.

> [I]solation is now unthinkable with the existence of modern mass media ... Thirty or even twenty years ago, such parallel activities as ours would have been nipped in the bud, and nobody would have been the wiser, as indeed happened in the past. (Abel 1990, p. 83)

By the time the revolution reached Czechoslovakia the political situation could be compared with a supersaturated solution merely requiring the smallest push to precipitate an upheaval. Czechoslovakian dissidents drew on the examples of the preceding months: public protests against an illegitimate government, a charismatic leader, and the necessary alliance between workers and intellectuals. It also employed the experience of the Prague Spring. The massive purges conducted after 1968 had driven over a third of the party into active opposition. These men became a disloyal opposition within the ruling party and supplied the dissidents with important inside information on party weaknesses.

Czech opposition forces mobilized around the loose coalition of personalities surrounding Václav Havel. On 16 January 1989 a group of Czech students attempted to commemorate the death of Jan Palach, a young man who had immolated himself after the fall of the Prague Spring. The repression of the demonstration by the police galvanized domestic and international opinion in support of Havel who was arrested at the site of the protest. Hungary's Prime Minister publicly disapproved of the CPCz's action, while Polish opposition leaders called for a hunger strike. Even in Bulgaria one hundred intellectuals signed a petition for Havel's release.

This pressure from within and without led to Havel's release in May. In the period that followed the Czech regime was increasingly undermined by international events. The negotiated surrender of the PUWP, East Germans passing through Czechoslovakia in trains bound for the West, and the reformers in Hungary created an atmosphere of political possibilities. As one Czech student put it "when we saw all those East Germans leaving, it told us anything could happen ... I myself helped more than forty East German students escape."

On 17 November 1989 Czech students applied for a permit to hold a demonstration commemorating Jan Opletal, a student murdered by the Nazis during the occupation. The official youth organization granted the students permission, but when the demonstrators left the cemetery and began a march toward Wenceslas Square they were attacked and beaten by police. After retreating to their campus the students waited for the police to storm the university, but the police did not come.

The student beatings brought the crisis out into the open and placed Havel at the center of events during the final collapse of the CPCz. All the familiar elements from the previous revolutions fell into place under the direction of the newly formed Civic Forum. On 23 November 1989 workers held a two-hour strike in support of Havel's forum. Said the strike leader, "the workers are no longer separated from the intellectuals. I respect Václav Havel as my leader" (Echikson 1990, p. 113). The next day, during a joint press conference held by Havel and Alexander Dubček, Miloš Jakeš and his Politburo resigned. Havel put Civic Forum support firmly behind Ladislav Adamec in order to strengthen him within the party. New Party Secretary Karel Urbánek, speaking at an emergency party meeting, warned that the CPCz would not "sell out to foreign capital" and refused to disband the Party's private army. Four days later the People's Militia was disbanded.

Hardliners within the CPCz were without support in the international sphere as well. A delegation from the Civic Forum was decorously received at the Soviet Embassy. Hungarian television rebroadcast an interview with Dubček in which he denounced Brezhnev as double-dealing and lacking in character. Both East and West were preparing to declare an end to the Cold War at the Malta Summit and neither would have tolerated the use of force in Czechoslovakia to maintain the CPCz. Gorbachev's statements while he was in Prague stressed that "minor repairs will not be enough. An overhaul is in order" (Abel 1990, p. 58). Following the successful Summit in Malta, the Warsaw Pact on 4 December 1989 denounced the 1968 invasion. Gorbachev held meetings with pro-Forum CPCz leaders and concluded that the Prague Spring was "right at that time and ... right now" (Abel 1990, p. 67).

The wave then moved on to well-entrenched communist parties in December of 1989 as holdouts Bulgaria and Romania experienced similar revolts. On 10 December 1989 a rally of 50,000 in the Bulgarian capital of Sofia forced the abolition of the leading role of the communist party. At the same time Ceauşescu in Romania was fleeing as his decades of dictatorial rule came to an end. As with oil nationalization once the movement for change gets underway there is a qualitative change in the character of the participants. Initial reforms took place in countries with experience in challenging the system, countries such as Poland, Czechoslovakia, and Hungary (East Germans tended to use the exit rather than the voice option); once these reforms were underway communist parties in other countries such as Bulgaria and Romania were threatened. Finally, well-established local communist parties in Albania, Yugoslavia, and the USSR itself succumbed to the movement for reform. For change to be truly explosive it appears that this stage must be traversed, since in the normal state of affairs status quo groups remain in the majority while reform groups are in the minority. But the model does suggest that reform groups can have an impact beyond their mere numbers. This was true within each of the East European countries as well as between them.

Conclusion

The beginning of the end came with the first recognition of Solidarity in Poland in 1980. Although later suppressed, a crucial principle had been abandoned: that the party maintain its exclusive leadership of society. The successive revolutions in 1956, 1968, and 1980 had already demonstrated that only the Soviet-backed system kept those governments in place. Until Stalin's death the system imposed by the Soviet Union did not allow any deviance from the stalinist model. After 1956 Moscow permitted more nationalistic governments so long as they did not tamper with the fundamental props of one-party rule. Foreign policy independence was granted to those states having strong domestic party organizations and less vital strategic positions in the bloc.

When uncertainty about Soviet policies arose, particularly during leadership crises in Moscow, local societies attempted to reassert themselves. As calls for reform mounted local elites fell victim to an international and domestic cross-pressure: Moscow demanded close adherence to bloc policy; workers, intellectuals, and students pressed for reform. Only leaders able to endure costly reprisals from Moscow could secure their independence. But whenever reform began to threaten the leading role of the party Moscow intervened.

In each confrontation with the Soviet system from 1945 to 1968 the reformers learned more about successful strategies for undermining it. However, it was not until the summer of 1980 that *ad hoc* political protest gave way to a more disciplined alliance of opposition forces. The PUWP's recognition of Solidarity showed how far such a strategic mobilization could go despite the international context.

After 1985 the fundamental character of the system changed. Policy decisions at the center removed the force that had dominated bloc relations since its formation. East European states responded to this new situation according to their levels of domestic legitimacy. The Hungarian party preempted the reform movements and reconstituted itself along social-democratic lines. In Poland the party negotiated a face-saving withdrawal. The East German communist party and the GDR itself disintegrated under the attraction of German reunification. And Czechoslovakia's CPCz failed to maintain itself in power by repressive means.

Barrier models provide some policy insights. For example, after Jaruzelski's coup in Poland there was discussion in the US about cutting off food supplies and other necessities of day-to-day life. Often the attitude in the émigré communities was "if they suffer enough they will revolt." Not to mention the hypocrisy of such an attitude coming from people sitting comfortably in the US, it ignored the fact that the people *already* wanted change. There was no need to incite them through physical deprivation to revolt, the issue of embargoes on food and medical supplies was completely irrelevant. The refusal of such supplies would only have hurt individual Poles without contributing to political change.

One conclusion that can be drawn from the study of the events in Eastern Europe is that revolutionary change in the international system cannot be explained solely in terms of a single variable such as the balance of power. Rather it must be analyzed in historical terms as a relationship between power and resistance. Focusing solely on the macro level obscures the process of testing and learning that leads reformers to adopt successful strategies for inducing change. It is not stretching the point to say that "why?" is less the issue here than "how?" Examining the multilevel relationship between actors and their environment in terms of political barriers helps explain the events of 1989. Taking the long view, the events of 1989 can be seen as the end of a continuous process of liberation – a long good-bye to a physical empire – but also a bow to the idea that popular pressure against a decaying barrier can produce dramatic change in a short period of time.

The last three chapters have investigated the problem of explosive change. I have suggested that barrier models explain one common – though not necessarily universal – kind of explosive change. I chose to apply this model to two examples which on the face of it are quite different: one is more economic the other political, the US is the barrier in one and the USSR in the other, and one involves Europe the other the Third World. Despite these surface differences the underlying dynamics are remarkably similar: it is the same sort of state that tests the barrier in the early years, the system is maintained by manipulating domestic politics in countries subject to the barrier, once the barrier breaks down reform spreads to conservative governments, and finally it is the increasing weakness at the center which allows the process to get underway.

The barrier model as outlined here has a number of defects. I have stressed the importance of learning but I have not provided a coherent learning theory. As opposed to Leng's maladaptive learning model, barrier models present a much more positive view of learning in world politics. I have also emphasized that preferences and goals change during the process. Though this runs against a long-standing tradition of assuming constant preferences for international actors I have not provided much of a mechanism for explaining such change beyond the allusion to group pressure models. Finally, barriers like all contexts in this book have remained exogenous factors, but explaining how barriers break down is crucial for a complete explanation of explosive change.

9 HISTORICAL CONTEXTS

> A world optimally adapted to current environments is a world without history, and a world without history might have been created as we find it. History matters; it confounds perfection and proves that current life transformed its own past.
>
> Stephen Jay Gould (1985, p. 54)

Introduction

The war diffusion model stressed the spatio-temporal environment within which states operate. It proposed that historical and current environments are crucial to understanding international war. The last three chapters explored one kind of situation where the current environment plays a central role in explaining behavior. States learned from what was happening to their neighbors, and their neighbors put pressure on them to conform. The spatial emphasis of the war diffusion framework found strong support in barrier models. This chapter and the next examine the second focus of the diffusion framework, the relation of the past to the present. How does what individuals or dyads do in the past influence what they will do in the future? Evidence for the spatial dependence of war and other phenomena exists. Does it exist for temporal dependence too? Or, are wars temporally "independent" events as many studies imply?

A more general way to pose the temporal dependence question is to ask about the relevance of history for explaining events. History has already appeared as an important context in this volume. The historical context was crucial in defining a valid military allocation indicator; the definition of overallocation depended on the historical period. States that face an international environment which puts barriers in their paths learn important lessons from the past that are essential to understanding their current behavior. History will also play an important role in the last two chapters on international norms where the strength of the norm of decolonization depends on past behavior.

That history matters for understanding human behavior may seem obvious. But there are theories which imply that the past is irrelevant, best illustrated by the rational actor school of analysis, whose models emphasize the present and future as the arenas for action. From this perspective the past is frequently not important, but the future can be fundamental in the decision-making calculus. Formal and empirical research in international relations, like in economics, has emphasized the current situation and future expectations in explaining state behavior. At the other end of the methodological spectrum, much of the international relations literature is historical and descriptive. The combination of explanation and narrative often provides little help for someone interested in general theories of the relation of the past to the present. Nonetheless, to give an explanation often involves giving a history. This chapter in particular, and my whole enterprise in general, attempt to investigate the tension between intuitions about history and formal, empirical analysis.

If an understanding of the historical flow of events is essential for a descriptive case study, in the quantitative literature on conflict, historical factors are noticeable by their absence. Studies using COW or events data are virtually all cross-sectional in nature. There is little evidence (though of course some, see below) of the longitudinal character of international conflicts. This is all the more curious given the widely acknowledged fact that somehow many of these conflicts are related to each other over time. Recent trends in both empirical and formal (particularly the latter) research have moved toward the reality of repeated interaction. Thus it is possible that the claim that much international relations research is ahistorical is belied by current research.

Rational actor and diffusion models provided two quite different approaches to the problem of war expansion. They will be important in the discussion of historical contexts as well. One variant of diffusion models is diffusion over time: the "addiction" as opposed to the "contagion" model. War may be addictive as well as contagious. Rational actor models generally argue that historical factors are irrelevant: rational actors ignore "sunk costs." The comparison of the two permits a clarification of the issues surrounding the importance of historical contexts.

It has been frequently claimed that formal, quantitative world politics is an ahistorical approach to the study of politics, an attack that comes from the traditional school of analysis (e.g., Bull 1966), or more recently from a "critical" tradition associated with post-structuralism (e.g., Walker 1990). Such claims are multifaceted and often difficult to unpack, but there are at least two simple, and perhaps simple-minded, interpretations. One is the empirical fact that formal and quantitative analyses rarely take the past into account. I suggest below that this is largely true, but with significant counter-examples. The other interpretation is that formal and empirical analyses are inherently ahistorical. That philosophical question is beyond the scope of this work, but at least a couple of restatements of what this might mean seem dubious if not patently false. One is that each historical sequence of events is unique. It is clear that there can be formal analyses and models of unique, specific historical events (e.g., Wagner 1989). A simple regression model can explain an infinite number of unique events if unique means different X values; for "unique" to carry any theoretical punch it must be interpreted as different parameter coefficients. In the final analysis, much of the question revolves around what "ahistorical" really signifies, which can vary widely and is often based on pre-theoretical or pre-philosophical intuitions. To anchor my discussion of this issue I shall propose in the next section a definition of ahistoricity.

In the latter part of this chapter I shall focus on the simplest and most common way that the past is related to the present, illustrated by concepts like tradition, conservatism, standard operating procedures (SOPs), incrementalism, and so forth. At heart all these ideas imply that behavior changes little over time, that human beings are creatures of habit. What they do today is the same as what they did yesterday and the day before. It turns out that despite its simplistic appearance the concept of "repeating the same action" poses important theoretical problems. As Wittgenstein has pointed out (1953, pp. 82–5, 116–17), the idea of the "same" is full of traps. The concept of context as changing meaning will be essential to this analysis. Many of the issues that arose in the discussion of military allocation ratios will reappear in new guises.

If the last three chapters posed the problem of explaining "dramatic change" then this chapter and the next pose the question of "no change." It may seem that no change in behavior requires no explanation, but I suggest that it poses significant theoretical problems (not to mention statistical; if there is no variation in the dependent variable then estimation is impossible). In fact, barrier models suggest one answer to the problem: various international structures and actors maintain the status quo. But there are other explanations to be explored as well, many of which come from sociology and organizational behavior. This chapter and the next on stability present a contrast with the previous three chapters on explosive change.

The question arises: individuals may be creatures of habit but are states? The discussion of habitual behavior is motivated by the fact that various states have repeatedly come into conflict with each other, e.g., France–Germany, India–Pakistan, etc. There is a widespread feeling that these conflicts are somehow related to each other. The rather abstract and theoretical character of this chapter leads into the following one where I shall give a detailed analysis of the concept of enduring rivalries (repeated militarized conflict between the same two states), demonstrate its empirical relevance, and discuss the theoretical and methodological implications of the concept for conflict research.

"Historical theories"

To say that the historical context matters is to say that we need "historical theories." One can ask whether there is something distinctive about "historical" theories in world politics. I propose a simple definition of historical theories; there are negative and positive versions:[1]

> Negative – If in order to explain or predict an event only current or future states or events are necessary then the theory or model is *ahistorical*.
>
> Positive – If past events or states are necessary in order to explain or predict an event then the theory or analysis is *historical*.

This definition eliminates a large number of theories of international relations as candidates for historical theories. Most structural theories are ahistorical (e.g., Waltz 1979). The system structure at the current time counts, what it was at time $t-n$ does not. Rational actor theories are also generally ahistorical; current preferences and power relations define expected utilities.

An analysis of a decision tree (figure 9.1) illustrates why most rational

[1] White (1943, p. 212) proposed a definition quite like this: "a historical explanation explains facts at one time by reference to facts prevailing at an earlier time." He rejected this because some natural science explanations would be historical. Instead of grounds for rejection I see this as an encouraging sign. Russell (1924) defined "mnemic laws" as earlier events causing latter events without an intervening causal chain.

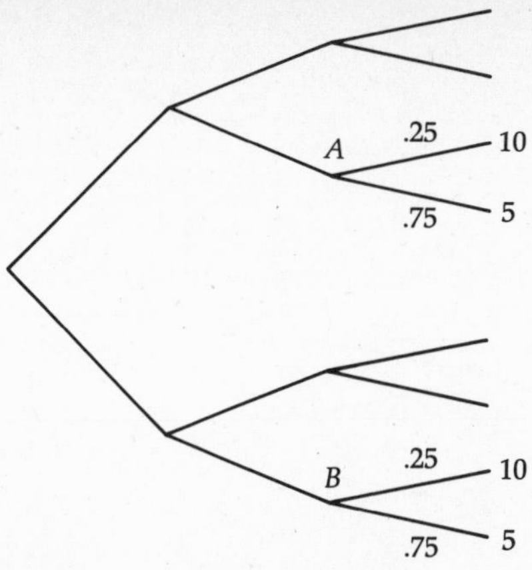

Figure 9.1 Historicity and decision theory

actor models are ahistorical. Only the branches that lead to the right – into the future – are needed to predict or explain what a player will do at any given node of the tree. How the player got to the node has no impact on that decision. The choices faced at nodes *A* and *B* are identical, but routes to these points are different: does this affect the optimal choice that decision theory proposes? No. It is only the part of the tree in the future that has an impact on the decision.

A decision tree also illustrates why historical narrative does not necessarily imply an historical theory. As the decision-maker works his way through the tree we can provide a narrative of his actions. We can give a history of how he got to node *A*, but this history only concerns his analysis of his present condition and future options at each node. We can write a history that does not involve historical facts at any point in the narrative. Thus according to my definition the explanation is ahistorical, even though it has the form of a historical narrative.

The property of ahistoricity is not unique to rational actor models, balance-of-power theory with its emphasis on flexibility and shifting alliances has the same character. It is the current strategic situation that determines a state's response, not a treaty signed in different circumstances. It is not surprising that diffusion models of alliance formation (McGowan and Rood 1975; Yamamoto 1974) in the nineteenth century find that alliance-making can be modeled by a Poisson model of independent events. Diffusion models frequently test whether current events are "independent" of past ones. It is this irrelevance of the past which characterizes ahistorical theories.

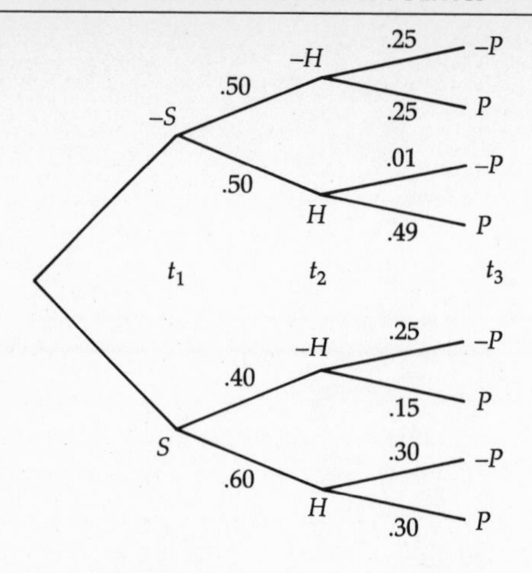

S = Smoking; –*S* = no Smoking
H = Heart attack; –*H* = no Heart attack
P = heart Pain; –*P* = no heart Pain

Figure 9.2 Path dependence and transitivity
Source: Eells and Sober 1983, p. 43.

One characteristic that differentiates ahistorical from historical theories is not the state of the world at time *t*, but *how the world arrived at its current state* that matters. Another common expression for this phenomenon is "path dependence" (March and Olsen 1984): current decisions depend on the route used to arrive at the present. While the concept of path dependence is quite well known, I have found no detailed analysis of what this might mean in practice. For example, North (1990) says about the concept: "path dependence – the consequence of small events and chance circumstances – can determine solutions that, once they prevail, lead one to a particular path." (p. 94) "Path dependence means that history matters." (p. 100) "Path dependence comes from the increasing returns mechanisms that reinforce the direction once on a given path. Alterations in the path come from unanticipated consequences of choices, external effects, and sometimes forces exogenous to the analytical framework." (p. 122). The definition of historical theories suggests one possible definition of this concept. As shown in figure 9.1 ahistoricity in decision trees means that the path taken to any mode has no impact on the decision made at that node. Path dependence then can be defined as the characteristic of choice such that the decisions made at nodes *A* and *B* may be different because the path used to arrive at those nodes is different.

Figure 9.2 illustrates the logic of path dependency (taken from Eells and Sober 1983). At time t_1 some people become smokers (*S*) while others remain non-smokers ($-S$). At time t_2 some smokers (60 percent) and some non-smokers (50 percent) have heart attacks (H). Path dependency is summarized in the fact that *given* that individuals suffer heart attacks the probability a smoker will have pain (P) is 0.50 (0.30/0.60) while that for a non-smoker is 0.98 (0.49/0.50). The two H nodes differ because the paths used to arrive at H differ, but in the decision theoretic case (figure 9.1) this is not the case, decisions at A and B can only vary if the nodes to the right – the future – vary. An individual in figure 9.1 is *pulled* by nodes in the future while an individual in figure 9.2 is *pushed* by nodes in the past.

The definition of path dependence has another important consequence: causes are no longer always transitive (in the probabilistic sense). I emphasized in chapter 2 that context as cause, and cause in general, are assumed to be transitive, but if we take the path dependence concept as characteristic of historical theories then we loose the transitivity property. This is also illustrated in figure 9.2. Smoking (S) causes (always in the probabilistic sense) heart attacks (H) because:

$$P(H \mid S) > P(H \mid -S), \quad \text{i.e.,}$$
$$0.60 > 0.50$$

Heart attacks (H) cause heart pain (P) for smokers (S) because:

$$P(P \mid H) > P(P \mid -H), \quad \text{i.e.,}$$
$$0.30/0.60 = 0.50 > 0.15/0.45 = 0.33$$

and for non-smokers ($-S$) because:

$$P(P \mid H) > P(P \mid -H), \quad \text{i.e.,}$$
$$0.49/0.50 = 0.98 > 0.25/0.50 = 0.50$$

Thus S causes H which causes P, but S does *not* cause P because:

$$P(P \mid S) \not> P(P \mid -S), \quad \text{i.e.,}$$
$$0.30 + 0.15 = 0.45 \not> 0.49 + 0.25 = 0.74$$

Eells and Sober proved (see their article for the details) the conditions for transitivity to be maintained. The first condition requires that effect at time t_2 (i.e., heart attack) is a cause of the effect at time t_3 (i.e., heart pain). The second is what they called in the "Markov condition" which states that the probability at any node of the tree *only* depends on what happened at the previous node. This is a common requirement of Markov chain models (Bartholomew 1982) and Eells and Sober take this condition to be unproblematic. It means that the path dependency differences are summarized in the different probabilities for H at different nodes. The third condition requires that all effects at time t_2 are *independent* of each other conditional on what can happen at time t_1 (i.e., smoking or no-smoking). This third condition essentially separates the paths of the tree from each other. The second and third conditions combined eliminate any dependence on other paths. Transitivity is maintained in path dependency only when paths are independent of each other and when the path dependency is summarized at each node of the path. One consequence of these results is that the notion of historical theories and path dependency, despite their intuitive validity, pose some deep theoretical problems.

This concept of path dependence thus stands in stark contrast to rational actor models (this contrast is often made in terms of "causal" versus "teleological" explanations, e.g., Braithwaite 1968). Such path dependence can arise because of adaptive and learning behavior, where because of selection, reinforcement, and learning processes an identical current and future situation, such as at A and B in figure 9.1, can produce different responses. As we shall see below many of the theories that stress historical contexts stand at odds with rational actor models.

Natural selection theories – and their cousins, functional theories – form an important class of historical theories. The existence of a feature (cultural or biological) is explained by its past success. Why the feature arose is often a mystery (it certainly was for Darwin), all that natural selection emphasizes is that it helped the actor (or at least was selectively neutral). There is of course nothing to guarantee that the feature is currently the best option. Given the freedom of rational choice another feature might be better and thus chosen, natural selection implies that such choices are not always made. As in figure 9.2 natural selection theories argue that the weight of the past pushes individuals in certain directions.

The path dependence concept implies that an emphasis on process distinguishes historical theories. The contrast between the power transition and the power parity hypotheses (Organski and Kugler 1980; Siverson and Sullivan 1983) illustrates the importance of process in the distinction between historical and ahistorical theories. The power parity hypothesis states that current power equality between two countries increases the likelihood of war. The power transition theory also predicts war in a situation of relative power equality; but power parity alone does not determine war, rather power parity plus the process by which power parity is achieved does. A static situation of power parity makes war less likely, but if power parity occurs as the result of a power transition then war becomes more likely. Events in the past are essential to the theory hence making it historical.

In general, static theories are ahistorical and dynamic models are historical. Barrier models illustrate a dynamic process; explaining the learning process requires the inclusion of past events into the explanatory framework. Another example of a dynamic model is Allan's (1983) concept of "diplomatic time." He argued that the rapidity with which events occur in a crisis has a special impact on decisions – the same situation not preceded by a crisis would produce a different response. Path dependency and process are both dynamic concepts. On the other hand, rational choice and structuralist models are usually static (much economic analysis falls under the rubric of "comparative statics").

Some of the important historical hypotheses in the world politics literature are dynamic, e.g., the power transition and arms race hypotheses. Both of these argue that war does not occur under static conditions of relative power or arms expenditure but as the result of a dynamic of change. The arms race and power transition hypotheses suggest that important changes in a certain direction are a cause of war. It is not the absolute level of variables but rather their change and the direction of that change that are crucial. The only way to know this is to compare the present to the past. As we shall see in the next chapter, the concept of enduring rivalries has been used to study power transitions and arms races. The hypothesis is that changes in power and in military spending mixed with a rivalry base is a recipe for war.

More generally, in most deterministic models (dynamic equation models are usually non-stochastic) all that is needed to predict the future are the laws of the system and the initial state: what happens in the future depends on the starting point. This situation characterizes the "covering law" philosophy of social and natural sciences:

> To give a *causal explanation* of a certain event means to derive deductively a statement ... which describes that event, using as premises of deduction some *universal laws* together with certain singular or specific sentences which we may call the *initial conditions* ... The initial conditions (or more precisely, the situation described by them) are usually spoken of as the *cause* of the event in question ... (Popper 1950, p. 262)

As I argued above, game theory, decision theory, and economics provide the best examples of ahistorical models. Hicks argued that what he called "contemporaneous causality" is the "characteristic form of causality in contemporary economics" (1979, p. 61). By this he referred to the equilibrium models that form the core of liberal economics. These models are static, a description that indicates well the lack of any real time component. He also argued that many actions made in the past, whose effects continue into the present, are not really to be considered as historical:

> The demand for petrol in the current period must be affected by the decisions that have been made to purchase cars in previous periods. But this does not mean that contemporaneous causality, in a demand study of this kind, has to be abandoned. It can be rescued (and in practice it clearly would be rescued) by replacing those previous decisions by the stock of cars, as it was at the beginning of the period, in which they are embodied ... We need do no more than reckon the opening stock of cars as one of the causes of the demand for petrol during the period. (pp. 70–1)

What Hicks calls contemporaneous causality I refer to as ahistorical theories, because past states that carry over into the present are not considered historical factors. Theoretically it is the existence of the cars that matters, not the act of purchase.

The concept of simultaneous causality is quite unusual because the concept of cause, at least since Hume, has included time as a central component. Effects occur *after* causes in time. Hick's claim to originality in his discussion of economic causality is the notion of *simultaneous* causality. Thus he argues, *pace* Hume, that causality does not have to imply a temporal ordering. The ordinary concept of cause is most frequently a temporal one, in the natural sciences as well as in the social sciences.

Typical quantitative regression analyses generally follow Hume's notions of temporal ordering and causality. The standard, but implicit, model considers that the X's occur just before the Y:

$$Y_t = \beta_0 + \beta_1 X_{1_{t-\epsilon}} + \beta_2 X_{2_{t-\epsilon}} + \ldots$$

The X's are the values of the explanatory variables just before the occurrence of Y. Usually data problems do not permit such accuracy so the values of X are taken at time t contemporaneous with Y. In cases where this would be clearly invalid, e.g., military expenditures during a war, the data are taken from time $t-1$. Thus this model for actual estimation purposes loses the subscript $t-\epsilon$ (see Bollen 1989 for a discussion of causality and regression models). However, the claim of historicity expresses something stronger than the cause occurring at ϵ before the effect; it argues for the cause occurring in the more distant past. This would be expressed in a regression model by lagged terms (i.e., $t-n$) representing events which took place in something beyond the immediate past. This suggests a simple rule for distinguishing between historical and ahistorical theories: if there are terms subscripted with $t-n$ then the model is historical, if there are no "t" terms then the model is ahistorical.

Another point of Hick's example is that the cause of the demand for gas is not the purchase of cars but the existence of cars. We have already seen this argument in chapter 2 in the discussion of how contexts can cause behavior. I suggested that the existence of gas could legitimately be the cause of an explosion, like the existence of cars may be a cause of the demand for gas (or like the existence of a bipolar system could be a cause of war). For some purposes all that is necessary for explaining the explosion is the existence of gas in the air: at time $t-\epsilon$ there was a lighted match and gas, hence at time t an explosion occurred. By my criterion this is an ahistorical explanation, but if for other purposes how the gas leak happened is important, then the explanation is a historical one:

> [I]f our goal is understanding, we will not hesitate to trace a puzzling event right back through one, two or many fully voluntary acts [intervening causes] done with the intention of bringing it about, to a much earlier factor, more obscure perhaps, but equally necessary and much more interesting. So some have said that the cause of World War II was the unfair Versailles Treaty; and others have found the cause of the Protestant Reformation in Julius Caesar's failure to conquer the German tribes.
> (Feinberg 1970, p. 166)

In other words, explanations of events have the "accordion" property of being shrinkable and expandable according to theoretical and pragmatic purposes. For theoretical purposes the cause is not necessarily the immediately preceding link in the causal chain. When Mary shoots Sally, her death is the result of a bullet damaging her heart, but for explanatory – and probably legal (Hart and Honori 1985) – purposes Mary's pulling the trigger is the cause of Sally's death.

It is the differing theoretical importance of past events that solves Elster's (1976) problem of "hysteresis" in the social sciences. Hysteresis in the natural sciences is when magnetic effects occur significantly after their causes. Elster asks how events in the distant past can be causes of current effects in the social sciences. I suggest that the answer lies in the accordion property of events. Not all links in the causal chain have equal theoretical importance. "The" cause frequently refers to the most important causal link which can occur in different places in the historical chain of events. It may be that how the gas leak occurred (at time $t-n$) is an essential part of *explanation*, while the existence of gas (at time $t-\epsilon$) when the match was lighted is a secondary link in the causal chain.

What Feinberg implicitly states is that we give different theoretical weight to different nodes of causal trees. The different nodes of figure 9.2 have no explicit theoretical weight assigned to them. We can use the probabilities in the figure to evaluate the relative importance of each, but other theoretical factors may also play a role in evaluating which links of the causal chain should receive the most emphasis. Path dependency could then also mean that the importance of a given node may vary from path to path. The importance given by Popper (see the quote above) to the initial conditions as the cause means that the initial node receives all the explanatory weight, since the succeeding links follow directly from those conditions.

Instead of causal factors historical variables are sometimes viewed as control variables. This becomes an issue in foreign policy analyses where the inertial characteristics of bureaucracies are potentially powerful influences. For example, Stoll (1984) examined the hypothesis that the prospect of presidential elections influences the incumbent president's use of force. In order to test this hypothesis adequately he had to control for recent US presidential commitments and actions; the past established a baseline from which to measure the impact of elections. Another example is Nincic and Cusack (1979) who in order to explain the political uses of military spending controlled for the incremental nature of budgeting. Conversely, for someone focusing on bureaucratic behavior (Wildavsky 1975), events such as elections are exogenous shocks that perturb the natural inclination of bureaucracies to budget in an incremental fashion.

In many ways the $t-n$ rule is a very weak one, so it is somewhat surprising that it eliminates much empirical and formal work in world politics. Though the rule seems simple enough not all cases are clear cut. This is particularly true when historical data are used to measure a current state of affairs. The theory is ahistorical but operational definitions are historical. This is the converse of the situation described by Hicks: if we did not know the current stock of cars but had data on car purchases we could use these as an indicator of current petrol demand. Bayesian methods have this character; previous events are used to indicate current knowledge. Current decisions are based on current knowledge, but this knowledge depends on information gained from previous events. But it may be that the updating process – learning – plays a theoretical role, then according to the accordion principle the past enters as cause in its own right. The ambiguity of past events that continue into the present – more properly termed "state" variables – opens up the possibility of alternative interpretations.

Using the $t-n$ criteria the following are some ahistorical theories in international relations:[2]

Power preponderance/parity.
Structural realism.
Expected-utility theories.
Sequential games.
Vast majority of COW studies.

Here are some examples of historical theories:

Learning, adaptive, and artificial intelligence models.
Power transition.
Dynamic models.
Arms race models.
Tit-for-Tat strategy.
Diffusion of war (addiction).
Contextual models:

Norms – the current strength and impact of a norm is a function of its evolution.
Barrier models – how nations act depends on what has happened in the past and what was learned from these events.
Military allocation ratios – the historical epoch is crucial in defining overallocation to the military.

The definition of historical theories leads logically to the concept of historical indicators. The long time temporal domain often used poses a potential problem in the quantitative study of war. Virtually all indicators used in this research are not historically anchored. In the case of military allocation ratios the meaning of overallocating was shown to be tied to the historical context. What "over" *meant* was a function of a period-dependent norm; what was "over" in 1850 was "under" in 1950, unless the historical period was explicitly taken into account. Historical indicators are sensitive

[2] In making such vast generalizations I am taking the "modal" study, it is possible there are historical studies in these categories.

to these issues and incorporate contexts that would otherwise invalidate cross-temporal comparisons.

I shall argue in the last two chapters that the importance of a norm is a function of its historical development. Norms change because of current events, but the inertia of the past is not easily overcome. Since norms change slowly, but other aspects of the world change more rapidly, conflict can arise between norms and self-interest. Underscoring this fact challenges some major aspects of realpolitik theories.

In barrier models history played an important role because leaders and societies learned and drew lessons from what occurred in the past; there is no way of understanding their behavior without including past events and how they were interpreted (learning is the intervening variable linking the past to the present). There is often pressure for change, but peoples and government often hesitate to press for change because they have seen what has happened to reformers elsewhere. The learning of new lessons takes time since past experience makes one cautious. An essential part of the current pressure on the barrier is associated with recent events and the changes in behavior that these events have incited.

The emphasis on the historical context raises issues relevant to the emphasis on prediction as the standard for evaluating theories (Freeman and Job 1979). The emphasis on prediction gives a biased view of the importance of historical factors. It is often the case that only the most recent information is needed for prediction: predicting an explosion only requires the knowledge of the existence of gas; an explanation of the explosion may require the cause of the gas leak. Or for example, predicting the outcome of a random walk only requires the most current information; however, if we would like to explain why or how the outcome was achieved the earlier information remains relevant:

> Later probabilities render earlier ones *predictively irrelevant* ... [but] later probabilities do not render earlier ones *explanatorily irrelevant*. (Sober 1984, p. 124)

The Markov condition means that the history of the process is summarized in all probablities. Knowing that an individual had a heart attack is sufficient to predict the occurrence of heart pain. But for other purposes knowing that he was a smoker is also relevant.

The emphasis on explanation stresses the importance of historical events while a priority given to predictions privileges the current state of affairs. The accordion principle expresses the same principle: causally relevant events may have occurred in the distant past, the predictively relevant ones may be the most recent links in the causal chain. The quote by Stephen Jay Gould at the head of this chapter is driven by the view that natural history is both *science* and *history*. Gould lays no claim to predictive theory, yet he sees his activities as science; he uses the standard tools of the "scientific method."

What is the "same" behavior?

Historical theories seem to come in two types: one that stresses the stability of behavior via metaphors like habit, inertia, custom, and tradition, and one that focuses on dynamic changes such as arms race and power transition models. Barrier models explain dynamic, explosive, non-linear change. In contrast, I concentrate in this chapter on the simplest historical model, that of repeated, constant, unchanging behavior (prediction may be trivial but all the theoretical problems remain). You can "explain" or at least predict behavior if it does not change. Most of the different metaphors and theories discussed below are variations on this theme, be they habit, inertia, momentum, or addiction. Some of these do not mean the same behavior but imply movement in the same direction at constant speed – inertia – but as in physics, not moving or moving at the same speed in the same direction differs radically from accelerating (which includes changing direction at a constant speed).

A fundamental problem in the analysis of habitual, repetitive actions is determining what "same behavior" actually means. The context of debate determines in large part its meaning, since the deceptively simple word "same" is heavily charged with theoretical significance. The natural, naive interpretation of doing the same thing is illustrated in figure 9.3. By doing Y_1 at time t_1 and t_2 the horizontal dashed line symbolizes that behavior is constant and unrelated to time. The corresponding naive view of changing behavior is when at time t_1 the state does Y_1 and at time t_2 it does Y_2, thus its behavior is changing over time.

The sophisticated view of sameness says that when the relationship is constant then behavior is the same; two behaviors that differ on face value are in fact the same since they lie on the solid line. A story to illustrate: A person (student) at t_1 buys a VW bug (Y_1) and later at time t_2 when she has become a businesswoman she buys a Cadillac (Y_2). From the naive point of view she bought a cheap car at time t_1 and an expensive one later. But from the sophisticated point of view she is buying the most expensive car she can

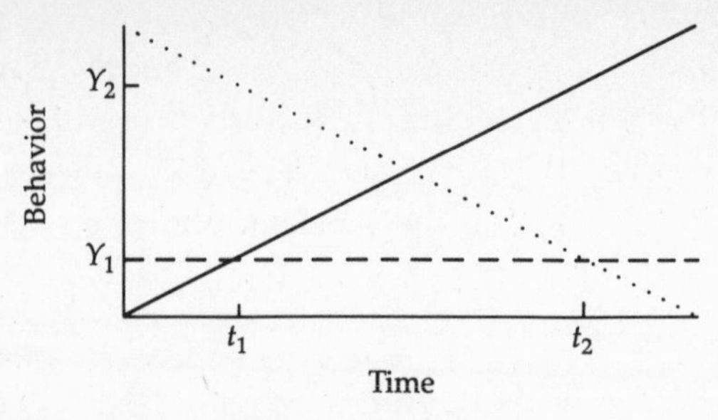

Figure 9.3 Continuity of behavior

afford at both times; or price as a percentage of her income is constant. That Great Britain changes frequently its alliance partners in the nineteenth century is not "inconsistency" but only following the prescripts of the balance-of-power theory.

The naive view argues that doing the same thing is repeating Y_1 at times t_1 and t_2. From the sophisticated perspective we have the paradoxical result that if in fact the behavior at Y_1 is explained at t_1 by the solid line and at time t_2 by the dotted one then *doing the same thing can be a radical change in behavior*. If the businesswoman buys a VW bug at time t_2 that may be considered a change in behavior but buying a Cadillac is not: buying a VW is normal for a student, but not for a businesswoman. This is in fact the definition of context as changing meaning: context – the person's economic status – changes the meaning of the act of buying a VW bug. What might be a statement of conformity (at least in the 1960s) becomes a statement of individuality in a businesswoman.

There are three possible explanations of behavior over time represented by the solid, dashed, and dotted lines in figure 9.3. The solid line represents the conformist behavior of a person who as a student (t_1) buys a VW and later as a businesswoman (t_2) buys a Cadillac. That constant relationship may be called conformity to social class norms. The dotted line stands for the opposite non-conformist rule, since as a student she buys a Cadillac and as a businesswoman a VW; she acts uniformly in a non-conformist fashion. The dashed line may be the ascetic ideal of always buying a modest means of transport regardless of social norms: the purchase of a VW is the expression of a moral ideal which pervades a person's life (this issue will arise again in the discussion of international norms). The same act of purchasing a VW at times t_1 and t_2 thus has multiple possible explanations, because in addition to the three given above, you can mix and match; for example, the person is a conformist as a student but *changes* and becomes a non-conformist as a businesswoman. This is exactly analogous to how spending 5 percent of GNP on the military can be underspending in the 19th century and overspending in the twentieth. The relationship between "sameness" and the assumption of non-changing contexts is of fundamental importance. For example, it is largely the assumption of no contextual change that can make habits, SOPs, and rules of thumb optimal.

If the dotted and dashed lines represent two systems we arrive at the same problems encountered in comparative research:

> The countries differ with regard to their levels of education, class structure, and family socialization, but they do not differ as *systems* so long as their patterns of relationships are the same. *Systems differ not when the frequency of particular characteristics differ, but when the patterns of the relationships among variables differ.*
>
> (Przeworski and Teune 1970 p. 45, emphasis is the authors')

It is clear that the issues highlighted by Przeworski and Teune are identical to the ones that arise in the VW/Cadillac story. All the problems of cross-sectional research apply to longitudinal research. Nations are on the face of it different systems and hence comparative problems seem more severe, but the same basic problems occur with events over time: How are we to know that we have the same system after the passage of years? Cross-sectionally the potential trouble spots are clear because they coincide with national boundaries, but over time potential problems are harder to spot. Though sometimes, as in the case of military allocation ratios, events like world wars provide obvious break points.

This said, I shall focus on the simpler and more common concept of the same behavior being the same act. Most of the little research on these issues in world politics has taken same behavior to mean the similarity of behavior from time t_1 to t_2 as represented by the dashed horizontal line (e.g., Huth and Russett 1984) and I shall follow this custom. It is in this sense that enduring rivalries are defined as repeated conflicts between the same two states. The analysis above shows that it is possible that each conflict takes place in a different context and reflects different laws of behavior. We need either a theory of changing contexts or one of continuity of behavior in a non-changing world (or some combination of the two).

Approaches to historical stability or, explaining no change

It is important to ask why the emphasis on the historical context so often leads to an emphasis on the continuity of behavior. A central question then is the relevance for the study of international relations of theories of stasis and their variants. Probably the most common interpretation of historical stability is that there is some consistency in behavior over time. Scholars have argued for the stability of societies even through revolutionary changes. De Tocqueville made this argument about the French Revolution and others have made the same case for the Russian and Chinese Revolutions. Now it is in some sense trivial to say that even with major revolutions not everything changes, but the argument is stronger than that: important or central aspects of the society and its politics did not change as a result of the revolution. However, here I shall limit myself to the problem of historical stability in the much simpler form of unchanging behavior by individuals, institutions, and states.

There are a number of ways of thinking about historical stability (the list is not intended to be complete):

conflict addiction.
habit, SOPs (standard operating procedures), and incrementalism.
preferences and norms.
unchanging circumstances: equilibrium and structuralism.

Conflict addiction

As discussed in chapter 5 addiction and immunization form one aspect of the war contagion theoretical framework. The fact is that certain states or pairs of states seem to be repeatedly involved in military conflict; these countries or dyads are "addicted" to conflict. This fact requires an explanation: why are these states involved in frequent conflicts while other countries are immune to them?

In spite of the spatial nature of most war diffusion research the basic methodology applies to diffusion over time. The usual procedure is to establish a null hypothesis model of "independent events," to which is juxtaposed a model of correlated or dependent events. This procedure can be applied to the individual nation, the dyad, or the international system as a whole. Often studies of spatial war diffusion will test the hypothesis of war addiction. The evidence has not been conclusive at the individual or dyadic level; typically only weak diffusion has been found over time as opposed to space (Stoll 1984; O'Loughlin and Anselin 1991). In contrast to the spatial diffusion model, the temporal diffusion literature has not gone beyond testing the hypothesis of correlation over time. Since the war diffusion studies have not found significant correlations over time, they have not looked for possible agents of temporal diffusion. In the next chapter I shall suggest that the concept of enduring rivalries provides a more satisfying framework for examining the conflict addiction hypothesis.

Habit, SOPs, and incrementalism

If rational decision-making requires a great deal of *conscious* effort, then the opposite end of the spectrum includes procedures that require little conscious work such as habit, standard operating procedures (SOPs), and incrementalism. We can perhaps rate decision procedures along a scale from hard, time-consuming, and conscious to easy, quick, and unconscious. A rational actor must work hard, order his preferences, calculate the probability of success, and gather information. Habitual behavior means at the limit there is no reflection; no decision is made but rather the actor behaves unconsciously, without effort and thought. The best examples of this come, of course, from the psychology of everyday life. Some people when they wake up in the morning put on the coffee pot. They do not think about this in any reflective sense, they just do it. It is quite reasonable to call repeated, unchanging behavior a habit (this is what drug addiction is colloquially called). The question for scholars of world politics is whether these psychological models can be applied to governments.

The natural organizational equivalent of an individual's habit is bureaucratic routines and procedures (Nelson and Winter 1982). The "rationalization" of modern life so dear to Max Weber involves bureaucracies creating efficient means to accomplish repetitive tasks. One relatively uncontroversial finding from the literature on organizational behavior is the tendency of bureaucracies to conceive and implement policies that are quite similar over time. Most of the literature drawing on Allison's (1969) analysis of the Cuban Missile Crisis has taken SOPs as a negative factor inhibiting rational decision-making, but they may be optimal in certain circumstances. They are best – and better than rational decision-making procedures – in situations that occur frequently without changes in important parameters. If the "same" situation occurs frequently then fine-tuned SOPs are the best solution, e.g., when your heart stops in the emergency room. Likewise in sports the goal is often to act "without thinking"; in fact, conscious thought often makes performance worse (see Elster 1989c for a discussion of phenomena, like "be spontaneous," where reflective thought impedes or deteriorates performance). The essential point is that it can be optimal to follow SOPs *if the context does not change*. The assumption of unchanging environments is crucial since it can be shown that learning (behavior modification) or trial and error will arrive at a maximum if the phenomenon remains stable (sophisticated trial and error is basically how computers calculate maxima). This optimal behavior has nothing to do with rationality since rats can achieve it (rats act "as if" they were rational). It has been suggested that inertia has an adaptive character even in changing environments; it allows organizations to survive over time (Freeman and Hannan 1975).

Wildavsky's (1975) study of the budgetary process is symbolic of how the inertia of organizations interacts with changing environments. He found that in the short term simple incremental rules modeled well the budgetary process in the US. However this smooth linear process was frequently disrupted by exogenous shocks of various sorts, which resulted in the need to reestimate regression lines. Under stable circumstances incrementalism is the "natural" bureaucratic mode of operation, but unfortunately (perhaps) the environment does not remain stable for long periods of time.

As the Gould citation at the beginning of the chapter states, the process of adaptation and incremental change may not in fact be optimal, but only optimal given the constraints of previous choices (Oster and Wilson 1984). One piece of evidence for the validity of natural selection as the explanation of biological evolution is the existence of non-functional, non-optimal holdovers (like appendices, spines more suited to walking on four legs, etc.) that are evidence that we were not designed by a rational god (who would have done a better job).

The emphasis on SOPs and rules suggests that individuals and organizations are not completely rational. Wittgenstein says that "When I obey a rule, I do not choose. I obey the rule *blindly*" (1953, p. 85e, emphasis is the author's). As Wittgenstein suggests, following a rule or habit means giving up reflective, conscious choice; following a rule is not rational in the classic sense. Choosing to follow a rule is like selling yourself into slavery, it may be the last free act (occasional, short-term slavery may have advantages, as the case of Ulysses and the Sirens illustrates (Elster 1979) or burning bridges behind oneself may have its advantages (Schelling 1960)).

The emphasis on this mode of behavior creates a tension with the image of a rational, free-choosing agent.

Preferences and norms

Organizations are inertial beasts, but it is also the case that nations and leaders *want* consistency in foreign policy. In the VW/Cadillac example, the horizontal dashed line represented the ascetic rule of behavior; buying a VW might be a moral response to the consumerism of American society. The US had a firm commitment to resisting the spread of communism after World War II. This commitment conditioned the Kennedy administration's response to the Cuban Missile Crisis (Anderson 1981). Commitments made in the past thus constrained (a word that Anderson uses frequently) the possible choices of the US in that crisis, but the US also wanted to maintain a consistent and credible commitment into the future. The desire for continuity and credibility has thus a historic and a future dimension.

Depending on the researcher's theoretical bias one dimension or the other receives prominence: traditional foreign policy analysis gives more weight to the past while rational actor models of reputation stress the future dimension. Norms may be freely chosen by actors but also they are frequently imposed on them from the outside, e.g., hegemonic norms. Over time norms may be internalized and incorporated into preferences. Norms have been most extensively investigated recently in the realm of international economics, where norms place limits or indicate appropriate behavior. Treaties or international organizations codify and embody norms, and states often conform to them. These norms, patterns of behavior, "usage and custom" are important parts of regime theory. "Patterned behavior accompanied by shared expectations is likely to become infused with normative significance: actions based on purely instrumental calculations can come to be regarded as rule-like or as principled behavior. They assume legitimacy ..." (Krasner 1983a, p. 18). Patterned behavior eventually is transformed into normative (this was Pascal's argument that one way to real belief in God was through the observance of religious rites).

There are cases when self-interest dictates following a norm. This is particularly true when achieving desired goals requires the cooperation of others. For example, the lending of private banks (public institutions often as well) to less-developed or troubled economies often depends on an agreement between those countries and the IMF. The quite well-established norm is that borrower governments must come to an agreement with the

IMF before being accorded loans. Many international organizations and treaties exist to help nations function well in their dealings with each other. As the literature on neo-institutional economics shows (see Eggertsson 1990 for a survey), rule and institution creation can be the result of self-interest maximizing behavior.

Structural and equilibrium explanations of constancy take the environment as a major "cause," it is an explanation from the "exterior." In contrast, an emphasis on norms and rules is a move toward an "interior" explanation. From a sociological perspective (Ikenberry and Kupchan 1990) norms are values that have been "internalized" through various methods of socialization. We come to *prefer* certain behaviors to others. In economic terms, it is the structure of our preferences that may be the explanation. If one "prefers" one action vastly more than the alternatives she will continue in that vein in spite of sanctions. Pacifists, often for religious reasons, refuse to kill regardless of the situation; they refuse a utilitarian calculus which says that killing one person is justified if many lives are saved as a result.

It is quite possible that current goals are a result of past wars and conflicts. Loss of territory in a war may create negative preferences in the future, or it may be the simple fact of having lost that creates a desire for revenge. One notable outcome of World War II was to change Japan and Germany from traditional enemies of the USA to close allies. Interaction over time can create and change values; they become endogenous. However, in general, problems with preferences have remained outside the purview of rational models (a modest literature exists on this topic, see Elster 1983). The focus on international norms brings this issue into the limelight. Understanding norms involves explaining the mechanisms of their creation and maintenance, which frequently emphasizes evolutionary factors and concepts like internalization and socialization.

Unchanging environments: equilibrium explanations and structuralism

One important fact suggested by the idea of "rational rules" is that it may be quite reasonable, and even optimal, to engage in the same behavior repeatedly over time. As long as the situation (game) remains the same, the best strategy is also likely to remain the same, particularly in games against nature (expected-utility models), though less so in more-than-one-person games. In Bueno de Mesquita's (1981) model as long as power relationships and preferences remain the same, repeated conflict could be a natural outcome of repeated expected-utility calculations. So, for example, enduring rivalries are not necessarily inconsistent with expected-utility models. If enduring rivalries are the result of self-interest maximization, then this implies that the concept of enduring rivalries is spurious and, in fact, misleading. From an expected-utility point of view repeated conflict is a "historical accident," the epiphenomenon of rational choice in a particular international system. To focus on the concept of enduring rivalries is to go down a primrose path leading nowhere.

More generally, the concept of equilibrium is fundamental to liberal economics. If an economy is in equilibrium then the system will continue in the same state until there is some exogenous shock, at which point actors readjust and a new equilibrium point is (maybe) achieved. Much of economics is comparative statics: the analysis of equilibria in different systems. Historical stability can be a market equilibrium, the result of self-interest and profit-maximizing behavior on the part of individuals and firms.

If equilibrium is the natural state of pure markets, it is not the natural outcome in situations of social choice. There equilibria may not exist or there may be cyclical majorities. This lack of stability and non-uniqueness has led to models of "structure-induced" equilibrium (Shepsle and Weingast 1981). Models with no constraints on choice are replaced by choice under the constraints of institutional rules. The rules thus produce a stable equilibrium. As its name indicates, structures promote stability, institutional constraints produce stable outcomes.

If enduring rivalries are historical accidents for an expected-utility model they are in some sense historical necessities from a structural perspective on world politics. Ironically enough, it is for basically the same reason. If structures are relatively determinant in explaining nation-state behavior, then to the extent that the relevant structures do not change one would expect to see the same behavior repeated: behavior in the same structural conditions should be relatively similar. Since structures generally change fairly slowly this implies that behavior also changes slowly over time.

Equilibrium and structural forms of stability have quite different characters. From the literature on system polarity it is clear that the argument for the stability of bipolar systems (Waltz 1964) is a structural one. In bipolar systems there is little change, hence stability, consistency, and continuity. In bipolar systems friends and enemies are well-known and change infrequently. The rigidity and stability of this system produces the same behavior over time. Multipolar systems, on the other hand, illustrate equilibrium explanations (see Sober 1983, who also stresses the lack of importance of historical factors in equilibrium explanations) where there are forces that maintain the system. In bipolar theories the forces maintaining the system are rigid while in multipolar systems the forces are fluid. Both are explanations of stability.

From the structuralist point of view enduring rivalries may start because of significant system-level changes and end with future changes (Diehl and Goertz 1993); but dramatic environmental changes also affect the calculations of a rational decision-maker. The Cold War started with the US and the USSR being the two most powerful countries on earth and ended with the collapse of the USSR. The usual intuition is that structures change slowly – otherwise why would we call them structures – while rational actors are prompt and ready to change their behavior. Because of these images rational actor models have trouble dealing with endemic conflict and structuralist ones have trouble with the rapidity with which friends become enemies. But if we examine more carefully the two paradigms behavioral stability is the result of unchanging environments in both. Nations behave in the same fashion because contexts have not changed.

Conclusion

In the section on barrier models I proposed that the phenomena of "explosive change" presented a challenge for students of international affairs. In this chapter I suggest the phenomena of "no change" poses problems as well. In exploring possible approaches to these problems contexts of all sorts have played important roles. The concept of "same" itself is context dependent. To say that two conflicts are part of the same enduring rivalry is already a theory of context: context as changing meaning is the tool that permits an analysis of that claim. At the same time this contextual mode showed how the issues of concern in comparative cross-sectional research apply longitudinally as well. This confirms in a more general framework a result of the analysis of military allocation ratios.

System structure plays a role in almost all approaches to the problem of repeated behavior. Be it structuralism, expected-utility, or habit, the stability of the environment is an essential consideration. If contexts do not change then behavioral constancy can be quite reasonable, but as soon as this is no longer the case following the old procedures becomes problematic. In this sense context is a necessary part of any explanation of repeated behavior, it must be controlled for or accounted for in some fashion.

There are a variety of approaches to the problem of "no change" but most come from outside international relations, be they psychological (habit), sociological (norms), organizational (SOPs), or equilibrium (economics) they are not at the core of international relations theory – though each has received some attention from scholars of world politics. The role of norms in explaining repeated behavior has not been developed at length, but it is perhaps the most obvious framework for explaining the consistency of state behavior in the international realm. Many of the issues raised by the concept of SOPs and organization theory fit well within a regimes framework. Nations act consistently because they sign treaties and it may be in their self-interest to follow the terms of treaties. All these issues arise in the last two chapters on the context of international norms.

Perhaps not unsurprisingly the emphasis on the historical context has resulted in a focus on *change*. Changing systems and environments are crucial; change is what distinguishes the power transition from the power parity hypothesis. What "same" means can change; even no change is a theory of change. As the examples of this book indicate an emphasis on context underscores the importance of behavioral dynamics. History does not just mean theories of change, but a certain kind of change. As the literature from game theory and economics shows, rational choice has its own dynamic driven by future prospects: a rational person is not bound by the chains of the past. The emphasis on history suggests a different kind of process: we are prisoners of our past. Historical explanations look to events in the past to explain why we are prisoners. Historical theories stress that path dependency affects the current situation; they include past events as fundamental aspects of explaining current behavior.

To emphasize the historical context puts many issues surrounding the formal and quantitative study of war into a new perspective. It focuses attention on linking conflicts together over time, to see one war as the cause of the next. The concept of enduring rivalries is one fruit of such a conceptual reorientation. The next chapter is devoted to exploring this concept and to arguing that much international war and conflict occurs within the context of enduring rivalries.

10 ENDURING RIVALRIES, OR PLUS ÇA CHANGE ...

[W]e should consider a bit further why organisms *do not* change when we all concede that their environment necessarily and inevitably *does* change ... What really happens to organisms when environments change?

Nils Eldredge (1985, p. 136)

Introduction

One island of "stability" in international politics is the long-term antagonisms between different countries. War and military conflict are rarely thought of in terms of stability, but there are pairs of countries that have repeatedly confronted each other for decades with irregular eruptions of crises and wars. The concept of enduring rivalry captures this long-term situation of more or less overt military hostility. The post-World War II era saw the US and the USSR in repeated conflict for about forty years (assuming this is now over); earlier, pairs like France–Germany and Japan–Russia were long-term rivals. Major powers have been quite involved in enduring rivalries – as in all kinds of international activities – and a large number of wars have taken place in the context of rivalries. Thus, on the face of it, the concept of enduring rivalry offers a good place to begin examining the importance of the historical context on military conflict between states.

Leng's work (1983) also leads one to suspect that the notion of enduring rivalry is of theoretical and empirical importance. Leng found that in repeated military conflict between two countries war was often the end result; war rarely broke out without preceding militarized disputes. He argued that this was due to a realpolitik learning process that incited leaders to use more force in the next incident, resulting finally in war. Also the power transition hypothesis (Organski and Kugler 1980) more or less assumes the existence of a rivalry, implying that a power transition on top of a rivalry is a volatile mixture. The concept of enduring rivalries hovers in the background of many theories that emphasize the historical context of behavior. It appears fundamental to understanding the process linking conflicts over time. The implicit, but important, role of rivalries in theories of learning, power transition, arms races (Diehl 1985), and deterrence (Huth and Russett 1993) underscores the significance of the concept.

In this chapter I would first like to discuss the theoretical and operational aspects of the concept of enduring rivalries. This is followed by a survey of the uses to which the concept has been made, in particular as a background condition for studying phenomena such as arms races, power transition, and deterrence. I then argue that enduring rivalries are an important context for understanding war, militarized disputes and territorial change by showing that a large – in absolute and relative terms – percentage of wars, disputes, and conflictual territorial change occurs within the context of rivalries. In the latter part of the chapter I discuss some of the methodological implications of the concept. One major weakness of virtually all quantitative research is that it considers theoretically and empirically each war or war decision as an independent event, the focus on repeated conflict between dyads over time means that standard cross-sectional analyses are not valid. The chapter ends with a brief discussion of how the concept of enduring rivalries relates to the wider issues of contextual analysis. My goal in this chapter is to take the concept of enduring rivalry out of the shadows and to examine it theoretically and empirically. The success of this enterprise will be indicated not by the number of questions answered but by the number of problems posed, problems concerning the beginning, end, and war-proneness of enduring rivalries that I can only suggest here.

The concept of enduring rivalries

The concept of an enduring rivalry has three components: spatial consistency, competitiveness, and time. The first component of an enduring rivalry is spatial: a consistent set of states participate in the rivalry. Given that most militarized conflict has thus far been dyadic (Gochman and Maoz 1984), one can anticipate that most enduring rivalries will involve only two states. Nevertheless, it is possible that by virtue of alliances more than two states might be involved in an enduring rivalry; the hostility between NATO and the Warsaw Pact might qualify as such.

When states are engaged in an enduring rivalry, they are competing over a scarce good. This good may be intangible such as political influence (as in "power politics" conceptions) or ideological/religious dominance. The competition may also be over more tangible goods such as natural resources or territory. In practice it is likely that individual enduring rivalries reflect varying mixes of these sources of competition. Intangible issues may be more conflict-prone and less divisible, and therefore less likely to be resolved easily or quickly (Vasquez 1983). Although enduring rivalries are competitions (often perceived to be zero-sum by the rivals), this should not imply that the source of the dispute is necessarily consistent over the life of the rivalry. States may fight over essentially the same issues during a rivalry, e.g., the Arab–Israeli conflict since 1948. Yet the specific issues may vary over time, e.g., Britain and France in the eighteenth century. States may compete over a series of goods and the confrontations may vary according to which goods are in dispute. Because of the varying specificity of the concept of issue, from the struggle for power to the struggle for a piece of land, consistent issue-based definitions are problematic.

The mere notion of competition is insufficient to constitute a rivalry (at least in the context of international conflict research). One could give any number of sports analogies that reveal that competitions can be friendly. Similarly states and corporations compete for the same markets, but there is usually little chance that such competition will result in war. In international conflict research an enduring rivalry connotes that military conflict is a part of that competition and war is possible. Thus competition in an enduring rivalry has a hostility dimension involving the significant likelihood of the use of military force.

The final component of enduring rivalries is a temporal one. The term "enduring" itself conveys the notion that rivalries are more than short-term or one-shot phenomena. International conflict that is either sporadic or brief does not qualify as an enduring rivalry. For a rivalry to be enduring, it must last longer than a few years.

That the concept of enduring rivalry involves time implies that fundamentally the concept is continuous. Rivalries can be more or less enduring, thus attempts to dichotomize all possible dyads into enduring and non-enduring rivalries must always be partially arbitrary. Since the major use of the concept of enduring rivalries has been as a case selection mechanism in order to test hypotheses on power transition, arms races, and deterrence, all current definitions (see below) are dichotomous. But any serious discussion of rivalries must deal with their continuity and how cut-off points are to be drawn through the continuum of "enduring."

If conflicts are considered part of the same rivalry the question arises

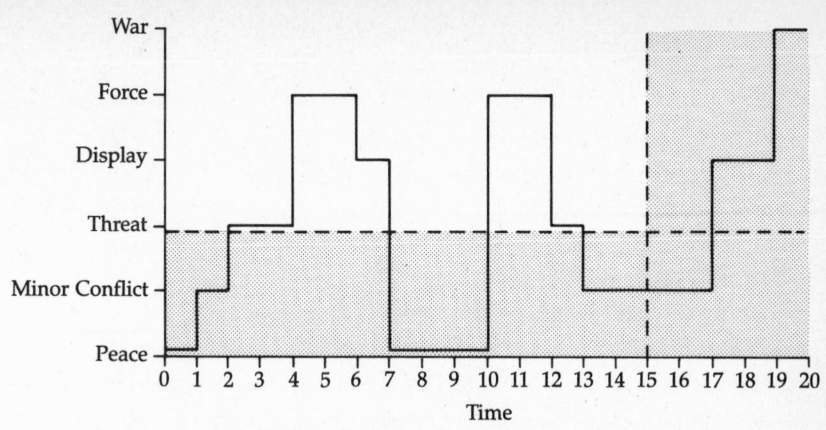

Figure 10.1 Hypothetical evolution of an enduring rivalry

about the stability or existence of the competition through good periods and bad. The difficult question is how "dormant" a competition can be and still remain a rivalry. The basic problem is whether a "rivalry" continues during periods of relative peace. This is illustrated in figure 10.1 where the rivalry is interrupted from times 7 to 10. We observe only what occurs above the horizontal dashed line. We see conflict from times 2 to 7 and 10 to 13. The figure shows that the underlying issues have been resolved so the countries are at peace with each other. In this case there is not one enduring rivalry but rather two separate rivalries, the second one beginning at time 10. The outward situation is the same from times 13 to 17, but since the underlying rivalry continues over this period of relative peace we have just one rivalry. The dilemma is whether we consider the interactions before and after time 7 or 17 to be part of the "same" rivalry. This is like the problem surrounding whether buying a VW at two different times is the same or different behavior. The indication of a "peaceful" period in the hypothetical rivalry of figure 10.1 means that the two rivalries might be explained by different theories, or in Przeworski and Teune's (1970) terms they constitute two different systems.

Implicitly the concept of enduring rivalries argues that different conflicts fall upon the horizontal line of figure 9.3. The concept is a theoretical, interpretive device that implicitly makes this argument. It is already a "pre-theory" of international conflict. There are approaches, such as the rational actor, that can challenge this pre-theory. Later I shall attempt to provide some prima facie empirical evidence in support of such a pre-theory, but the jury is still out.

Operational definitions

There have been few systematic attempts to define enduring rivalries. This is not to say that scholars have not studied rivalries or conflict phenomena that can be labeled as rivalries. Some cases, such as the Anglo–German conflict at the beginning of the twentieth century or the US–Soviet conflict after World War II, are consistent with conventional wisdom on what constitutes an enduring rivalry.

But the case study method does not result in systematic criteria useful for a general definition of an enduring rivalry. Most quantitative literature on enduring rivalries has originated from associates of the Correlates of War (COW) Project. There have been a number of separate, but not independent, efforts to develop a list of enduring rivalries. Not surprisingly, all have relied on the COW list of militarized interstate disputes (see chapter 4 for a discussion of this data set) to operationally define enduring rivalries. Each effort has established some threshold for the frequency of disputes involving the same pair of states over a given time frame in order to distinguish sporadic conflict from an enduring rivalry. The existence of militarized disputes indicates competitiveness, temporal proximity indicates issue-connectedness, and the stability of the actors indicates spatial consistency.

If isolated conflicts are by definition *one*-time affairs, then the smallest enduring rivalry involves two disputes not too distant from each other in time. Wayman (1982) took this minimalist approach by defining an enduring rivalry as any instance in which two states oppose each other in two or more disputes within a ten-year period. If reinforced by further disputes then the rivalry continues. A ten-year dispute-free period signals the end of the rivalry. Thus a rivalry lasts from the onset of the first dispute until ten years after the last dispute.

If we move along the severity continuum we arrive at a criterion using three disputes and a longer period of time. Diehl (1985) defined a rivalry as any situation in which two nations engage in at least three militarized disputes within a period of fifteen years. He argued that once established, enduring rivalries need a lesser frequency of dispute occurrence for their maintenance. As in the Wayman definition the rivalry continues until the end of a ten-year dispute-free period.

Moving along the time and dispute continuum, we arrive at the five dispute and twenty-five year minimum of the recent work from people associated with the COW project (Jones 1991; Geller 1992, 1993; Huth and Russett 1993). Because of its origins I will refer to this as the COW

Table 10.1 *A comparison of enduring rivalry definitions*

Definition	Min. num.	Min. time	Termination criterion	Multi-lateral
Wayman	2	11	10 yrs.	yes
Diehl	3	15	10 yrs.	yes
COW	5	25	10 yrs.	sometimes
Goertz–Diehl*	6	20	15 yrs.	yes
Gochman–Maoz	7	none	none	yes

Note: * See below for a discussion of this definition.

definition. However, each person or group uses a slightly different but closely related list of enduring rivalries – in fact the same person can use slightly different lists from one study to the next (Huth, Bennett and Gelpi 1992; Huth and Russett 1993). As a result the exact definition varies somewhat from study to study, but these variations are relatively minor (at least in superficial terms). First, the definition specifies a severity condition: for an enduring rivalry to exist, there must be a minimum of five militarized disputes involving the same two states. It also stipulates that the two rivals must be the primary initiator and primary target of the dispute respectively or there must be direct and prolonged military confrontation between the rivals in a multiparty dispute in which they were not the primary parties. This clause eliminates third-party interventions in which one rival is not in direct confrontation with the other. Another stipulation is that the dispute must be reciprocal and last longer than thirty days. The duration condition of the COW definition requires that there be at least twenty-five years between the outbreak of the first dispute and the termination of the last dispute. The final stipulation is the intensity condition: in order for any two disputes to be part of the same rivalry, there must be a period of no more than ten years between them or the issues over which the disputes revolve must be the same and unresolved, if the underlying "issue" remains unresolved then this overrides behavioral rules. States must consistently be challenging one another either through frequency of conflict within a narrow time frame or through the same disputed issue over a broader period.

At the other end of the enduring rivalry continuum there is the Gochman and Maoz definition which, however, is somewhat vague. They consider enduring rivalries as "the pairs ... of states that most often have engaged in disputes with one another" (1984, p. 609). In practice this turns out to be a minimum of seven militarized disputes over the 1816–1976 period. The temporal limit has been eliminated altogether; no period of relative peace ends the rivalry. Disputes may be years apart and involve wholly different issues, the only thing they have in common is the participants.

Table 10.1 compares the four definitions, plus the one I shall propose below, on a number of conceptual and empirical criteria. Most of the definitions rely on temporal proximity to indicate an interconnection between the disputes. Without specified theoretical underpinnings three of the definitions use the somewhat arbitrary ten-year dispute-free period as terminating an enduring rivalry. The COW definition is the only one to specify an issue component, but even in that case the temporal interconnection criterion (i.e., frequency of disputes) can override the issue condition.

One fundamental difference between behavioral and issue definitions of enduring rivalries is that the behavioral ones only focus on the effect – military conflict – while issue ones implicitly include a "cause." If the US and the USSR have disputes over time about "different" issues then these conflicts do not qualify as part of the same enduring rivalry. Thus it would seem logically possible for two states to engage in several *simultaneous* enduring rivalries. For example, do the conflicts between the US and China over Korea and the Taiwanese islands constitute two enduring rivalries or one? Of course it depends on what level one situates the "issue," from the relatively concrete territorial ones to the general "struggle for power in Asia." The advantage of a purely behavioral definition is that it remains fairly agnostic about the mechanism of cause, but, on the other hand, it risks putting apples and oranges together. There are risks and assumptions associated with both positions that need to be made as explicit as possible.

As figure 10.1 illustrates there are rivalries that contain peaceful periods. In a number of cases, such as Turkey and Greece, there are rivalries that end according to various termination rules (e.g., ten years without a dispute) and then start up again later The question is whether the rivalry is really the same one as existed before, a new rivalry, one in hibernation, or one just below some threshold of military conflict. (The same issue arises in the analysis of the post-Cold War conflicts in the Balkans; many trace them back to World War I.) The behavioral definitions of Wayman and Diehl consider these as new rivalries. The COW definition discriminates, it allows enduring rivalries to have no significant behavioral signs (i.e., militarized disputes) for an extended period of time and still be considered an enduring rivalry. Unresolved issues connect temporally distant disputes. The extreme case is the Gochman and Maoz definition that classifies all disputes between the states as part of the same rivalry; there are no such things as interrupted rivalries.

An easily forgotten problem concerns the termination of the rivalry. It is often easier to see a rivalry begin, because usually the start is marked by a crisis or some other dramatic event, than to understand when it is over. None of the definitions really provides termination criteria distinct from those related to the maximum time between disputes. The problem with this is that although states might resolve their major differences through war and/or international agreement, the definitions will not recognize the end of rivalry until years after this resolution.

It is clear that each of the definitions occupies a position along the continuum of rivalry severity. The two main components of this continuum consist in the number of disputes, which goes from two to three to five to seven for the four definitions, and the minimum duration, which goes from ten to fifteen to twenty-five to unlimited. Each definition may be quite reasonable for the purposes for which it was devised, but are there any "natural" breaking points that might separate *enduring* rivalries from less severe conflict? Although the concept of enduring rivalries is continuous, the empirical distribution of rivalries along this continuum may not be smooth. One possible starting point is the Wayman definition which includes virtually everything that could plausibly be called an enduring rivalry. Table 10.2 gives a breakdown of the number of rivalries and their average duration by the number of disputes in the rivalry (using the Wayman definition).

Although one can comment on the validity of the cases included or excluded by varying the dispute standard, *ceteris paribus*, there is a dramatic drop in the number of rivalries and a big jump in their average duration as the severity of the rivalry increases. Empirically, the number of rivalries drops as one moves from six disputes, where there are fourteen rivalries, to seven disputes with only five rivalries. Beyond this there are no more than five rivalries at any level. In terms of average duration the big break comes between five-dispute rivalries with an average duration of thirteen years and six-dispute rivalries with a twenty-year average duration.

The big break between five and six disputes in table 10.2 provides the framework for my conclusions about the four operational definitions. The duration time for five-dispute rivalries is thirteen years which jumps dramatically to twenty years for six-dispute rivalries. Would a simple requirement of six disputes produce a list considerably different than the

Table 10.2 *Changing thresholds and enduring rivalries*

Number of disputes	Number of rivalries	Average duration (years)
2	133	4
3	62	7
4	32	11
5	20	13
6	14	20
7	5	21
8	5	17
9	5	22
10	1	25
11	3	24
12	2	26
15	1	46
16	1	28
18	1	24

COW list with its complicated criteria? I compared the COW list (as represented by Jones's definition) to one generated by the six-dispute minimum (with a ten-year termination rule). The latter results in an identification of nine more rivalries. The shortest one is thirteen years, and four of the nine fall below the twenty-five year minimum of the COW definition. The shortest rivalries (Laos–North Vietnam and Zambia–Rhodesia) are the result of long wars. Good definitions should exclude these cases because one does not want to make long wars coterminous with enduring rivalries.

Using this empirical information in conjunction with the theoretical considerations above, a compromise between simplicity and validity is an operational definition of an enduring rivalry as:

1 A minimum of six militarized disputes.
2 A minimum duration of twenty years.
3 A fifteen-year termination rule.[1]
4 Multilateral disputes are counted.

With this definition – that I shall call the "Goertz–Diehl"[2] definition – I arrive at almost the same results as the COW group with the advantage of

[1] A fifteen-year termination rule was adopted because there are a number of cases where there were eleven- to thirteen-year non-dispute periods in what one would consider enduring rivalries.

[2] Much of my work on enduring rivalries has been in conjunction with Paul Diehl.

the list of rivalries being easily replicable and omitting the number of minor conditions that encumber their definition. From this point on I refer to this operational definition when I use the word "enduring rivalries."

The empirical evidence suggests that the class of enduring rivalries (the Goertz–Diehl definition or similar ones) does constitute a separate phenomenon. Although the concept of an enduring rivalry is continuous, empirically the large drop in the number of rivalries and the significant increase in average duration suggest that these cases form a class apart. The list of rivalries in the appendix to this chapter includes almost all long-standing rivalries that frequently come to mind. This definition does not dramatically differ from the COW definitions which are based on intuitive notions of enduring rivalries. It remains an open question if slight differences between definitions have a profound impact on hypothesis tests. (It is quite possible that a few observations influence strongly the results of a regression analysis; these observations are said to have "leverage" (Belsley, Kuh, and Welsh 1980).

Enduring rivalries as a background context

The concept of enduring rivalries has been hovering around the consciousness of scholars of international conflict for some time, but only recently has it emerged from the shadows. The enduring rivalry concept made its first appearance in the early 1980s (Wayman 1982; Diehl 1983; Gochman and Maoz 1984). These early papers suggested the outlines of the operational definition and also illustrated the most common use of enduring rivalries: case selection. The concept served to choose cases for analysis in order to test hypotheses that assumed a background of hostility. (It was not until the 1990s that enduring rivalries began to be investigated in their own right, e.g., The Workshop on Processes of Enduring Rivalries, 1993, Bloomington, IN).

Thus for most of its history the concept of enduring rivalries has been used as a secondary concept, as a component in research programs designed to test other hypotheses; and this has remained its principal use. For example, Organski and Kugler (1980) in their original study claimed there must be some underlying hostility between the two countries for the power transition hypothesis to apply; they used the terms status quo and dissatisfied powers. To determine if there was underlying dissatisfaction they used Bueno de Mesquita's (1981) alliance alignment measure. Since then there have been a number of attempts to extend this hypothesis beyond its original domain of serious confrontations between major powers to all dyads. Enduring rivalries replace the alliance alignment measure to verify the underlying hostility requirement. Wayman's definition was designed in order to test the power transition hypothesis; Geller (1993) has studied this same hypothesis using the more restrictive COW definition of enduring rivalries.

In a similar fashion, enduring rivalries form the background for the study of arms races. Nations may be increasing rapidly their military expenditures but the competitor in the race must be identified (military spending can, of course, be driven by internal forces as well). This may be a pretty simple problem to solve since it is usually quite obvious from inspection who the rival is. Even though it may require no fancy procedures to identify the rival, the concept of rivalry underlies all procedures. Arms races make no sense without some rivalry component. As Vasquez states: "There is a consensus that arms races presuppose rivalry, at least at some level, and intensify that rivalry once they are underway" (Vasquez 1993, p. 177). Thus the concept of a rivalry is implicit in the concept of an arms race.

The identification of the rival can be based on inspection, but perhaps a more rigorous and replicable procedure is to operationally define a rivalry. Diehl (1985) developed his definition just for these purposes. An enduring rivalry constituted the context within which he examined the likelihood that arms races lead to war. He argued that using the concept of a rivalry was necessary since looking at just rapid increases in military spending produced cases that were not appropriate (e.g., Smith 1980). An analogous problem arises with power transitions between non-rivals.

The problem arising in the study of power transition and arms races also occurs in the empirical study of deterrence. Again, deterrence is only an issue if there is some underlying hostility or expectation of future conflict between two countries. An interesting example is Huth's work on deterrence. In his early work (e.g., Huth and Russett 1984) he examined extended deterrence within a universe of cases where there had been an explicit threat to be deterred. In his recent work (Huth, Bennett, and Gelpi 1992; Huth and Russett 1993) he now examines deterrence and other phenomena in the context of enduring rivalries. The concept of enduring rivalry has become an integral part of Huth's research design, but its function remains a case selection one: "the concept of Great Power rivalry is critical because it identifies the population of cases to be used for testing the model's propositions" (Huth, Bennett, and Gelpi 1992, p. 483). So while progress – if this is to be measured by more sophisticated operational definitions of a rivalry – is being made in defining lists of rivals, its theoretical uses have not changed.

The growing interest in enduring rivalries has incited researchers to come up with more elaborate and restrictive definitions of the concept. As we have seen above there exists a wide range of choice for the operational definition of an enduring rivalry. As two Wayman papers indicate (Wayman 1982; Wayman and Jones 1991), there now arises the problem of justifying minimalist versus maximalist definitions. One might suppose that minimalist definitions are used for background conditions like Wayman did for the power transition hypothesis or Diehl for arms races, but in fact this is not the case. The trend has been away from the minimalist definitions of the mid 1980s to the maximalist ones which find favor in the early 1990s. To my knowledge no one has theoretically justified the use of a more or less restrictive definition of a rivalry (though Diehl 1985 gives reasons to prefer his definition to Wayman's). Nor has anyone investigated the empirical consequences of the use of maximalist versus minimalist definitions of enduring rivalries.

Enduring rivalries also provide a context for theories of crisis behavior. Embedded in the concept of enduring rivalries are crises; most of the disputes that constitute an enduring rivalry are in fact crises. Here there is an interesting contrast between *short-term intense* conflict within a larger context of *long-term enduring* conflict. How are we to relate the two? Enduring rivalries constitute an important context for understanding crises. One might suspect that when a crisis breaks out between long-term rivals it differs from an isolated crisis. At the same time there may be something about how crises end that leads into the next crisis. Like in contextual analysis we need to understand how the context of a rivalry affects a crisis, but also how each crisis redefines and changes the enduring rivalry.

From a contextual perspective what is interesting about this literature is its use of enduring rivalries as a background context to study power transitions, arms races, and deterrence hypotheses. It is perhaps time for the concept to leave the closet and be incorporated as a factor in its own right in these various hypotheses. Context as changing meaning provides one theoretical tool: characteristics of enduring rivalry may mediate the relationship between, say, an arms race and war. This permits a much more theoretically informed analysis of the role of enduring rivalries in the arms race phenomenon. The choice of spatial–temporal domain (case selection) is a theory of context: the use of enduring rivalries in this vein is a striking example of how theoretically important this implicit theory of context can be.

The empirical importance of the concept of enduring rivalries

I propose that beyond its auxiliary uses in case selection, enduring rivalries are worthy of study in their own right. There are many important questions that the power transition, arms race, and deterrence approaches have left unexamined which the concept of enduring rivalries throws into the spotlight. One obvious question is why enduring rivalries start; when enduring rivalries are used as a background condition this question and other similar ones never arise. Another assumption in the arms race literature is that if an arms race leads to war then the case is closed. But a focus on rivalries questions this, it implies that wars can start arms races, and can even be in the middle of them.

This section is devoted to an analysis of the empirical importance of enduring rivalries. I would like to investigate if there are some *empirical* grounds for claiming that this concept is significant for the study of international conflict and war. To do this I examine whether important phenomena such as war, militarized disputes, and territorial changes occur frequently within the context of rivalries.

As we saw in an earlier section the concept of enduring rivalry is fundamentally continuous but all current operational definitions are dichotomous. In order to examine how frequently wars, disputes, and territorial changes occur within a rivalry a continuous definition of an enduring rivalry would provide the most information. Using the current definitions I can cobble together a continuous one suitable for my analysis. At one extreme is isolated conflict: one-dispute, zero minimum duration, and zero-year termination criterion. This connects to Wayman's definition: two-dispute minimum, ten-year minimum, and ten-year termination criterion. Following this I use Diehl's definition: three to five disputes, fifteen-year minimum, and ten-year termination criterion. Finally, I define full-fledged rivalries according to Goertz–Diehl: six or more disputes, twenty-year minimum, and fifteen-year termination criterion. This "continuous" definition increases gradually the criteria for a rivalry along the three dimensions. Since the number of disputes forms the core of the definition I shall refer to the severity of the rivalry by the number of disputes it contains.

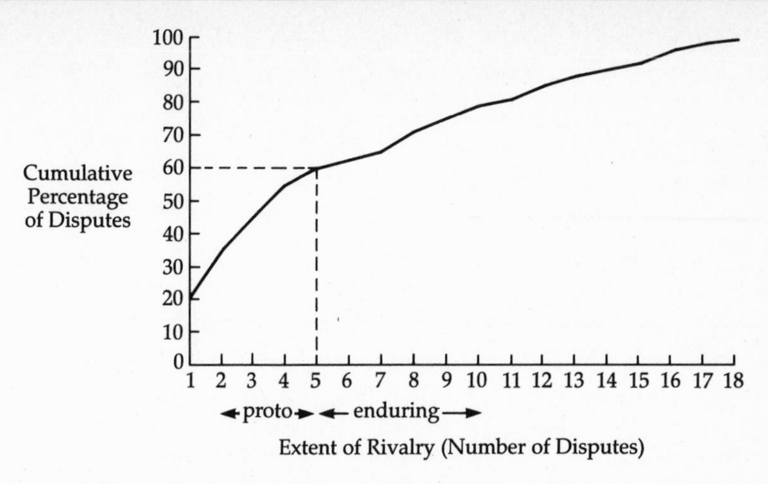

Figure 10.2 Non-war disputes within enduring rivalries

For grosser comparisons I shall refer to one-dispute rivalries as "isolated conflicts," two- to five dispute rivalries as "proto-rivalries", and reserve the term "enduring rivalry" for six-or-more dispute rivalries.

One test of the empirical relevance of the concept of enduring rivalries consists in the extent to which important phenomena occur within this context. If the rivalry context matters then I would expect that a large percentage of non-war militarized disputes occur within it and that isolated disputes would comprise a small fraction of the universe of cases.[3] Figure 10.2 shows that less than one-fourth of militarized disputes occur in isolation, hence the vast majority of disputes may be connected over time in some fashion. (This and other graphs present the cumulative distribution, e.g., 60 percent of non-war disputes occur in rivalries of five or fewer disputes.) Thirty-nine percent of disputes occur in proto-rivalries, while 40 percent occur in enduring rivalries proper, which is all the more significant since the number of rivalries is relatively small. Somehow rivalries are "dispute-producing" out of all proportion to the number of conflicting or all possible dyads.

Figure 10.2 shows that a large number of non-war disputes occur within rivalries. It is natural to ask whether rivalries include the more severe conflicts between nations as Leng's results suggest. Isolated conflict may occur between normally friendly states (e.g., a fishing dispute between Iceland and Great Britain or British–American confrontations over Latin

[3] A dispute or war may be part of more than one rivalry in which case it is placed in the most severe rivalry.

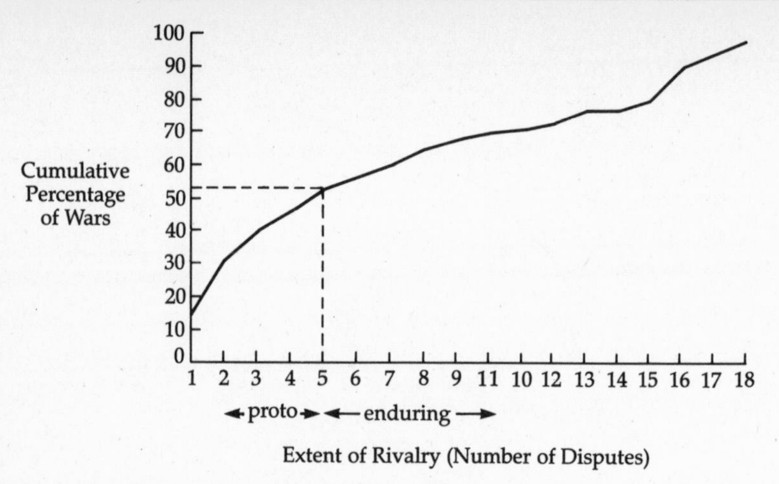

Figure 10.3 Wars within enduring rivalries

America at the turn of the century). States involved in isolated disputes may not want to escalate tensions, which might move relations to a totally hostile level. The converse can also arise because there may be domestic political conditions which incite a government to take a hard line against a traditional enemy.

Two variants of this hypothesis are (1) a large number of wars occur in rivalries and (2) the likelihood of war increases as the severity of the rivalry increases. A rivalry sets the stage for escalating tensions in a dispute to culminate in war. Disputes without a violent past are more likely to be resolved peacefully, or at least without resort to all out force. Figure 10.3 gives the occurrence of war within rivalry contexts. Only 16 percent of wars occur as isolated events whereas 47 percent occur in a serious rivalry context; like non-war disputes, most war occurs in some rivalry context (84 percent), be it enduring or proto. This indicates that the more severe the conflict the more likely it is to occur within a rivalry context: 25 percent of non-war disputes were isolated while for wars it is 16 percent, 47 percent of wars occur in enduring rivalries against 40 percent in non-war disputes. The curve in figure 10.2 for no-war disputes is higher than that in figure 10.3 for wars, which means that more severe conflicts (i.e., wars) are associated with more serious rivalries.

Instead of taking the war or dispute as the unit of analysis it is perhaps more appropriate to ask about the likelihood of war given that there is an enduring rivalry. Figure 10.3 indicates that most wars occur within some rivalry context, but does the existence of a rivalry imply the likelihood of at

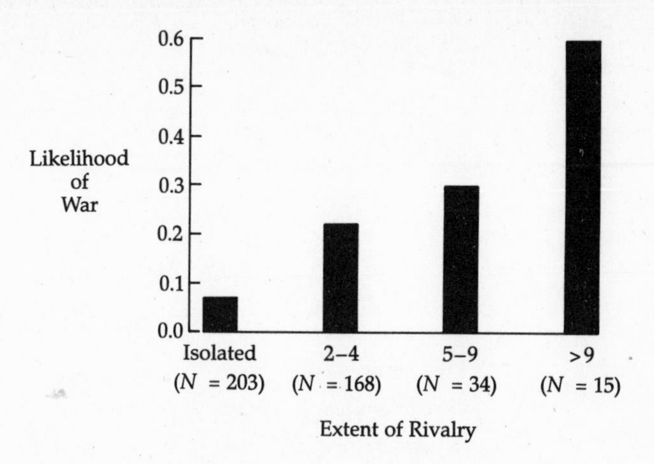

Figure 10.4 Likelihood of war in an enduring rivalry
Note: This is the likelihood of at least one war.

least one war? Figure 10.4 shows that the likelihood of war in an isolated dispute is 0.07, which more than doubles to 0.22 in proto-rivalries, which then increases to 0.60 in rivalries involving ten or more disputes.[4] Thus not only do most wars occur in rivalries but as rivalries get more severe war becomes more likely.

Beyond the greater frequency and severity of military conflict, I suggest that other related phenomena also occur frequently within the context of enduring rivalries. One such phenomenon is territorial conflict and change. It has been argued that territorial issues are themselves the source of much international conflict, in fact, according to some (Holsti 1991; Vasquez 1993) the primary source of interstate conflict over the past five centuries. If territorial changes occur with more frequency in enduring rivalries than in isolated disputes then this is further evidence for the importance of the concept.

Figure 10.5 shows the distribution of non-war territorial changes within rivalries of increasing severity (the data on territorial change are described in Goertz and Diehl 1992a).[5] Here, however, there is no evidence that

[4] I aggregate rivalries into categories in order to have a sufficient number of cases for the averages to make sense.

[5] Some territorial changes occur outside any conflict or rivalry, these are considered "isolated" rivalries in this analysis. Only territorial change between recognized states of the system as defined by the COW project are included.

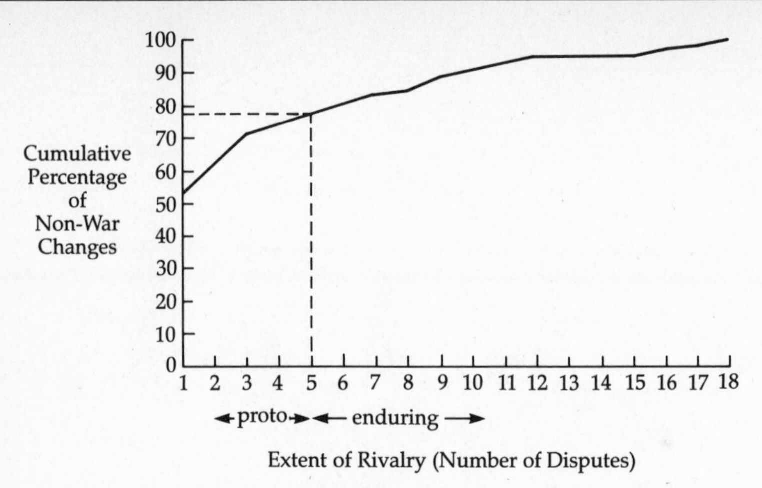

Figure 10.5 Non-war territorial changes within enduring rivalries

non-war changes occur with particular frequency within rivalries.[6] In fact 53 percent of non-war territorial changes occur outside any rivalry context. Only 23 percent occur within enduring rivalries, this does not reach the levels of militarized disputes and war. Indeed, most – over 75 percent – territorial changes are transacted peacefully (Goertz and Diehl 1992a). On the other hand, striking is the number of territorial changes involving military conflict which occur within the context of a rivalry (shown in figure 10.6). In this case only 22 percent of changes involving military conflict occur in isolation while 38 percent occur within serious rivalries. Here again enduring rivalries provide the framework for militarized conflict, this time over territory. Territorial changes occurring in proto or enduring rivalry contexts are over three times more likely to involve military conflict than isolated changes and include three-fourths of all war-related changes. Rivalries influence less the frequency than the modality of territorial change.

This brief analysis indicates that a large portion of militarized conflict takes place in the context of rivalries, especially enduring rivalries. Enduring rivalries are the setting for almost half of the interstate wars since 1816. They are also at the extreme eight times as likely to experience a war as a pair of states in an isolated conflict. Territorial changes did not occur disproportionately within this context, but changes involving military conflict did;

[6] "War" over territory is defined as the military conflict between organized forces from both sides of the exchange.

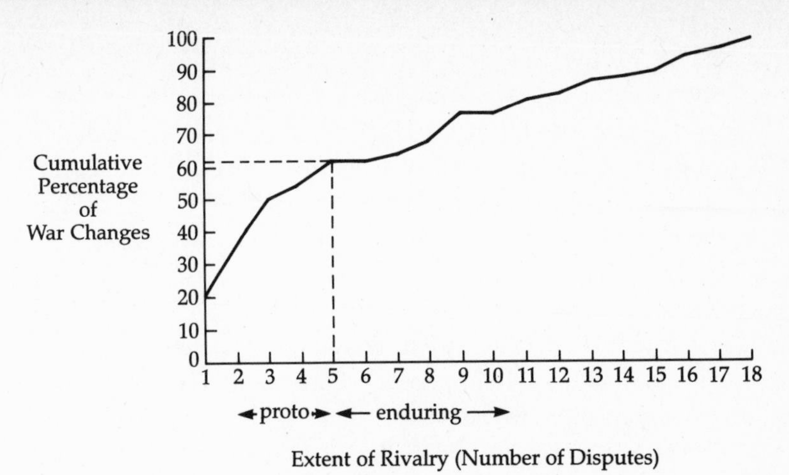

Figure 10.6 War territorial changes within enduring rivalries

in fact they were three times more likely to involve conflict than isolated changes.

Given that rivalries have been used to study power transitions, arms races, and deterrence it is perhaps not surprising that so much international conflict occurs within this context. What these studies fail to capture, with their use of the concept as only a case selection tool, is that the rivalry context may play a *causal* role in determining which arms race, power transition, etc., escalate to war. The analysis showed that the more severe the rivalry the more likely war was to occur. The rivalry context is both the result of historical conflicts and the anticipation of future ones. That past conflicts condition current ones and future expectations, that leaders learn realpolitik lessons, and that peoples learn to hate each other all mean that theories of enduring rivalries are historical theories. This means recourse to historical theories and a stress on the historical context.

Methodological implications

It would be foolish to assume that between crises relations among states cease to exist. By using dispute data we capture events that score high on the conflict "Richter" scale. It is likely that there continues to be low-level conflict between rivals. In order to be included as a dispute in the data set one state needs to have made at least a serious threat to use military force, conflicts which do not reach this level are not counted. In statistical terms, the data are *truncated* from below. The dashed horizontal line in figure 10.1

represents the minimum level of "force" that the data set picks up, all interaction at a lower level remains subclinical. The COW definition of rivalries increases the truncation threshold by requiring that the disputes be reciprocal and last at least thirty days. Ordinary least squares procedure used on truncated data underestimates coefficients (Judge *et al.* 1985). This problem is not unique to enduring rivalries but is a concern when comparing wars with non-war conflicts. The COW definition by pushing up the truncation level risks underestimating the importance of the factors explaining rivalry behavior.

The inability of the dispute data to detect low-level conflict means that they cannot distinguish it from peace. The assumption is that during the enduring rivalry relations remain on the conflictual side, that they never dip down to peace. In figure 10.1 from time 7 to 10 there is peace and in "reality" the rivalry has ended, however from time 13 to 17 the rivalry continues at an unobservable level. The cutoff rules assume that after ten years of no military conflicts relations have become peaceful. The truncation problem means that it is difficult to determine the end (and also symmetrically the beginning) of the rivalry. According to the various behavioral definitions a rivalry begins at time 2 but in fact it has already begun at time 1. The problem posed by the militarized dispute coding scheme is that since the minimum threshold is set quite high, we know neither about the relations between rivals during the interdispute periods nor before or after the first or last codable dispute.

A banal aspect of enduring rivalries is that they do not last forever. They are born, flourish – some more than others – and then die. There are important questions associated with each aspect of the life-cycle of a rivalry. What certain conditions are conducive to their birth? When do they flourish and how long-lived are they? How is it that they die; is it quick and painless or slow and lingering? One way to talk about enduring rivalries is through the life-cycle metaphor. If one looks at enduring rivalries from this perspective there are a number of consequences that follow.

One of the consequences is methodological. In virtually all studies of disease there exists a situation where some of the experimental subjects still have the disease at the end of the study, some have died, and some have recovered well. This is true of enduring rivalries as well; as of 1976 some rivalries have ended, some have ended and restarted, and some are still going on. A similar situation arises at the beginning of the temporal domain since some rivalries are already underway in 1816. In statistical terms the data are *censored*. In the Appendix to this chapter all rivalries beginning before 1831 are censored as are all rivalries or potential rivalries with disputes after 1960, twenty-four of the forty-five cases. In figure 10.1 all the information after time 15 is censored. While it appears at time 15 that the rivalry has ended, in fact, it will flare up again at time 17. Censoring means that we do not always know the beginning or the end of the story; for some dyads we know the complete history, for others not. This presents certain statistical problems, since with censored data ordinary regression underestimates the strength of relationships (Judge *et al.* 1985).

The dotted area in figure 10.1 covers all the information unavailable to the militarized dispute data set. The move toward more restrictive definitions of rivalry, as in the COW definition, enlarges this area. Of course, events data could be used to lower the truncation level but the problem is a theoretical one as well. A key to the theoretical definition of enduring rivalries is the possibility of war between rivals. As one lowers the truncation boundary this probability also goes down. But one may also be interested in conflictual patterns where the probability of war is lower: enduring rivalries can also be a tool for the study of security regimes, conflict management and conflict resolution. For these purposes one might want to enlarge the coverage of the enduring rivalry definition. Though the enduring rivalry concept has only been used to study war it has potential also for the study of conflict management, and peace.

Probably the most fundamental methodological shift implied by the concept of enduring rivalries can be summarized as the one arising when moving from completely *cross-sectional* research to quasi *time-series* situations. This move has technical, statistical implications as well as more substantive ones.

The error term (customarily denoted by ϵ) contains most of the statistical assumptions in the regression analysis of time-series data. One standard assumption is that the error terms are independent. It is well known that the residuals in time-series analyses (the estimates from the data of the ϵ's) are often highly correlated (when they are plotted against time a clear pattern emerges). If this is the case parameter estimates are not correct. With cross-sectional data this issue does not arise so easily (there is nothing like time against which to plot the residuals, though the same assumption holds). But once one begins to see a temporal relationship between conflicts this means that any regression-type analysis of these data must begin to deal with the problem of correlated residuals. The quick fix used by economists dealing with purely time-series data (only one time series and not several) is to assume that ϵ_t is correlated (this is called the autoregression coefficient usually denoted by ρ) with ϵ_{t-1}. One can then estimate this correlation (ρ) which corrects the parameter estimates. If this does not solve the problem there exists a wide range of techniques (Box and Jenkins 1976) devoted to time-series problems.

Unfortunately, the case of enduring rivalries involves more than the analysis of just one rivalry. If the goal is to establish patterns common to all rivalries then the research design is *cross-sectional time-series*: the focus is on over-time relationships in different cross-sectional units. In this situation various kinds of assumptions can be made, but a common approach is to calculate a different autoregression coefficient (ρ_i) for the error term of each enduring rivalry in the sample, formally:

$$\epsilon_t = \rho_j \epsilon_{t-1} + \mu \quad \mu \sim i.i.d.\ N(0, \sigma^2) \tag{10.1}$$

for all different rivalries j in a series t of conflicts.

These kinds of techniques are fairly common in econometrics but as far as I am aware there have been few attempts to apply them, at least in spirit, to problems of international conflict. O'Loughlin and Anselin (1991) used a related approach to study the spatial dependence of conflict. Spatial dependence has its own set of particularities due to the two-dimensional nature of geography. They used models based on ideas similar to equation 10.1; the difference lies in that instead of having j different enduring rivalries they consider all dyads in a spatial fashion. Their study, including models based on the Poisson modeling technique outlined in chapter 5 (modified by their spatial concerns), regular ordinary least squares models, and models incorporating equation 10.1 and equation 10.2 (below), found that generally ordinary least squares did the least well, followed by the Poisson models, with the spatial–temporal models (equations 10.1 and 10.2) doing the best in capturing the relations between conflict and cooperation in African dyads. While they emphasize the geographic context, the same methodological techniques apply to my temporal concerns. O'Loughlin (1986) provides an example of how traditional regression analysis misses the spatial nature of international conflict data. I suspect the same exercise would yield similar results for the temporal data of enduring rivalries.

It is important to notice that I have not mentioned any particular explanatory model. The discussion has centered on problems of the error term (ϵ) in the regression model. The error term is the focus because this is the main area where statistics comes into play. I have not dealt with the *substantive* reasons why conflicts are related over time but only with these nebulous error terms. In fact, there is no a priori reason why there should be a problem with the error term; it all depends on the model and the data. These problems are "technical," their solutions are technical, and there is no reference to the substance of the problem of enduring rivalries.

A better solution to this problem requires the production of good *substantive* reasons why conflicts are related over time. Instead of assuming correlated error terms, it is better to think about how conflicts are connected over time; these factors can then be entered into the regression model – and may well correct at the same time problems with the error terms. This is also better political science, since what we are really interested in is the regression model not the structure of the error term. It is possible to give a substantive interpretation to the autoregression coefficient (ρ), but this is very rare. Williams and McGinnis (1992) did something that has this flavor by modeling US and Soviet behavior through spectral analysis, arguing that there is an underlying rivalry dimension (something like a ρ) that better explains US and Soviet behavior than arms race models and the like.

One simple way to model conflicts related over time is to include a lagged endogenous variable in the model – in rivalry terms, the previous conflict is a cause of the current conflict:

$$Y_t = \gamma Y_{t-1} + \epsilon_t \quad \epsilon_t \sim i.i.d.\ N(0,\sigma^2) \tag{10.2}$$

The γ is the dependence of conflict (Y) at time t on the conflict at time $t-1$. This is a more substantive approach to the problem than one focusing on error terms but is still quite atheoretical. It is quite like the diffusion studies that ask if conflicts are correlated across time or space. Davis, Duncan, and Siverson (1978) used a similar approach in their analysis of the diffusion of conflict across time in the international system as a whole. In their case Y_{t-1} is not the previous conflict but rather the waiting time between the past and present conflicts (they actually used Y_{t-4} to Y_{t-1}) for all warring dyads in the system. If short waiting times follow short waiting times then conflicts cluster, evidence of positive infection.

Most of the work using the diffusion framework has concentrated on spatial diffusion, but at the same time hypotheses on temporal diffusion have also been tested. However, this testing has not gone beyond the hypothesis of correlation over time. Most of the findings whether at the system (Levy 1982) or state (Stoll 1984) level of analysis have found weak correlations. The results presented above confirm that the basic intuition of the temporal diffusion metaphor is correct. What has been lacking is the proper framework within which to investigate the problem. Instead of focusing on the nation or the system the appropriate unit of analysis is the dyad. Also conflict addiction studies have correlated conflicts on the assumption that they occur within a few, fixed number (typically one to five) of years of one another. Conflicts in enduring rivalries do not necessarily occur on a periodic basis, nor do conflicts necessarily succeed each other in a rapid fashion as most previous diffusion work has implicitly assumed. The enduring rivalry framework reflects the irregular but connected patterns of conflict over long periods of time, and, in fact, the results of my analysis indicate very significant correlations of conflict over time.

If γ in equation (10.2) is statistically significant[7] then diffusion of conflict across time is one possible conclusion. However, this gives us no clue about *how* or *why* these conflicts are related. Frequently the recourse is to metaphors such as inertia and momentum (correlations over time are often described as inertia, e.g., Johnston 1972, Bartholomew 1982) as well as diffusion. What we need are some good mechanisms for relating conflicts over time. This can be illustrated formally by (where the X is also a good symbol of the unknown factors):

$$Y_t = \gamma_0 + \gamma_1 X Y_{t-1} + \epsilon_t \quad \epsilon_t \sim i.i.d.\ N(0, \sigma^2) \tag{10.3}$$

X represents *substantive* factors that link Y_{t-1} to Y_t.

To include Y_{t-n} in the model is to historicize it (by the definition of the previous chapter). Conflicts in the past cause conflicts in the present. The X variable in equation 10.3 is what links the past to the present. For example, it can represent the learning that takes place over time. Depending on the learning patterns of different governments (different X values) there is a different impact of Y_{t-1} on Y_t. We also saw in the last chapter that theories of inertia, incrementalism, and momentum explain the present by reference to the past. The autocorrelation type coefficients are one formal representation of these concepts in the statistical and econometric literature. This seems natural since autocorrelation reflects how similar (dependent) the past is to the present. In short, the concept of enduring rivalry pushes theoretically in the direction of historical theories. There are a wide variety of statistical techniques that link lagged effects to current ones; what is needed are theories which determine which technique is appropriate.

[7] Lagged dependent variables present special statistical problems of their own, these are treated in most econometric textbooks (e.g., Judge *et al.* 1985).

Enduring rivalries and context

From the discussion of the previous chapter and this one there are several possible means by which conflicts may be related to each other over time:

Irrelevant question – states repeatedly conflict if it is rational for them to do so in the present.
Issue – there is some contentious problem that remains unresolved, like many territorial issues.
System structure – since system structure determines much conflict, if it does not change conflicts recur.
Preference formation – States change their preferences because of the outcome of previous conflicts.

The first three of these have the same theoretical structure. Both rely on the idea that if the cause, be it structure or issue, does not change then conflicts recur. In short, they state a fairly obvious position, "same cause, same effect"; behavior does not change if the context does not. Habits, rules of thumb, and SOPs can be quite reasonable – or even optimal – if the relevant parameters do not change. Expected-utility calculations produce repeated conflict if preferences and power distributions have not changed. It appears that the assumption of unchanging contexts will be crucial to the analysis of enduring rivalries. This assumption cuts across approaches and in all constitutes a critical factor.

The system structure explanation of enduring rivalries exemplifies the context as cause mode of analysis. Certain kinds of systems encourage the formation of enduring rivalries. For example, bipolar worlds may generate enduring rivalries since the two blocs are in constant conflict with each other. On the other hand, one might expect few enduring rivalries in multipolar systems due to cross-pressures and a larger variety of interactions. Bipolar situations imply repetitive conflict and multipolar ones imply changing conflict.

By the same sort of logic environmental change and shocks may be related to the emergence and demise of rivalries. Theories of repeated behavior imply that actors often continue along the same path until some exogenous shock forces a change. Well-entrenched enduring rivalries may be subject to these external shocks. The end of the Cold War has seen the resolution of a number of conflicts in different parts of the world. From these considerations arises the hypothesis that significant changes in the international system may bring rivalries to an end and/or establish the conditions for new ones (Diehl and Goertz 1993). World wars, for example, seem to be the ending and beginning points of some notable rivalries. It is not that there are not significant internal dynamics to the rivalry, but that these dynamics are subject to changes in the outside environment. The fundamental fact is that enduring rivalries have deep roots; the question then becomes how well-established habits change. One answer is systemic shocks.

The concept of enduring rivalries focuses on issues, tangible and intangible, over which nations conflict. When looking at different rivalries these conflicts may be over territory, over regional influence, etc. so that each rivalry appears quite unique. There may be different issues over which rivalries occur but they all may have the same functionality. The variable "issue" varies from rivalry to rivalry but may play the same basic role in understanding the course of rivalries in general. Perhaps one reason why no one has developed a general theory of enduring rivalries is because historical inspection makes them seem too disparate. Context as changing meaning provides one methodology for dealing with the problem of multiple issues. These issues may play the same role or have similar effects in explaining the rivalry, their face differences are subsumed in a model that gives them the same meaning.

In a recent conference (Peace Science Society 1991, Ann Arbor MI) there was a roundtable and general discussion of the problems and implications of the study of enduring rivalries. One of the interesting aspects of this discussion was that the discussants and the audience, mostly formal theorists and researchers of the quantitative empirical school, frequently used words like "hate," "dislike," and other expressions of an emotive flavor. The concept of enduring rivalries brings to the fore in a way familiar to traditional policy analysts, but foreign to behavioralists, the importance of preferences and values other than "power" or "utility" maximization. How this fits into a potential theory of enduring rivalries is not clear, but one "naturally" and "intuitively" talks this way about these conflicts. This is not to say that there are not conflicts over territory between the Arabs and the Israelis, but that this conflict has created dislikes above and beyond the concrete issues at hand. The French and Germans no longer fight each other, but certainly negative stereotypes still exist. Thus norms and preferences may play an important role. The converse has been argued by Maoz and Russett (1991) for democracies; there are normative values shared by democracies which prevent them from becoming involved in war with each other. Williams and

McGinnis (1992) argued that underlying the US–Soviet relations exists a "rivalry" dimension that explains why arms race models and domestic politics models cannot account for the behavior of either side.

Barrier models stressed the role of social pressure (spatial context) in preference formation, the concept of enduring rivalries emphasizes the temporal aspects of desire creation. In terms of equation 10.3 current preferences ($P(t)$) are a function of previous conflicts ($P(t) = f(Y_{t-1}, Y_{t-2}, \ldots)$). Theories of preference formation are almost always contextual and historical. Using the enduring rivalry concept brings these issues to the fore.

There are certainly many hypotheses and theoretical frameworks that address the enduring rivalry puzzle. Structural, cyclical, diffusion, and game theoretical analyses of war are all potentially applicable. The explanation of enduring rivalries provides an important testing ground for the many theories of international war.

Appendix: Goertz–Diehl Enduring Rivalries

Rivals	Begin	End	Disputes	Wars	Censored
USA Haiti	1869	1891	15	1	
USA Mexico	1836	1893	15	1	
USA Ecuador	1952	1972	7	0	C
USA UK	1837	1861	9	0	
USA Spain	1850	1875	10	1	
USA Russia/USSR	1946	1973	12	0	C
USA China	1949	1974	10	1	C
Ecuador Peru	1893	1955	14	0	
Peru Chile	1871	1920	6	1	
Brazil UK	1826	1862	6	0	
Bolivia Paraguay	1906	1938	9	1	
Bolivia Chile	1857	1884	6	1	
Chile Argentina	1873	1900	7	0	
Chile Argentina	1952	1967	8	0	
UK Germany	1900	1939	5	1	C
UK Italy	1911	1940	5	2	
UK Russia/USSR	1877	1923	12	0	
UK Ottoman Empire	1876	1922	10	1	
UK Japan	1932	1954	6	1	
Belgium Germany	1912	1939	7	1	
France Germany	1905	1939	8	1	
France Ottoman Empire	1880	1920	6	1	
France China	1860	1914	6	2	
Austria-Hungary Italy	1843	1915	4	4	
Italy Ottoman Empire	1880	1926	13	2	
Greece Ottoman Empire	1829	1919	11	5	C
Greece Ottoman Empire	1958	1976	6	1	C

Appendix: Cont.

Rivals	Begin	End	Disputes	Wars	Censored
Russia/USSR Iran	1911	1945	6	0	
Russia/USSR Ottoman Empire	1876	1921	7	2	
Russia/USSR China	1898	1929	8	1	
Russia/USSR Japan	1895	1976	13	4	C
Somalia Ethiopia	1960	1975	7	0	C
Zambia Zimbabwe	1966	1976	8	0	C
Zambia South Africa	1968	1976	6	0	C
Iraq Israel	1948	1973	3	3	C
Egypt Israel	1948	1973	7	5	C
Syria Israel	1948	1976	13	3	C
Lebanon Israel	1965	1974	6	0	C
Afghanistan Pakistan	1949	1974	6	0	C
China Japan	1874	1937	9	4	
China India	1950	1975	8	2	C
India Pakistan	1947	1971	14	4	C
India Nepal	1950	1969	6	0	C
Thailand Kampuchea	1953	1976	11	0	C
Laos N. Vietnam	1958	1971	9	0	C

Note: Any militarized dispute before 1830 or after 1961 could be a part of an enduring rivalry that extends before 1816 or after 1976 (the problem of censored data). I only include rivalries that had six or more disputes in the 1816–1976 period.

11 THE CONTEXT OF INTERNATIONAL NORMS

> Late in the century [nineteenth] landlords and employers were urged to install running water toilets in their tenements or factories. The sales pitch was aimed less at the health of the labouring classes than at morality. The water closet was, among other things, intended as an architectural structure that would ensure the privacy of bodily functions, a natural extension of walls to separate the sleeping quarters of parents and children, a final material codification of the rules of the nuclear family. When combined with safe water disposal, however, it was also a significant health measure. It is hardly an exaggeration to say that morality and health were always combined in the utilitarian mind.
>
> Ian Hacking (1990, pp. 119–20)

Introduction

An analysis of normative contexts forms a fitting conclusion to this book because all the modes of context and substantive contexts play important roles. Norms are usually quite stable and hence can explain behavioral consistency; they emphasize historical, temporal contexts. Norms are important when many people hold them; spatial contexts come into play. International regimes are system-level structures that influence state action. Norms are frequently referred to, particularly by economists (Koford and Miller 1991), as a constraint or barrier. Normative contexts help determine behavior (context as cause) and serve as a guide to interpreting behavior (context as changing meaning). Many of the contrasts between diffusion and rational actor models have analogues in the contrasts between norms and self-interest. Pressure to conform to a norm comes from the surrounding environment, but self-interest can also dictate following norms. Both substantively and methodologically context plays a major role in the analysis of norms.

The normative context forms an important part of the international contexts that are the subject of this book. Norms are part of the international environment – a frustratingly intangible part – within which all nations live. Decision-makers largely agree about the international rules of the game; even those who try to change the rules recognize the normative force of the system in place. The existence of dirty tricks departments in all governments attests to the felt need to violate the rules. Rules may be violated, but the concept of violation itself depends on the existence of rules that are widely accepted. States use norms to justify their actions, even though this is often just the tribute vice pays to virtue. But nevertheless some actions are harder to justify than others.

Norms present an interesting context because they cannot be reduced to the level of the individual, they are created by individuals and affect them simultaneously. They exist as a creation of international society, created by the actions, words, and treaties that are such an important part of international life. Norms are like the market price; the market price is the creation of innumerable individual bargains made by individual economic agents, yet we can talk about it as an independent entity. Likewise individuals make normative decisions; it is through these decisions and interactions between individuals that norms come into existence. Norms pose many difficult questions: How do we model the relations between individuals and norms? What are the dynamics of norm creation? Do norms, like Frankenstein's Monster, take on a life of their own? Are they "sticky" like prices?

Norms play dramatically varying roles in the different social sciences. Anthropologists constantly use norms to explain behavior while economists tend to ignore them preferring self-interest maximization. Students of international relations who emphasize the struggle for power find themselves closer to the economists than to the anthropologists. With realism as the dominant position in world politics since World War II, norms have had only a bit part in explaining state actions (see Cusack and Stoll 1990, Vasquez 1983, and Wayman and Diehl 1994 for analyses of realism). The traditional image appears clearly depicted in the description of international life as an *anarchical society*; the international system is a "society," but one without effective rules of behavior, the classic Hobbesian state of nature where life is nasty, brutish, and short. Each state uses whatever means are at hand – most notably military force – to gain its ends. The state maximizes its own power, all action is instrumental and chosen for its efficiency; rules or "oughts" do not guide behavior (though norms can be seen as a self-interested "solution" to the state of nature problem, e.g., Gauthier 1986).

Traditional realism has been increasingly challenged over the last fifteen years. The question: "Do norms influence nation-state behavior?" has been answered in the affirmative by a growing number of people, particularly in the case of international economics and international organization – though doubts remain in the area of security affairs (Jervis 1983). The affirmative answer has centered around the concept of regimes as "sets of implicit or explicit principles, norms, rules, and decision-making procedures around which actors' expectations converge in a given area of international relations ... Norms are standards of behavior defined in terms of rights and obligations ..." (Krasner 1983b, p. 2). The definition of a regime includes norms, but as a relatively unambiguous and unproblematic primitive concept. As Finlayson and Zacher (1983) illustrate, norms are fundamental principles, not necessarily non-contradictory, that underlie most regimes. While they discuss the different norms of GATT, they assume that the concept of a norm itself is clear. Their discussion is symptomatic of the regime literature where little subtheory exists about the norms which constitute regimes.

I am not interested in regimes themselves, but in these underlying principles, and the extent to which they influence state behavior. I suggest that until we understand the characteristics of individual norms an analysis of "sets" of norms is premature. For this reason I refer to norms rather than to regimes. The two are obviously related, and any theory of norms must have important implications for theories of regimes, but I am only interested in regime theory when it suggests different theories of norms, not for its own sake.

Norms pose analytic problems because of their elusive nature. The standard approach to them in regime literature utilizes the case study. Methodologically I shall take a different tack by estimating a statistical model in the next chapter of what I call the norm of decolonization. My theoretical model takes explicitly into account self-interest and power politics considerations which are essential to understanding if and when norms are important. In addition I develop an explicit behavioral measure of the norm of decolonization, which I then use to assess the norm's impact on behavior. In this chapter, however, I sketch a prolegomenon to a theory of normative contexts in order to provide the foundation for the empirical analysis of one particular norm in the following chapter.

Four elements for a theory of international norms

In this section I discuss the nuts and bolts of a theory of norms. In the following section I shall use these nuts and bolts to construct different kinds of norms based on varying configurations of my building materials.

Norms present in many respects the polar opposite of rational choice. Rational choice concerns itself particularly with efficiency, norms only on occasion. Norms define the desirable in human affairs, rational choice takes preferences as exogenous. Rationality focuses on the decision-making process, norms on the action itself. Norms are constant, rationality is ever changing in response to new situations. Norms are situation independent, "do not commit adultery"; rationality is context sensitive, "commit adultery if she is pretty enough." Despite these differences their paths cross frequently, which has important theoretical and methodological consequences for a theory of norms.

Norms frequently prescribe or proscribe certain actions. Behavioral consistency and regularity characterizes norms, but not rational choice. As opposed to the means–ends calculation of rationality, norms often are only about the means. Norms proscribe many possible means or prescribe a certain action regardless of efficiency considerations. Thus the first element for a theory of norms is regularity and consistency of behavior. States following norms regularly perform certain actions and avoid others. If when a norm applies a state acts differently from one time to the next then the norm probably does not guide its behavior.

Behavior in an anarchical society may not be at all "erratic," "random," or "disordered." As rational actor theories show, rational behavior can be quite consistent with rule-like behavior. It is rational to stick with a dominant strategy. There is no incentive for actors to move from an equilibrium point in a situation of perfect competition. Rational behavior can appear quite like norm-following behavior depending on the situation. *Norm-like behavior may be driven by pure self-interest.* Thus it is often impossible to disentangle the two. It is well known that for most behavior, justifications based on norms can be found. Hence the widespread opinion that these claims are merely justifications and not real reasons. Also, given a choice between self-interest and norms as an explanation of behavior, the external observer – particularly if she is a political scientist or an economist – almost always chooses the self-interest explanation over the normative one.

That rational behavior may be norm-like can be seen by noting that one category of "norms" are more rightly called conventions (Lewis 1969). It does not matter which side of the street we drive on as long as we all agree. It is in our best self-interest to respect this convention, if we do not, we risk sanctions like traffic accidents. Many of the successes of international organizations lie notably in the domain where it is in the parties' best interest to agree. Especially more technical organizations like telecommunications and the Postal Union succeed because self-interest corresponds largely with normative behavior.

Robert Keohane takes self-interested rationality as a basis for studying international regimes of which norms are an essential part: "I explore ... how we can account for fluctuations in time in the number, extent and strength of international regimes, on the basis of rational calculations under varying circumstances" (1983, p. 142). As suggested already by Luce and Raiffa (1957) norms can solve coordination problems (see also, Schelling 1960; Snidal 1985; Sugden 1986). The establishment of rules, regimes, and norms can result from a self-interest maximization process. The literature on neo-institutional economics is devoted to explaining rules and organizations based on utility maximization (Eggertsson 1990). Keohane's project springs from the same source: keep the self-interest maximization assumption, but introduce other concepts like transaction costs to explain institution formation.

I shall take the opposing position and state a basic axiom:

> If it is in one's best self-interest[1] to follow a norm then the norm has no independent impact on behavior.

This is a conservative position on norms. It may well be the case that the norm and not self-interest motivates behavior, but this principle expresses quite well the "null hypothesis" place that realism holds in world politics. Elster argues a variant of this: "If some are to be altruistic, others must be selfish, at least some of the time, but everybody *could* be selfish all the time" (1989b, p. 54). The interesting cases will be when an actor departs from narrowly self-interested behavior.

> A more difficult question arises when a person's choice happens to coincide with the maximization of his anticipated personal welfare, but that is not the *reason* for his choice. If we wish to make room for this, we can expand the definition of commitment to include cases in which the person's choice, while maximizing anticipated personal welfare, would be

[1] Acting for the "public good" is not considered self-interested in the usual formulations. A related problem is altruism (Nagel 1970).

> unaffected under at least one counterfactual condition in which the act chosen would cease to maximize personal welfare. (emphasis is the author's, Sen 1977, p. 327).

Thus the second element in conceptualizing a norm is its position *vis-à-vis* self-interest as a motive for action.

Characteristically in social systems violations of norms, rules, and customs are sanctioned. Axelrod (1986, p. 1097) takes sanctions as central in his definition of a norm:

> A *norm* exists in a given social setting to the extent that individuals usually act in a certain way and are often punished when seen not to be acting in this way.

Axelrod does not assert that the individual acts self-interestedly in following a norm, but since he applies his definition in game situations the self-interest assumption applies. Norms require sanctions because self-interest reasons to violate the norm exist. Sanctions change the self-interest calculation making the norm the dominant choice. Axelrod, like Snidal (1985), emphasizes one obvious characteristic of many norms: some kind of sanctioning system is necessary to keep individuals on the straight and narrow path. In contrast, sanctions do not come up in Keohane's analysis: "sanctions" or "enforcement" does not appear in the index of *After hegemony*. If norms correspond to self-interest then there is no motivation to violate them.

Sanctions imply power relationships, the existence of sanctions means that powerful groups are willing and able to use coercion to enforce the norm. Yet Axelrod never states the reason why someone should sanction a norm violation. From one point of view we can consider sanctions as exogenous constraints and focus only on the maximizing behavior, but it may be equally important to explain the sanctions. Sanctioning means paying costs. One possible explanation of sanctions is that a cost–benefit analysis makes them a paying proposition; this is one rationale behind hegemonic regime theory (see Pettit 1990 for an argument for costless sanctions). I shall argue below that ethical and political values provide another reason to sanction norm violations.

The emphasis on sanctions as affecting cost–benefit analysis naturally occurs to someone with an economic turn of mind, but Axelrod's formulation alludes to sociological theories of norms. Over time norms are "internalized," and hence sanctions become less important (Parsons 1968; Scott 1971). But do states internalize norms? Can an organization internalize a norm or can only individuals do this? The internalization process is one where the teacher or parent sanctions incorrect behavior, which results in the child learning and internalizing the norm. At some point sanctions become less important because values have been inculcated into the individual; he has become well socialized. Sanctions play an indirect role via the socialization process. The question for international relations is whether the internalization model applies to states or decision-makers (Ikenberry and Kupchan 1990).

In international relations the relative diffusion of sanctioning power dramatically changes the mechanism of norm enforcement. In domestic politics the central government holds exclusive use of force, and the issue of diffuse sanctioning power does not arise. In hegemonic regime theory we have an analogous situation since the hegemon sanctions rule violations. But generally in world politics sanctioning power is decentralized and diffused throughout the system. How decentralized sanctioning systems work has received surprisingly little attention in the regime literature (though see Martin 1992), though examples like environmental regimes illustrate its potential relevance. The dispersion of sanctioning power constitutes an essential dimension to any characterization of an international norm. If we assume that most norms require sanctions to be behaviorally effective, the major distinction between systems of sanctions in international relations rests on the degree of centralization of sanctioning power. The degree of centralization of sanctions thus represents the third element for a theory of international norms.

Definitions like Axelrod's fall into the category of behavior modification norms: behavior is "learned" or "modified" via sanction – a rat could be following a norm by his criterion. This brings us to the fourth element of norms not to the liking of many behavioralists and which the regime literature has failed to deal with: norm often means *normative,* theories of justice and rights express themselves in norms of behavior. Religious and ethical systems consist in norms of behavior. This makes norms much harder to deal with, because they are tied to peoples' cultures and because they evolve over time. The presence or absence of the deontological factor differentiates between different types of norms. In the particular norm investigated in the next chapter, the "right" of self-determination of peoples, the commitment to democracy and self-government are values whose wide acceptance had an impact on the decolonization of the world. The final element for a theory of norms is thus whether the norm has any deontological force.

The deontological facet of norms points to something crucially lacking in many rationalist theories of international relations, the problem of preferences or national goals, which are often based on normative considerations. The desire for self-rule, that democracy is the most legitimate form of government, cannot be derived from rational calculations of efficiency. A *complete* rational theory of international relations needs to take seriously the problem of preferences, what they are and how they change, which implies a theory of norms.

To summarize there are four elements that are the building blocks for a theory of norms:

1 behavioral regularity conforming to the norm.
2 the extent of conflict with self-interest.
3 the extent to which sanctions are centralized or decentralized.
4 the role of deontology in its justification.

Behavioral regularity has a different status from that of the other three elements. Different types of norms (see below) take different positions with regard to self-interest, sanctions, and deontology, but all concepts of norms assume behavioral regularity. By definition any normative system contains the first element. It distinguishes normative theories from other theories of behavior, but does not distinguish between different kinds of norms. This element will not immediately concern us, but it will be important later when I discuss the methodology of studying norms.

A typology of international norms

Using the nuts and bolts outlined above I can describe five major types of norms (see table 11.1 below for a complete list) based on the presence or absence – or less dramatically, the relative presence or absence – of the three central elements that distinguish between norms: self-interest, sanctions, and deontology. The first type of norm, which I shall call a "cooperative norm,"[2] has characteristics:

the norm corresponds to the self-interest of the actors.
no sanctions are necessary, the norm is "self-enforcing"; in this sense sanctions are decentralized.
the deontological aspect is absent.

[2] Nardin (1983) refers to something like cooperative norms as "purposive associations," and Oakeshott (1975) calls them "enterprise associations."

These norms form the core of functional theories of international regimes (e.g., Keohane 1984) as well as some versions of international law (McDougal *et al.* 1987). All see order and regularity as the result of nations cooperating to solve *common* problems. (Rawls 1971 also sees the existence of a social group as requiring cooperative action in view of the realization of "shared final ends.") Because goals are common and require joint action, nations make international law and found international organizations. Since nations have common purposes there is little incentive to defect, hence no need for sanctions. Centralized control serves to coordinate not to enforce, so international organizations need not be powerful. The deontological component is absent because the realm of common goals tends to be low politics rather than high.

The second kind of norm, which can be called "hegemonic norms," has characteristics:

> conflict between self-interest and the norm for some, but not for the hegemon.
> sanctions are centralized in one body – government or hegemon – and play an important role.
> no deontological character.

This norm can "solve" problems, such as providing public goods, where there are reasons to cooperate and reasons to defect. Sanctions play a much larger role since self-interest pushes toward rule violation (defection in prisoners' dilemma terms). Several forms of sanction have been proposed, the hegemon being the most prominent (Gilpin 1987; Keohane 1980). Sanctions are possible because it is in the hegemon's self-interest to apply them (Olson 1965). The costs of sanctioning norm violations may be less than the benefits that the hegemon gains from the existence of the norm. Deontology does not play a role since the norm promotes the hegemon's self-interest and other actors include hegemonic sanctions as part of their cost–benefit analysis.

The third type of norm, most important in the discussion of security regimes, has characteristics:

> conflict between the norm and self-interest.
> decentralized sanctions.
> no deontological component.

This norm offers one potential solution to the classic prisoners' dilemma problem and more generally to the problems of national security. There are reasons to cooperate, but each side is afraid that the other will be tempted by the possibility of major gains from defection. No centralized sanctioning system exists: it is the self-help standard, each state is responsible for sanctioning violations. The question is whether there are strategies – rules or norms – that can overcome the dominant solution to defect. Axelrod (1984) showed that the tit-for-tat rule can produce cooperation. Tit-for-tat falls under the general rule of reciprocity. Hence I propose that this type of norm be called the "pure reciprocity" norm ("pure" in the sense that the rule is chosen for purely instrumental reasons; but reciprocity also has moral value (Becker 1986)).

"Pure reciprocity" presents an interesting case since it represents a research goal of public choice theorists. The important research question is how and when norms can arise and be effective in a system of egoists, where self-interest alone motivates behavior. Axelrod's work with repeated prisoner's dilemma suggests that there may be strategies, like tit-for-tat, which can produce cooperation among self-interest maximizing agents. But here, as in hegemonic norms, sanctions remain self-interested.

Pure reciprocity, cooperative, hegemonic norms lack any deontic force; they are purely norms for maximizing self-interest. These economic/game theoretic norms can be contrasted with the more sociological and psychological norms where legitimacy, values, and internalization play a role in the well functioning of the norm.

The first norm where deontology plays a role (the fourth type) I have termed "legitimate government" and has the characteristics:

conflict between norm and self-interest.
sanctioning power is centralized.
the deontological aspect is important.

These characteristics typify a stable, legitimate government. The central government has the exclusive and legitimate monopoly on force. It relies on both sanctions and legitimacy for its strength. Since this situation does not arise in international relations I shall not treat it any further.

The fifth kind of norms – for which there is no obvious name – I call "decentralized norms" and it has the following characteristics:

conflict between norm and self-interest.
sanctioning power is diffused and decentralized.
the deontological aspect is important.

As opposed to hegemonic regimes that come from the top down, decentralized regimes are bottom-up. Individual actors must be willing to sanction violations of the norm. In purely behavioral systems like Axelrod's sanctions are exogenous, but one must ask why sanction a norm violation? Hegemonic norms suggest that self-interest can be one motive, but deontological values propose another. Because actors hold some values dear they are willing to make sacrifices, of their persons and finances, to punish violations. A widely and deeply held norm creates "moral pressure" through bad publicity and public opinion. The deontological component motivates directly the power politics of sanctions. Hence values can close the circle and explain why certain groups are willing to pay the price to sanction norm violations. Environmental action and human rights show how relatively powerless groups that represent powerful values have an important impact on the creation and effectiveness of international norms.

Because this norm depends on widely held values and decentralized sanctions it is the case where context plays the largest role. The second half of this chapter and the next chapter are devoted to an analysis of this type of norm.

Decentralized norms may be more typical of international relations since they emphasize the lack of a central enforcement agency, but less typical as they stress the deontological component. The real world of international politics lies perhaps somewhere between the hegemonic and the decentralized one, what one might call the "oligarchic norm." Since a very large percentage of system power is concentrated in few hands an agreement of these few can be imposed on the rest. But hegemonic theory underestimates the support necessary from other actors for the norm to work. It is important to consider what we know about the legitimacy and the efficiency of dictatorial systems in domestic politics. If in these situations where the government has overwhelming power compliance proves difficult to achieve, an extrapolation to the international arena implies even greater difficulties without some normative support for the regime.

Summary

Table 11.1 gives a summary of the different types of norms based on the three critical elements: self-interest, centralization of sanctions, and deontology. As the table indicates – and as the reader will have realized – all possible combinations of the three basic elements gives a total of eight (2^3) different norms (assuming that any element can take on two values).

Table 11.1 *A typology of international norms*

Type	Self-interest	Sanctions	Deontology
Cooperative	Agreement	Centralized	Important
Cooperative	Agreement	Centralized	No
Cooperative	Agreement	Decentralized	Important
Cooperative	Agreement	Decentralized	No
Legitimate government	Conflict	Centralized	Important
Hegemonic	Conflict	Centralized	No
Decentralized	Conflict	Decentralized	Important
Pure reciprocity	Conflict	Decentralized	No

The first four norms I categorize as cooperative. My discussion of cooperative norms focused on only the last of them because agreement on goals is sufficient to create effective norms. Essentially the other types are "overdetermined" cooperative norms, effective sanctions and value consensus contribute perhaps to make the norm more effective, but sufficient grounds already exist.

Scholars of jurisprudence have debated issues of sanctions, morality, and the creation of norms, and many of the arguments found here have analogues in a theory of international law. For example, hegemonic regime theory is similar to Austin's (1954) notion of law as the command of the sovereign. Raz (1980) and Kelsen (1967) emphasize the necessity of centralized sanctions for the existence of international law. McDougal's (1987) view of international law as an association for common purpose corresponds to cooperative norms. Customary law emphasizes behavioral regularity as a source of law. To the extent to which this literature addresses the problem of effective rules of behavior, it addresses the same issues as a theory of international norms. When theories of international law emphasize law creation, such as Hart's (1961) "rules of recognition," or methods of arbitration they move away from the behavioral aspects of norms that concern me here. Thus to the extent that one can distinguish substantive from procedural – this should not be pushed too far since all procedural rules have substantive qualities – this distinguishes a theory of international law from a theory of international norms. International law institutionalizes many important norms, but it is the behavioral significance of this not the legal aspects that occupies a theory of international norms.

The five types of norms appear to cover the major kinds of norms, regimes, and rules that have drawn the attention of regime analysts. The advantage of the classificatory scheme[3] is that it uses an elementary morphology of norms. One argument for the sufficiency of the elements of self-interest, sanctions, and deontology is that it produces the types of norms that exist "in nature." There are other potential elements that could be proposed such as permissive versus mandatory (Raz 1990), regulative versus constitutive (Searle 1969), or primary versus secondary (Hart 1961). Perhaps a more refined systematics of norms will require additional elements, but for my purposes the three elements and the five types of norms provide the necessary framework to discuss the context of international norms.

Modes of context and norms

In this volume I basically consider only contexts as exogenous variables. In barrier models system structure was partially endogenized because pressure from below increased the rate of barrier breakdown, and we shall see the same kind of process occurring with international norms. Nevertheless, my concern is with contexts as causes (or counteracting causes) rather than with contexts as effects. The different types of norms divide themselves into two categories: norms which are effects and norms which cause. To put it simply, if self-interest drives the norm, the norm is an effect; if values drive a norm, the norm is a cause. Since I am interested in contexts as causes I shall focus in my detailed analysis on the only type – decentralized norms – that has a causal impact on behavior and is relevant to international relations.

Norms as effects

From the typology of norms it appears that some norms are not causes but rather *effects*; norms sometimes result from self-interested behavior. Nations have common goals, coordination problems which are solved by the

[3] Other proposed typologies of norms include Puchala and Hopkins (1983) who proposed the following types: (1) specific versus diffuse, (2) formal versus informal, (3) evolutionary versus revolutionary, and (4) distributive bias. Young (1983) suggested three types of regime formation: (1) spontaneous, (2) negotiated, and (3) imposed. These correspond in many ways to my cooperative, decentralized, and hegemonic norms. Kegley and Raymond (1990) proposed a typology based on the three elements: (1) substantive versus procedural, (2) formal versus informal, (3) partner-specific versus actor-universal. Martin (1992) defines a limited four-game typology of regimes. Giddens (1984, p. 22) gives four elements for a typology of norms: (1) intensive/shallow, (2) tacit/discursive, (3) formalized/informal, (4) weakly sanctioned/strongly sanctioned, but nowhere does he justify these choices.

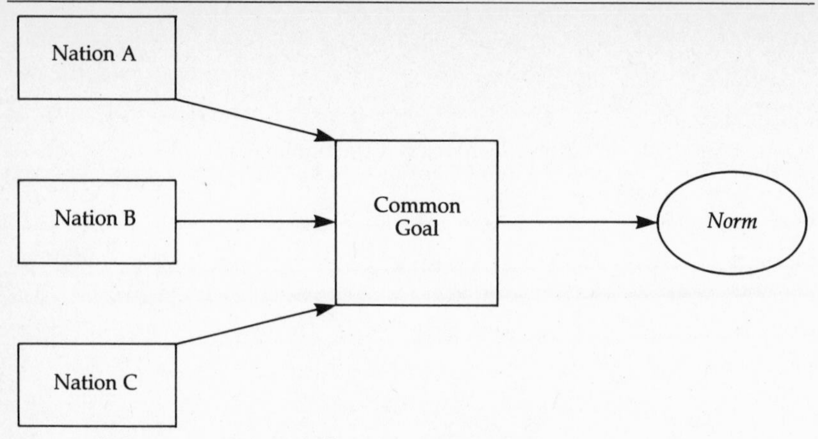

Figure 11.1 Norms as effects: cooperative norms

erection of international norms and regimes. This is illustrated in figure 11.1, where the common goals are the cause of the norm. *Because* of common goals nations create a regime. The argument from effects is typical of functional theories, and typical of much regime theory (Haggard and Simmonds 1987).

Hegemonic norms represent a more ambiguous situation. In the pure self-interest version, the norm is a function of hegemonic self-interest. As illustrated in figure 11.2 the norm is an intervening variable between "hegemon" and "behavior." (This could be represented algebraically by a recursive system of equations.) The question is whether the norm has any independent effect: would the behavior be the same if the norm box were removed from the chain?[4] If the norm does have an additional effect – through mechanisms yet to be identified – then ignoring the norm in the analysis has the effect of increasing the estimated impact of hegemonic self-interest; hence overestimating the impact of realpolitik factors.

Part of the confusion surrounding the possibility that norms have independent effects arises from considering either just the left two-thirds or just the right two-thirds of figure 11.2. Consideration of just the left part means that norms are the effect of self-interested behavior, but if one examines only the right two-thirds then norms become a cause. But tracing back the arrows makes it clear that norms are an effect not a cause.

Pure reciprocity norms are also not causes. The tit-for-tat strategy has been of great interest not because it reflects the moral value of reciprocity but because it is instrumentally useful in maximizing utility. This norm is a

[4] One possible scenario is that a hegemon imposes a norm, say free trade, which other actors then learn to value thus transforming it into another kind of norm.

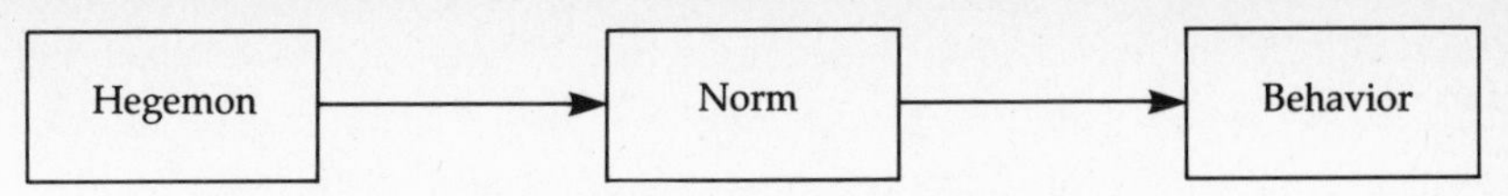

Figure 11.2 Norms as intervening variables: hegemonic norms

tool, it is a cause like the gun that Mary used to kill Sally, it is a means to an end: it intervenes between Mary and Sally's death.

In discussing various contexts I have avoided to a large extent the problem of "context creation." Although hegemonic, cooperative, and pure reciprocity norms are important phenomena, I focus on norms that are causes of behavior.

Norms as causes

Norms are a cause when the deontological element is present. "Legitimate government" is stable in part because it is fair and just; sanctions are not sufficient for the well functioning of domestic society, as the recent experience with authoritative regimes of the right and left has shown. Decentralized norms are a cause because the values represented in the norm are essential in explaining its impact. Decentralized norms are not necessarily functional, they depend on deeply entrenched value systems, which may not be efficient. These values explain why actors would want to act in accordance with the norm. Reference to these norms is also crucial in explaining why actors sanction violation, even at fairly high cost to themselves.

I suggest that *prescriptive* norms that order positively a particular behavior may appropriately be seen as cause. The norm is a *reason* to act in a certain fashion, and a reason that may override other good self-interested reasons (Raz (1990) argues that norms in general exclude and override other reasons, notably self-interest). The influence of the norm depends on the level of support for that norm both in producing sanctions as well as the support for the value in the preferences of the decision-maker. One hypothesis is that the influence of the norm on producing the prescribed behavior is proportional to the conjunction of these factors. The effects of the norm – the prescribed behavior – are proportional to its deontological force.

For materialists, such as realists and marxists, norms do not matter because they are mere words. But words are mechanisms of control; words have power to make us act (Minsky 1986). Words are not "materialistic" and can often be easily manipulated, but normative values are sometimes just as hard to hammer into certain forms as any material substance. Normative systems limit the possible justifications decision-makers can use. Walzer in discussing justifications of war emphasizes that this talk is in fact more than just talk but also "coerces" (1977, p. 12). His wide range of examples shows there is some consistency in the way nations have justified war.

If norms affect behavior, we need to find the mechanism that connects norms with actions: *how* do words exercise their control function? One aspect of social and group life is the pressure to act in accordance with group values. This manifests itself through phenomena like fashion and groupthink. We have already seen that conservative monarchies were under pressure to nationalize their oil. Leaders usually desire reelection, this makes Bush an "environmental" and "education" president. Social opinion constitutes a powerful context for the propagation and enforcement of norms (Pettit 1990).

Another mechanism widely explored by sociologists and psychologists is internalization. If group pressure is an external force then internalization is the internal pressure to conform. The extent to which states and organizations can internalize values is unclear. Does it come through institutional change (procedures)? Is it value change of individuals in the institutions?

Norms as barriers

Proscriptive norms have different characteristics from prescriptive ones. Since they exclude certain actions, they do not determine behavior to the same degree as prescriptive norms. Here the normative environment acts as a *barrier* to action, or as a *constraint* on behavior (see Nozick 1974 for an analysis of deontological rules as constraints). Gauthier illustrates well the standard view of rational choice theorists on the status of ethical values: "Morality ... is traditionally understood to involve an impartial constraint on the pursuit of individual interest" (1986, p. 7). For example, the vegetarian rule excludes meat dishes from the menu, but within this rule an individual chooses what tastes best. Those who consider norms as rules of the game that regulate individual pursuits of different ends view norms as barriers. Certain means are forbidden, but these rules contain little positive or prescriptive content; the vegetarian rule does not say what to eat, but what not to eat. Nardin sees international norms, what he calls "practices," as fundamentally negative, as limiting and excluding certain options, but otherwise allowing for the free play of conflicting goals and values: "authoritative practices [norms] are more properly regarded as limiting or constraining that pursuit [of particular ends]" (1983, p. 8). This implies that the frequency of the forbidden event should be less than that of the various allowed options. Norms do not account for the frequency of the allowable choices just for the rarity of forbidden ones.

The concept of norms as constraints is congenial to economic thinking (Koford and Miller 1991); constraints are part of any economist's tool box. Norms as constraints are exogenous factors; economic agents maximize within those rules. After the Civil War landowners in the South had to minimize labor costs under the no-slavery rule. From the economic point of view why there should be such a rule usually does not come up (however, neo-institutional economics attempt to explain constraints as the *result* of maximizing behavior). The constraints may be more important than the maximization process in explaining behavior: norms may be explaining more of the variance than self-interest maximization. The relative importance of each is an empirical question, but a question that must be posed.

"Permissive" norms destroy barriers instead of creating them, but nevertheless they work in the same fashion as proscriptive norms. They do not oblige individuals; actors are free to perform the permitted action or not. When the barrier crumbles, governments still have the choice of whether to nationalize oil, or of whether to overthrow communist governments. Permissions are necessary but not sufficient conditions. Children need permission to stay out late, but that does not mean that they will always do so.

Prescriptive and proscriptive norms are *powerful* because they represent deeply held values and beliefs. In many cases governments do not hold these values but individuals and pressure groups do. Opposed to the power concentration of hegemonic norms, the power of decentralized norms comes from individuals, non-governmental organizations, scientists, etc. Functionalist theories cannot easily explain these norms since they represent values not functions. Decentralized norms represent the most interesting normative context (for intrinsic reasons as well as for the contrast they provide to most of the regime literature). Therefore for the rest of this chapter and the next I shall focus on this type of norm.

The methodology of decentralized norms

Little has been written on the methodology of studying norms, its particular problems and perils. In the international regimes literature this is due to the very wide agreement on the case study as the principal mode of research. Rare are studies in world politics that do not adopt this technique, the notable exceptions being the work of Kegley and Raymond (1990) and Martin (1992). From a theoretical point of view there is important work from the social choice perspective (see the special issue of the journal *Ethics* (July 1990) for a good sample of this literature), but this provides few tools for the empirical examination of an individual norm.

Psychologists and anthropologists often formulate the problem of norm versus self-interest in terms of the contrast between attitudes and behavior. Their methodology consists in surveying participants about their attitudes and values, which then can be compared with their behavior (Tittle and Hill 1967). For example, Cancian (1975) surveyed Mayan attitudes and behavior, and found that there was no relationship between them. She correlated statistically a dependent variable "behavior" with an independent variable "norms."

This technique of correlating beliefs with behavior takes advantage of the characteristic of norms which prescribes consistent behavior. Hence one can investigate whether action followed the relevant norm. However, this combined with the fact that self-interest can coincide with the norm means that correlation can really only show that norms do *not* influence behavior. (I do not want to suggest that this comparison is easy, in fact correlating beliefs with actions is notoriously problematic.) As in the Cancian study, the fact that words and deeds do not correspond provides stronger evidence for the irrelevance of norms than a significant positive correlation provides for their impact. Positive correlations are always subject to the counter-claim that normative behavior corresponds to self-interest. Of course if the number of cases is large and varied and the relationship close then it is unlikely that self-interest matched the norm, but nevertheless doubt remains. Thus the first methodological principle for the study of decentralized norms is that:

> Comparing norms with behavior can only demonstrate the *irrelevance* of norms.

Internal versus external approaches

One of the fascinating, as well as frustrating, aspects of the study of norms is that much of the phenomenon occurs in people's heads. This situation produces two quite fundamentally different approaches to analyzing norms. The "external" or "objectivist" approach uses only behavior and avoids trying to get into heads. The opposite approach emphasizes just this aspect and can be called "internal" or "subjectivist." This is not the place to review the pros and cons of Verstehen or ethnomethodology versus external or behavioral perspectives, but these two positions have important methodological consequences for the study of norms. These can be illustrated by the standard story of a driver sitting at a red light at 3:00 A.M. with not a car to be seen. The law does not allow the running of red lights at 3:00 A.M., but, on the other hand, it seems a bit silly to waste time at a light when one wants to get home to bed. The external approach looks at just the behavior of the driver, if he (driver) runs the red light then she (social scientist observer) concludes that self-interest has prevailed. If, however, he waits then she is not so sure – because everyone knows that there are always cops around the corner. The external approach can show the irrelevance of a norm, but is less well suited to give evidence of its impact.

The subjectivist, on the other hand, would like to be able to get inside the head of the driver to look at his rationale for action. If the driver does not stop at the light then there is perhaps little doubt about his reasoning, but if he stops the subjectivist wants to know his reasoning. If he believes that one should obey the law then he follows a norm, but if he does so for fear of being caught then it is self-interest. As all anthropologists and survey researchers know, self-reports are not unproblematic (Nisbett and Wilson 1977; Goleman 1985), but they are still stronger evidence for the impact of the norm than can be marshaled by the external point of view. Since norms and values are intangible, internal approaches have a certain advantage over the external approach. They try to get directly at the phenomenon as opposed to inferring it from outside behavior. From this we get a second methodological principle:

> External/objectivist approaches can only *infer* the importance of a norm, internal/subjectivist approaches can provide direct evidence.

Norms and self-interest

As I hope it is clear by now, the grand methodological principle in the study of decentralized norms is controlling for self-interest alternative explanations. In international relations since Morgenthau the basic assumption has been that states struggle for power and to promote national interest. For anyone who wants to argue that norms matter he or she must continually refute arguments based on self-interest. For example, I shall argue that the norm of decolonization had an impact on the level of military conflict during the transition to independence. I shall be constantly faced with self-interest counter arguments. Neo-colonialism in its many forms argues that direct control over colonies was no longer necessary, the gains from indirect control were as great as under direct colonization, hence the transfer of control could be quite peaceful.

One aspect of the internal versus external distinction is that the external approach cannot provide evidence for the impact of a norm but can only provide disconfirming evidence. We are now in a position to amend that with the proviso that the external approach can provide evidence *only if* self-interest is taken into account. In fact, this applies not just to the external approach, but to any approach that tries to demonstrate the impact of a norm on behavior (this is not an issue if only negative evidence is desired). This main principle is thus:

> To demonstrate the independent impact of a norm it is necessary to include self-interest in the analysis.

This principle applies regardless of whether the methodology is case study, statistical, or survey because more than a methodological principle it is a statement about human behavior.

Rarely is the world so neat that determining the relative importance of norms and self-interest is clear cut. The relative weights of the two vary from case to case. In figure 11.3 the horizontal arrow reflects the rigidity of a behavioral rule. The bottom curved line indicates behavior dictated by self-interest. The curved line in between shows the compromise between the two. This illustrates one of the pitfalls of assuming that a norm has no effect when it is not strictly followed. Even though the norm does not override self-interest, by the same token neither does self-interest have complete control. In a statistical setting one interpretation is that the norm explains 40 percent of the variance and self-interest 60 percent.

Something like this occurs in my statistical analysis of the norm of

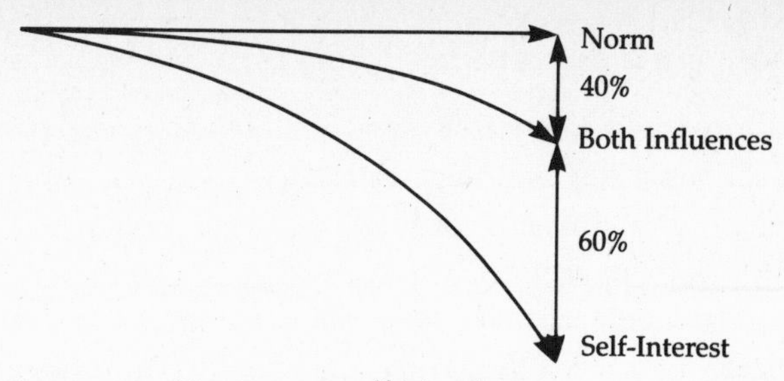

Figure 11.3 Norms versus self-interest

decolonization where *both* the self-interest and the norm variables are significant. Uvin has said of the food aid regime: "Approximately one-quarter to 40 percent of all food aid can be said to be donated only for reasons the traditional interpretation would expect: manifestly self-interested ones" (1992, p. 307). Food aid constitutes an issue where the distinction between self-interest and humanitarian motivations can be more clearly drawn. Both between countries and over time the relative mix of self-interest and norms varies:

> The contrast between norms and rationality need not generate a distinction between different kinds of actions. Both types of motivation may be among the determinants of a single action. Often, norms and rationality coexist in a parallelogram of forces that jointly determine behavior. When the norms require me to do *X* and rational self-interest to do *Y*, I may end up with a compromise. Or rationality may act as a constraint on norms: I do *X* provided that the costs – the direct costs of doing *X* and the opportunity costs of not doing *Y* – are not too high. Conversely, norms may constrain and limit the pursuit of rational self-interest. (Elster 1990, p. 866)

For cooperative norms self-interest makes the state follow the regime. Behavior is an overdetermined because rule and self-interest dictate the same thing: vice and virtue coincide. For example, I interpret Weber's (1958) hypothesis about Protestantism and the rise of capitalism in the sense that self-interest and religious values were pushing in the same direction. I think this also helps explain the attractiveness of the tit-for-tat strategy, it is moral (Becker 1986) as well as efficient. I am interested in the *independent* impact of norms. Norms are not about cooperation per se at all, but rather about conflict, the conflict between them and self-interest.

Measuring a decentralized norm

A norm is a rule of behavior, either what should be done, or acts that are forbidden. The consistency and wide-spreadness of the behavior indicate the existence of a norm. Any attempt to examine behaviorally the evolution of a norm must identify behavior that corresponds to the rule or that strengthens it. To the extent that actors follow the norm one can suppose that it is strengthened (even if this is done purely from self-interest) and vice versa for behavior that contravenes the norm. Norm-driven behavior should be consistent over time and space.

At the beginning only a few may propose or act upon a norm, but as time goes on the norm may spread. Thus, in part, the current strength of a norm is a function of its history. Any measure of a norm must take into account the norm's historical development with its ebbs and flows.[5] The measure should reflect the historical nature of norm creation. The strength of the norm for any nation at any given time t depends on how it and other nations have acted until this time, i.e., from t_0 to $t-1$. Custom, an important source of international law, depends on the frequency of past action. Understanding and measuring the current strength of a norm is in part knowing and measuring its history.

International norms result from the combined action of many states, organizations, and individuals. Yet at the same time international norms must be present at the domestic level since individual states must finally implement them. The impact of the international normative structure is not necessarily uniform in all times and places, thus any measurement approach needs to consider the relationship between the international norm and its impact in different countries. The impact of a norm on state behavior is a function of its strength in the international community and its degree of acceptance in individual states. The rush to decolonize Africa affected all European countries but Spain and Portugal. That military dictatorships ruled these two countries and they were quite isolated from the currents of international life is not unrelated to the lack of impact of the decolonization movement on them.

Governments do not just act but also justify their actions. As certain actions become modal they must fit into some value system; a successful fit means that actions have become legitimate. Governments will certainly

[5] One might say that a norm is established when it becomes the most common behavior. Barkun (1968) argues that one can think of norms as "modal behavior."

continue to contravene norms, but these jobs will be given to the *secret* service or the official rationale will conform to accepted values. As Rawls (1971) emphasized, norms and values are public, norms do not work under the cloak of darkness (as self-interest sometimes does). Since decentralized norms are "ought" statements we need to be sure that the intellectual history, public debate, and international treaties surrounding the norm correspond in their basic outlines to any behavioral measure.

Thus there are four elements of a behavioral measurement approach to decentralized norms:

1. Identify behaviors that strengthen and conform to the norm.
2. The current strength of the norm is a function of its development.
3. There must be links tying the international norm to the individual states that must implement it.
4. The deontological history of the norm embodied in public documents, treaties, and philosophical works should correspond to behavioral assessments.

Any satisfactory measure of the strength and evolution of a decentralized norm should have the four properties listed above. In the next chapter I develop a measure of the norm of decolonization with these properties.

There has been one attempt (Kegley and Raymond 1990) to systematically measure an international norm. Kegley and Raymond were interested in the variation between two competing and opposing norms, one – *pacta sunt servanda* – that emphasizes the bindingness of alliance treaties, the other – *rebus sic stantibus* – that stresses the freedom to abrogate those treaties. They examined systematically standard international law textbooks in order to chart the variations in the relative strength of these two opposing norms:

> Evidence on the content of international norms may be derived from what publicists *report* about them in the legal treaties they publish. That is to say, by focusing on what these eminent writers actually *observed* rather than on what norms they thought members of the international community ought to follow, quantitative indicators of alliance norm formation and decay may be constructed by means of content analysis. (emphasis is the authors, p. 82)

They argued that textbook writers reported beliefs about norms. In this sense their approach is a subjectivist one, because it indirectly tried to get into the heads of statesmen. The elements of "ought" and "beliefs" that these jurists identify in statesmen are probably not clearly specified; they are probably in part what statesmen are doing and in part what they are saying. International law texts also serve as a basis for determining international law, so the normative component is not lacking either. The sources present a complex mix of observation and normative statement. Kegley and Raymond found that different legal observers in a given period reported similar perceptions (though they gave no numerical measure of this) of the relative strength of each norm. This is important since if actors disagree then each plays by his or her own rules, and a coherent international normative context disappears.

In contrast, I emphasize an external, behavioral approach. Instead of trying to examine the beliefs of leaders as evidenced in legal texts, I look at behavior that corresponds to the norm or strengthens it. Hence I make a significant inferential leap from these external signs to the existence of the norm. I try to mitigate this leap by emphasizing that the political and intellectual history of the norm corresponds *grosso modo* to the behavioral measure, but an inferential leap it still remains.

Conclusion

In this chapter I have outlined a pre-theory of norms that suggests different ways norms form an important context of state activity. Cooperative norms exist as long as there are common goals to be achieved. Hegemonic regimes exist as long as there is a hegemon around to pay for them. Pure reciprocity is an important norm as long as the situation is such that it is a successful strategy. Decentralized norms rely on values to motivate or sanction behavior. Of all the norms investigated by scholars of international relations decentralized norms remain the least studied, but in many ways they differ the most from the other types. They also depend the most on various contexts for their existence and effectiveness. Since sanctions are decentralized the reactions of individuals, organizations, and states are all relevant.

Decentralized norms are not created without conflict nor in a short period of time. They are historical creations, their current strength is a function of acts in the past that created them. Norms are a very important means by which continuity is maintained in international politics. Sociologists have argued that people internalize norms. The strength of a norm in the present is then a function of how widely and deeply it has been integrated into the personalities of persons and institutions. The system of social reproduction implies a complex mix of present and historical factors in explaining behavior. This explains why norm-guided behavior is more stable – in the sense of unchanging – than rational behavior.

International law traditionally relies heavily on the notion of customary practice in determining the content of international law. Very roughly, the strength of a norm depends on the length of time a norm has been in practice, the frequency with which it is observed weighted by the importance of the actors involved (the practices of Great Britain count more than those of Belgium). The important point is that what nations do – often from self-interest – can define rights and obligations in law that will constrain them in the future. The United States has been very careful not to sign treaties – even though there is no enforcement mechanism – that create dangerous precedents. The notion of precedent itself implies that historical commitments and actions influence events in the present (Anderson 1981).

Not only does historical practice create norms, but certain norms are "historical" in the sense I have given to theories. To believe in the rule that promises should be kept – *pacta sunt servanda* – means that previous actions determine current behavior. People keep promises that they have good reasons to break because they believe in the promise-keeping norm. Similarly the norm of reciprocity can take on a moral character in addition to its purely instrumental value. Reciprocity means that obligations are created that must be repaid.

National goals and preferences are not created *ex nihilo*. In most societies, domestic and international, powerful groups generally create and impose norms. Many aspects of our everyday life were historically practiced only by the rich and powerful. What we wear, how we eat, and how we conduct our romantic lives all come down to us through relations of power. Power creates norms. But once created norms have "inertia." While their creators may have withered away, the norm continues to exist. The founding fathers would have been appalled that the principle of one man one vote be applied to blacks, not to mention women. The values embodied in the American Revolution influenced the way the US treated its future colonies and the colonies of other powers, sometimes in ways that may not have corresponded to its pure power interests.

In international norms, like in international law, it has always been difficult to conceive of decentralized systems of rule that effectively regulate behavior. For this reason conceptions of norms have most frequently been tied either to the model of the centralized domestic state – hegemonic norms, or to the notion that there are common purposes being pursued – cooperative norms. I would like to suggest a metaphor to make more plausible the notion that decentralized norms can work as well: that metaphor is language (I am not the first to propose this, see Ruggie 1982).[6] We all know that language is a system of rules since we are taught, often painfully, the rules of grammar in school. Members of society generally follow grammar rules, but the rules constitute a system created by no one. We think of grammar as existing independently of any person or organization. We learn it from parents, peers, and institutions. The system works partly through internalization, partly because of sanctions. In academia a new norm of politically correct, non-sexist, non-racist language has been created. This norm has been created through struggle, partially because individuals have sanctioned violations, partially because people believe in values expressed by this new norm. In general no centralized institution arbitrates, creates, or enforces rules of grammar (of course there are institutions like the French Academy, but they tend to follow as much as lead). In spite of the lack of centralized institutions, the system works, not perfectly, but adequately nonetheless. Unlike economists who firmly believe in invisible hands, students of world politics have found it difficult to conceive of a system that acts invisibly, it is perhaps not that the action is invisible but that the analogies have been borrowed from the wrong place.

Postscript: normative realism

A common misconception is that norms are either independent of power politics or opposed to it. The discussion in this chapter has underscored that norms are a source of power and the result of power. This intimate connection I would call *normative realism*. Along with Gramsci normative realism emphasizes that powerful groups create norms; because of power, norms are internalized. But in addition, individuals, groups, and states value certain norms highly and act to preserve and propagate them. Norms also constrain the powerful from the bottom up. Popular values influence decision-makers in issues such as abortion, the environment, and decolonization. As long as values are exogenous norm-induced sanctions remain just another cost and we have an incomplete theory of international politics. Morgenthau thought power maximization was "natural" universal behavior since it was a part of human nature (1973, pp. 104–5). Normative realism

[6] Elster (1989b) uses this same metaphor as an example of a cooperative norm arguing that we use correct grammar since we have the common goal of communication, but he overlooks the fact that children learn grammar as much from being taught, corrected, and imitating others as through a desire to communicate. We do not now use the generic "she" to improve communication.

argues that preferences and values are not the same for all states, institutions, and individuals, and that directly or indirectly different values explain variation in state behavior. Figure 11.3 suggests that the conflict between self-interest maximization and norms may result in compromise. Normative realism does not argue for one at the expense of the other. Two different forces are at work, it is not just self-interest and not just norms, but their interaction that characterizes normative realism.

12 THE NORM OF DECOLONIZATION

> Moral acceptance of rights (especially rights that are valued and supported, and not just respected in the form of constraints) may call for systematic departures from self-interested behavior. Even a partial and limited move in that direction in actual conduct can shake the behavioral foundations of standard economic theory.
>
> Amartya Sen (1987, p. 57)

Introduction

Decentralized norms are supra-national structures that cut across boundaries. Not just national governments but many other forces combine to maintain them and keep them effective. They are in the most basic sense of the word a context within which states act. They are interesting structures because, *pace* power structures à la Waltz (1979), they cannot be reduced to any state attribute, but are the result of domestic political factors, the spread of ideas, and the formation of non-governmental pressure groups. The decolonization norm is one such structure.

This norm stipulates that colonies and dependent territories have a right to self-determination and eventually to political independence. By 1980 the norm is virtually uncontested, signaled by the fact that the whole topic is considered primarily in historical terms. Around 1800 politicians, philosophers, and peoples created it under the auspices of the American and French Revolutions. The notion of *self-determination* for Caucasian settled colonies and the idea of *nation*-states combined had by 1980 conquered the whole world.

Throughout the nineteenth century the norm of decolonization developed, notably in Great Britain, for European-settled colonies such as New Zealand and Australia. National independence was envisaged for these colonies, but not at all for the non-Caucasian peopled colonies of the world.

This distinction based on racist theories – racist in the two senses of being based on race and against certain races – allowed the competition for colonies in Africa while at the same time permitting more self-government to other colonies. But the limits originally placed on the norm gave way and the norm broadened to ever-wider classes of nations until it became applicable to all dependent territories.

The history of decolonization is a history of changing values in the international system. Part of the British "loss of will" to rule was the increasingly common view that colonies were no longer appropriate. The norm of national self-determination spread from one country to another until it covered virtually all of Europe and North America. That Spain and Portugal retained some of their colonies symbolized their political and cultural isolation from the rest of Europe.

Obviously not all norms start from a minority position to become universal, each norm has its own history and evolution. But there are a number of norms that have established themselves as dominant reference points for large parts of the world. For example, democracy was not widely accepted in 1800, but by 1990 it had become virtually the only *legitimate* form of government. Even communist countries are – or rather were – "People's Democracies"; they as well as many authoritarian governments hold nominal elections. Though the norm is frequently violated in practice these elections attest to the normative strength of the idea of democracy. The norm of democracy ties into a normative system including "universal" human rights (Donnelly 1989) and ecological values, all of which have also become pervasive in the industrialized world. Related to the development of human rights is the disappearance of slavery, which was common in many Third World countries (and some industrialized ones), but which came to be viewed as completely immoral and is now illegal almost everywhere.

The decolonization, democracy, and anti-slavery norms show how norms form structures that influence their mutual development (see Harman 1986 for a coherency view of belief systems, and Dworkin 1986 for how this plays a role in jurisprudence). Systems of norms are articulated structures, the establishment of one norm bootstraps its less-established cousin. Factors such as changing attitudes in colonies, changes in attitudes in the colonial powers, the real political struggle between different groups, such as women and blacks, in the colonial powers as well as the general development of social-democratic ideas are all aspects of decolonization. The norm of decolonization flowed naturally out of the continual struggle in Europe to extend democracy to more than wealthy white males: if women should have a say in their governments why not Africans? Granting independence to non-European peoples formed part of the same movement that gave the vote to women. The arms that European states forged to gain their independence or unification were available to be turned against them. The French Revolution created tools that the Algerians could use to dismantle easily the claims that Algeria was just another part of France.

Because of normative structures powerful groups cannot impose arbitrary norms. Power in the long run can only establish norms that articulate with existing structures. Sanctions may be necessary for legitimate governments but they are not sufficient. Centuries of slavery never convinced slaves of the justice of their servitude, nor did forty years of communist rule create legitimate governments in Eastern Europe. Powerful groups can influence values but they nevertheless do not have complete freedom to create them.

The norm of decolonization provides a good example of a decentralized norm. It is clear that the norm prescribing independence for colonial territories conflicts with other political and economic interests. Neo-colonialist theories argue that this conflict was minimal, that political and economic benefits could be retained while granting independence. But it is not obvious that self-interest coincided completely with granting independence. Also typical of decentralized norms is that sanctioning power was diffused throughout the system. From the most powerful to the least, diverse groups supported the norm. The USA and the USSR, often for reasons of self-interest, but also because of their own revolutions against oppressive governments, favored independence movements to a certain degree. At the other end of the spectrum, revolutionary groups were founded in the colonies to demand independence. Support for decolonization arose in the colonial countries, often from socialist and communist parties. These sanctions, sometimes self-serving sometimes selfless, all contributed to changing the normative context within which these issues were debated. In a self-reinforcing fashion the strength of the norm increased the level of sanctions which increased the legitimacy of the norm.

In a rather one-sided fashion I shall only be concerned with decolonization but not colonization. Though without a doubt the two are related, I am interested in a prescriptive norm and not a permissive one. The decolonization norm prescribes a certain behavior with regard to dependent territories. The colonization norms allows their acquisition, but in no way makes that obligatory. In doing so I use the distinction made in the previous chapter between norms as causes and norms as barriers. The colonization norm functions like a barrier because of its permissive character: colonization is permitted as part of the rules of the game. The decolonization norm prescribes a certain behavior *vis-à-vis* dependent territories: it does not regulate, but commands that dependent territories be given self-government. Practically this means that in the empirical section I shall only investigate cases of national independence ignoring the acquisition of new dependent territory.

In the next two sections I give a brief political history of the decolonization norm and then present a behavioral measure of the norm. I argue that the two parallel each other, that the measure corresponds to what we know from political and intellectual history. The last sections of the chapter are devoted to evaluating the norm's impact on the transition of the dependent territory to an independent state. I show that even including self-interest and realpolitik factors the norm was a significant factor in reducing the level of military conflict in the evolution of 119 dependent territories to recognized members of the international system.

The historical development of the norm

My measurement model of a decentralized norm has a behavioral component as well as a deontological component. To see how the norm of decolonization evolved implies charting these two facets of its existence. Furthermore there must be some coherence between these two realms. To start out let me sketch out how attitudes about colonies and dependent territories have changed over the last 200 years. Below the question will be whether the behavioral measure corresponds to what we know of the deontological history of the norm.

The norm of decolonization developed along with the norm of democracy, both tied to the idea that states represent peoples. The American Revolution started the history of the decolonization norm because they were the first major colonies to gain their independence, and whose independence was accompanied with a justification based on norms of self-representation. The revolution was a bloody affair and the idea that colonies should eventually become independent was not accepted by the British or other colonial powers. This jolt to the system was quickly followed by the French Revolution which forcibly and permanently changed the relations between states and their peoples. One off-shoot was the independence of Haiti.

During the nineteenth century European peoples struggled for a voice in government and at the same time ideas about colonies were also slowly changing in the same sense. In Britain there was the growing realization that the English-settled colonies such as Canada, New Zealand, and Australia would eventually become independent. This change was vaguely starting also to be felt with regard to non-European countries. Paradoxically, this was evident in the Berlin Conference of 1885 which divided Africa among the colonial powers. The agreements suggested that colonial domination might only be temporary, although no one thought independence was going to happen soon.

The first real cracks in the colonial system happened as a result of World War I. It had been common practice in previous wars for the victorious power(s) to incorporate some of the territory of the defeated states into its own. After World War I, some of this certainly occurred, but perhaps for the first time the victorious coalition decided to put some of those areas on the path to self-rule. The League of Nations Mandate System removed dependent territories from colonial domination and provided a means for them to attain independence peacefully. The international community noted that colonial territories had an economic and political impact and therefore the community of nations had an interest in protecting the well-being of those territories.

Decolonization under the Mandate System was however quite limited. First, it applied only to the colonies of defeated powers in the war. Second, the colonies would not immediately receive their independence, but would pass through a transitional phase under the tutelage of another state – often resembling colonialism. Nevertheless, the notion that dependent peoples should be free to determine their own government received tangible recognition at the international level.

The United Nations and its Trusteeship System was a major turning point in the development of a norm of decolonization. The UN Charter explicitly recognized a right of "self-determination of peoples" and expanded on the League mandate system with the creation of the Trusteeship Council. The UN system and its underlying principles had the potential to apply to all dependent territories; the United Nations could not and would not seize existing colonies, but the moral justification for colonial domination became much less tenable.

The twenty-five years following the founding of the UN witnessed a tremendous number of territories gaining their independence, most through peaceful means. Various UN resolutions accompanied this movement, the most important of which was probably the General Assembly Resolution 1514 passed in 1960. This resolution equated colonial domination with a violation of human rights and stated that such domination is contrary to the UN Charter. Over time both UN resolutions and opinions of the International Court of Justice have consistently cited this resolution and the principles contained in it. Some legal scholars argue that decolonization has become so embedded in international society that it constitutes a "peremptory norm of international law" thereby giving it legal standing.

This thumbnail sketch of the changes in attitudes toward dependent territories over the last 200 years is a story about how ideas regarding the character of nation-states changed and about how relations between Europe and the rest of the world changed. The evolution was neither smooth nor always peaceful, it is a history of conflict – typical of the history of most norms. But norms are not only attitudes, they are also related to behavior. I now turn to a behavioral measure of the development of the decolonization norm.

A behavioral measure of the norm

Two indicators illuminate behavioral aspects of the norm's development. One is the extent to which colonies become independent; as more and more colonies gain independence the norm is strengthened. As ex-dependent territories form a larger percentage of states in the system, more states support decolonization and sanction violators of the norm. Nations can perhaps "forget" their heritage, but more frequently it is enshrined in national belief systems. Hence, once a dependent territory has become independent, its support for the norm is assumed to continue into the future. Following this logic one measure of the strength of the norm consists in the number of ex-colonies in the system. This indicator signals the potential sanctioning power in the system as well as the extent to which the decolonization value is widespread.

The second indicator is whether the independence was the result of significant military conflict. One can infer that if an independence occurred peacefully the norm of decolonization was stronger than in cases where the independence was simply the result of military victory. If the colonial power granted independence without being obliged to do so by military force then this is a sign that it had accepted (internalized) to a certain degree the norm. Self-interest may dictate the choice, but at the same time by granting independence peacefully the colonial power creates chains and precedents that can later bind it. This indicator thus reflects the acceptance of the norm by the colonial powers, while the number of ex-colonies reflects the number

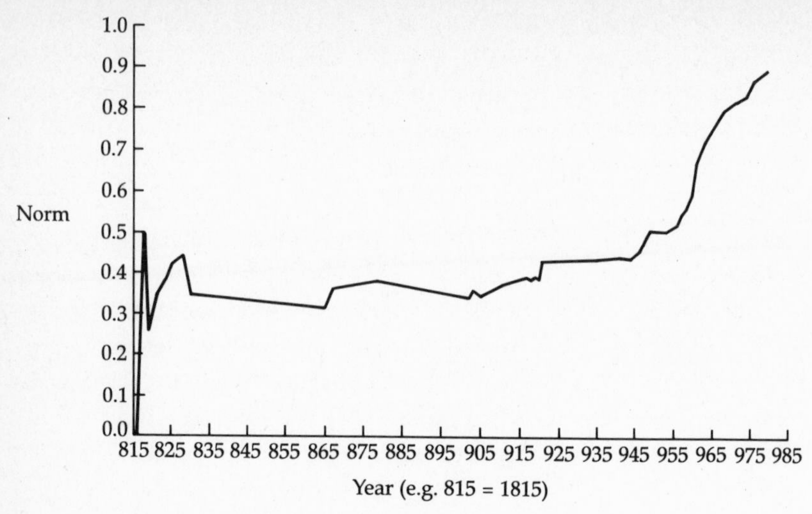

Figure 12.1 Evolution of the international norm

of states that have successfully gained their independence and that may be assumed to value the norm and to sanction violations.

Goertz and Diehl (1992a) provided the data on the number of independences and whether they involved military conflict. An "independence" is defined as the transition of a dependent territory of a "recognized" (Small and Singer 1982) state to the status of a recognized independent state. This excludes states that just "enter" the international system such as Japan. "Military conflict" over independence is defined as military combat between *organized* militaries from *both* sides within one year of independence. This eliminates rioting and other forms of violent protest that often precede independence. It also excludes cases where there was notable fighting early in the colonial period, but where decolonization itself was peaceful, e.g., Morocco.

If one plots the average[1] of the two indicators together, its evolution over the years from 1816 to 1980 follows in its general outline the political history sketched above. The curve in figure 12.1 rests fairly flat during the nineteenth century and starts to grow slowly around World War I reflecting changes such as the Irish and Canadian independences as well as the creation of the League Mandate system. It increases slowly until after World War II when it takes off under the impetus of the numerous independences in the 1950s and 1960s.

[1] The number of ex-colonies is standardized by the total N of 119 and the military conflict indicator is the percentage of independences involving military conflict.

The results of this attempt to measure an international norm appear to correspond to the intellectual and political history of decolonization. Thus our knowledge of two of the elements of a measurement model of a decentralized norm, one deontological and one behavioral, seem to reinforce each other indicating the same general pattern of growth and development.

These two indicators give us some idea of how the norm develops on the international level, but each state has its own history and domestic political forces. One of the problems with international norms is how their impact is felt at the state level. We can think of international norms as having a relatively independent existence, but states must implement them. Each nation reacts differently to a common environment; its reaction is determined partially by that environment and partially by local factors. The impact of the normative context varies from one colonial power to another: Spain's response to the norm differs from France's because of its different political history and politics. One can chart the development of the norm at the state level by using the same two indicators: the number of independences granted by the colonial power and the extent to which they were peaceful. This gives an idea of the local evolution of the norm.

The final measurement model includes both international and nation-specific factors. It utilizes to a modest degree the context as a changing relationship mode of analysis: different national experiences and realities mediate the impact of the international norm. The complete model includes two indicators of the international norm and two indicators of the evolution of the norm at the state level (figure 12.2). These are *not* independent since the international norm is the sum of all the state-level norms. This is as it should be, the international norm should not be completely unrelated to what individual states do.

Finally, international norms are the creations of states and more importantly the leading powers in the international system. This is reflected empirically in the measure by the large number of cases involving the major powers, notably France and the UK, which has a strong impact on the evolution of the norm.

To examine the evolution of the norm of decolonization I have four indicators, two domestic and two international, and data on all independences since 1816. I have used the LISREL statistical technique to estimate the underlying development of the norm based on the four indicators (Bollen 1989; Hayduk 1987). This technique constructs an "unmeasured" concept – norm – which has various manifestations, i.e., the number of ex-colonies and the military conflict over their transition to independence.

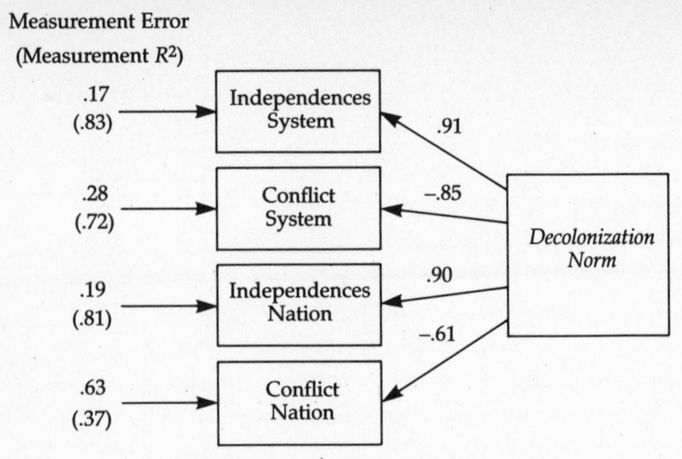

Figure 12.2 The decolonization norm measurement model

LISREL permits the strength of the relationship between the unmeasured concept and its manifestations to vary. The results, presented in figure 12.2, show that the model works quite well as shown by the measurement R^2's on the left of the figure. The signs of the coefficients linking the indicators with the latent norm variable are in the appropriate direction, positive for the number of independences and negative for military conflict over them. The norm is more related to its international aspects, the number of decolonizations in the system and the conflict over them than to the domestic history of the individual colonial power, but it is still reasonably related to all four indicators.

The measure of the decolonization norm has all the characteristics that an indicator of a decentralized norm should have:

1 It identifies behaviors that strengthen and conform to the norm.
2 The current strength of the norm is a function of its development.
3 There must be links tying the international norm to the individual states that must implement them.
4 The deontological history of the norm embodied in public documents, treaties, and philosophical works should correspond to behavioral aspects.

When colonial powers peacefully "grant" independence to dependent territories they "conform" to the norm, while independences of any sort "strengthen" it. The value of the norm at any given time is the cumulative impact of developments until that time. The final model has elements measuring the overall development of the norm plus nation-specific factors. Clearly the weakest link is my extremely brief description of the deontological history of the norm and its correspondence to the behavioral measure. Ideally an analysis like Kegley and Raymond's would indicate through a systematic analysis of legal texts and other documents the changing character of thought about colonies and dependent territories. The measurement model of the norm of decolonization appears to have the minimal theoretical and empirical characteristics of a valid model of an international norm.

But the question remains: Does it all matter? Can we say that the decolonization norm affected behavior?

The impact of the decolonization norm

To test the impact of the decolonization norm I propose to examine the extent of military conflict at the time of independence. As the norm of decolonization develops over time, as independence movements become more legitimate, one would expect there to be less military conflict over independence. The hypothesis is simple: the stronger the norm the less military conflict at the time of independence.

The dependent variable in the model – military conflict over independence – is however also one of those used to measure the norm variable. But the norm as I have modeled it is the behavior from 1816 to time $t-1$ and thus does not include the independence in question at time t. The independence at time t contributes either to strengthening or to weakening the norm at time $t+1$.[2] This represents the ways norms are created over time, how the inertia of past behavior can influence current actions.

At the time of independence of any given territory the development of the norm at the international level and at the level of the colonial/imperial power indicates the strength of the norm at that particular point in time and space. If one correlates the strength of the norm with the extent of military conflict at independence the correlation is -0.6, and statistically quite significant. The correlation is not -1.0, but also not negligible. The correlation means that when the norm of decolonization was strong there

[2] There is a potential problem with autocorrelation since one of four indicators of the independent norm variable is the dependent variable. However, it should be noted that among the four indicators of the independent variable three are completely different variables and that the fourth indicator is not just the dependent variable at time $t-1$ but is a function of all the previous dependent variables from 1816 to time $t-1$.

was less military conflict over independence. This suggests that the norm had an impact on the amount of military conflict at the time of independence. I do not argue that norms are the whole story, just an important part of it.

Nevertheless, correlation is not causation. One can argue that this is a case where self-interest coincided with norm-guided behavior – in statistical terms, a spurious correlation. One essential component of the methodology of decentralized norms is that they must be distinguishable from self-interest. Thus any test for the impact of a norm must take into account self-interest arguments.

In order to assess the independent impact of the norm I consider economic self-interest – trade and the "intrinsic" importance of the colony, and a power politics argument that claims that decolonization was a transfer of control from declining colonial powers to new dominant powers.

To measure the economic importance of the colony for the metropole I use two variables. One is the dependent territory's relative importance to the metropole as indicated by the colony's imports and exports as a percentage of its total imports and exports. This reflects the relative importance of the dependent territory in terms of the metropole's foreign trade. The second aspect of the economic importance of the territory is its intrinsic value, as measured by its area and total population. Using the LISREL technique I estimate two latent self-interest variables: the relative economic importance of the colony (trade) and its intrinsic importance (area and population).[3] It should be noted that I only examine the benefits generated by dependent territories, not the costs. If data were available it would be useful to include variables measuring the administrative and other costs involved in maintaining control of these territories (Manning 1974; Betts 1985; De Schweinitz 1983).

Norms are intimately tied to power politics. A realpolitik argument for decolonization is that in the post-World War II period there was a transfer of hegemony from the UK, France, Germany, and Japan to the US and the USSR. According to this explanation, independence was a transfer of control to the US or the USSR. The superpowers encouraged and supported decolonization as a means of extending their spheres of influence. The US and the USSR by virtue of their power facilitated the transfer of control from the colonial powers to local elites, who were then susceptible to US or Soviet influence.

[3] The data on the area and population of the territory come from Goertz and Diehl (1992a). Trade data were kindly furnished by Bouda Etemad and Paul Bairoch of the Center of International Economic History (University of Geneva, Switzerland).

To include realpolitik power explanations in my model I look at power changes in the colonial power in the period before independence. I have data on the change over the ten years previous to the independence of the metropole's percentage of the colonial system's (all colonial powers) total for: (1) GNP, (2) military expenditures, (3) military personnel. (The GNP and military data come from the sources described in chapter 4.) I use the various indicators together to estimate with LISREL a power-decline factor. This measure to some degree indicates the increasing costs – at least political – of maintaining dependent territories.

Other factors contributing to making colonies less attractive were independence movements which sprang up in many dependent territories. The strength of these movements varied quite dramatically from one colony to the next. Clearly these movements made continued colonial control less interesting, but rarely were liberation armies a match for colonial forces, with notable exceptions such as Algeria and Vietnam.[4] But to focus only on this "cost" would leave out the reason for its increase: the mounting strength of the decolonization norm that made peoples more willing to contest – violently and otherwise – continued domination. Arguments which take costs as exogenous are typical of what I have discussed as the norm as constraint model. But if increasing costs are the result of normative values then these values are an important causal variable. Recall that norms can act either through internal value change (changing values in colonial countries) or through norm-driven sanctions (value changes in the colonies). From the colonial power's point of view increasing costs can be just another constraint on power maximization, what is needed is to endogenize sanctions which then brings norms into the picture.

A complete analysis of the impact of the norm includes economic self-interest, realpolitik, and norm variables. This allows me to examine the influence of the norm while including other explanatory factors.[5]

Figure 12.3 gives the results of the analysis for 119 cases of independence since 1816. The overall fit of the model is modest with an R^2 of 0.50. The only insignificant variable is the intrinsic importance of the territory. The

[4] Since the dependent variable is military conflict over independence I cannot include an independent variable measuring the strength of independence movements which often include organized military units.

[5] Normally with a dichotomous dependent variable one would use logit/probit analysis. This is not possible within the LISREL framework; however, linear regression does approximate the middle of the S-shaped probit curve. Malhotra (1983) surveyed regression versus probit analyses and maximum likelihood techniques. He found that linear regression was generally a good approximation.

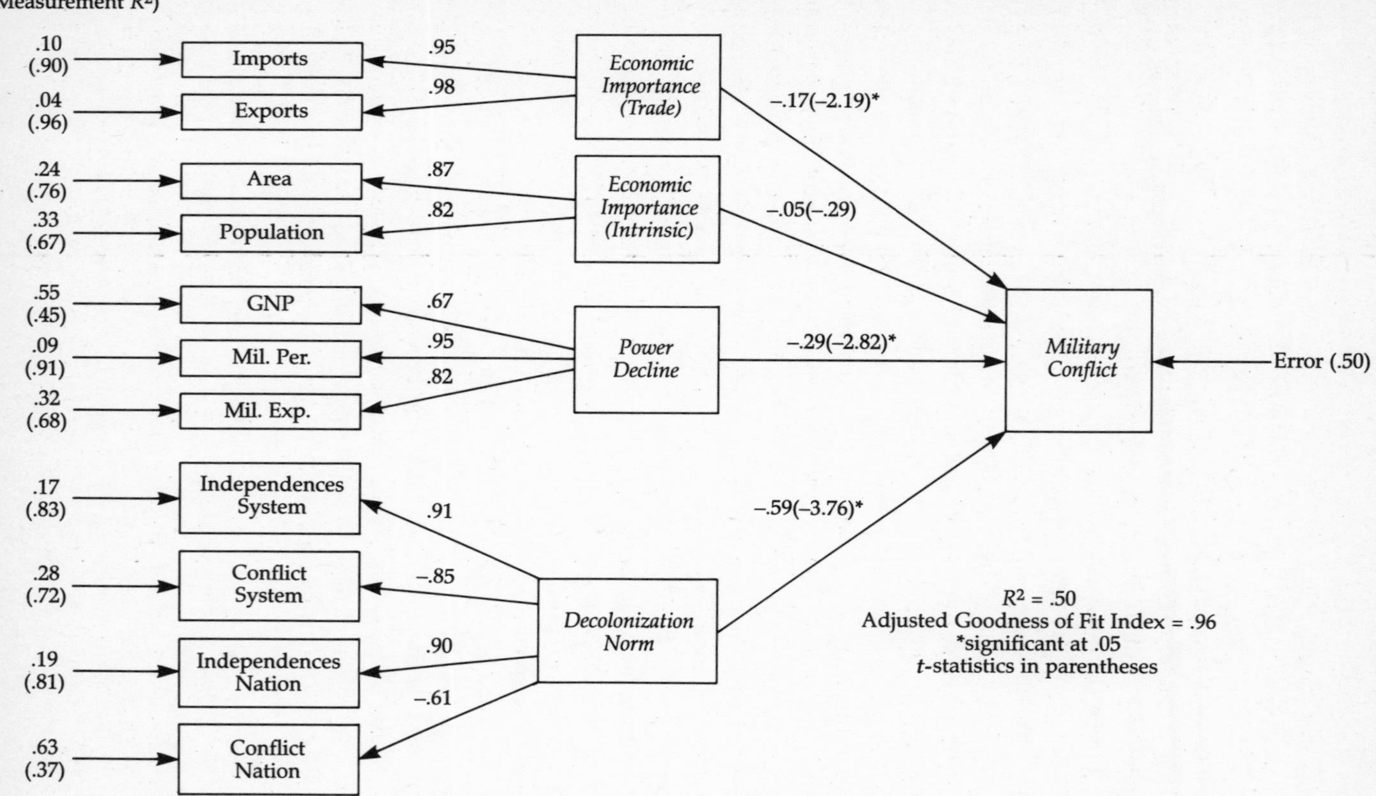

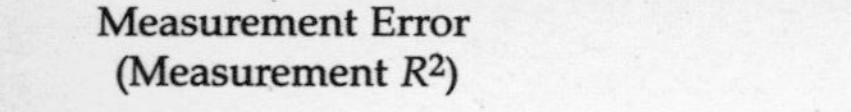

Figure 12.3 The impact of the decolonization norm on military conflict over independence

standardized structural coefficient of the norm variable is very significant with an approximate *t*-statistic of -3.76.[6] It is negative, meaning that as the norm gets stronger there is less military conflict. So even when including self-interest and realpolitik factors the norm appears to have had a significant impact on the amount of military conflict at independence.

Since the norm is the largest standardized coefficient it contributes significantly to the explanatory power of the model. The goal is not to explain all the variance but rather to show that the norm was important even when including other relevant self-interest factors. Economic self-interest in the form of trade and the power-decline variables were also significant. We have a situation like that illustrated in figure 11.3 where *both* self-interest and norms play an important role.

The results indicate that while empirically the norm was important, self-interest and sanctions also played a role. The self-interest of the metropole as represented by foreign trade was significant. The positive sign means that the more important the trade relations the more likely the metropole was to resist independence by military force. The realpolitik variable is also significant, the negative sign meaning that powers in decline were more likely to resist independence militarily. Thus the theoretical emphasis on self-interest and realpolitik in decentralized norms is confirmed empirically in this case.

Conclusion

All the themes that have played an important role in understanding contexts of international politics have made an appearance in the last two chapters on international norms. Normative realism uses a variety of substantive contexts and contextual modes.

The concept of a norm is quite entangled and intertwined with other related concepts, but some of this intertwining is essential to understanding norms. Norms give power and are the product of power. Power is present at the creation, one cannot consider norms just as a series of oughts. Norms and their impact on behavior cannot be studied apart from issues of power. Only where there are some sanctions – hence power relationships – will we

[6] The analysis reported in figure 12.2 was performed using unweighted least squares, a more conservative procedure than maximum likelihood, but one which does not provide significance values. The *t*-statistics are for the maximum likelihood estimates which were quite close to the unweighted least squares ones.

see norms in action (even violations of coordination norms are usually sanctioned). Moral and political values provide the motivation for many sanctions. Often the tendency is to emphasize either the strategic aspect of behavior to the exclusion of the deontological aspect or vice versa. However, we can only progress when we try to understand their interactions.

That norms are a form of power naturally suggests the use of the context as cause mode of analysis. As Durkheim (1937) argued: contexts coerce. The norm of decolonization demanded that dependent territories be given the choice of independence. The norm was a positive, causal force pushing colonial powers.

More common perhaps is the view of norms through the context as barrier mode of analysis. This is the view taken by many economists and theorists of international law. Norms place limits within which individuals and states maximize their self-interest. As the section on barrier models showed, barriers can place severe limitations on the maximization calculus. The traditional view of international relations, on the other hand, sees states as not very limited by normative constraints. The relative weight of these two factors will vary from issue to issue, but the problem cannot be swept away through assumptions of exogeneity.

Much needs to be done to understand the methodology and mechanisms of counteracting causes and barriers. Standard regression models are not necessarily the best choice. Given that barriers are necessary, non-transitive, and multiplicative the use of regression models that are sufficient, transitive, and additive does not appear appropriate (unless special care is taken). The mechanisms of barriers and constraints also remain unclear. Most regime theorists believe that regimes have some effect on decision-making, but how is not always so clear. For example, because norms imply behavioral consistency they allow the formation of stable expectations. But to assume at the same time that the decision-maker is rational means that one should *not* assume that she will continue to act according to the norm, only present and future considerations influence her choice. It would not be sensible for a rational leader in a balance of power system to base her expectations on previous alliance commitments. In addition, consistency of behavior in changing environments suggests that the assumption of rationality should be investigated.

Norms usually remain quite stable. Cooperative norms are stable as long as common goals exist, pure reciprocity is stable as long as it remains an effective strategy. If norms are occasionally subject to rapid change, most of the time they do not vary much. The norm of decolonization changed little throughout the nineteenth century, pressure was building up but nothing that could shake well-established procedures and values. Likewise today it seems unlikely that the norms of national self-determination are likely to change. Attitudes toward the break-up of the USSR and Yugoslavia confirm them. For internal and external reasons norms evolve slowly.

Because of this stability to understand a norm is usually to give a historical explanation. Customary international law depends on the past behavior of states. To base expectations on norms is to explain them using what governments did in the past: what one expects in the future is a function of what happened in the past. Thus norms are one of the major types of historical theories.

Theories of international contexts are about how states related to their environments, they are theories about the level of analysis. Self-interest is essentially an individual-level phenomenon – this is why economists are frequently methodological individualists, but norms are not tied to any state (hegemonic norms excepted, and even these change over time). They are a global phenomenon – a context. The concept of self-interest makes *no sense* independent of an individual; norms and rules do. We can easily discuss rules and norms that are followed by no one. But a *behavioral* norm by definition means a norm that influences – either through internal or external mechanisms – a state's behavior. For this reason a theory of norms must be about the *interaction* between norms and individuals. Norms are like the other contexts I have examined in this volume, they are theories of the interaction between states and international systems.

Context as changing meaning was used to relate the international norm to its implementation (or not) by various colonial powers. Contextual analysis must provide links between the system and state levels of analysis, context as changing meaning provides one general theoretical tool for making those connections. Norms also provide contexts for interpreting other norms. Legal systems could not function without unwritten norms of interpretation (Sunstein 1990). Rules about rules often have this interpretative character, for example, rules about which rule violations are acceptable (e.g., GATT rules, see also Edgerton 1985).

Barrier models stressed the importance of social pressure and learning. The same kinds of mechanisms come into play with decentralized norms, which emphasize the spatial context of norm creation and enforcement. In the decolonization norm measurement model this was indicated by the number of ex-colonies in the international system, in the oil case it was the number of recent nationalizations and the number of nationalist regimes in the world. The spatial context plays a role in regime theories that rely on expectations; following a norm may only be rational if it is reasonable to assume that most other actors are doing likewise. Depending on the context this may or may not be a reasonable assumption.

The emphasis on spatial and temporal contexts was a strength of diffusion models. Most theories of norm formation rely on spatial models (social pressure) or temporal ones (internalization). In contrast, rational actor models usually assume preferences are exogenous and stable. Through the discussion of context, diffusion models and rational actor models have served as points of comparison. These contrasts are in some ways even more clear in the case of international norms, because normative explanations of behavior are often of a different, and incompatible, kind.

States live in a normative world that is their joint creation, often through a process that evolves over centuries. At the same time these norms come to constrain their creators since they and others come to believe in the norms. Decentralized norms frequently involve deontological components that cannot be reduced to calculations of efficiency. Norm violation can lead to quite negative reactions. The demands of that normative world often conflict with the immediate short-term interests of the state. Self-interest often prevails, but we need to examine the counterfactual proposition about how it would have prevailed in another international system with different norms. What we need is a theory of the struggle between self-interest, and normative constraints and imperatives.

The analysis of the norm of decolonization suggests that economic self-interest, power politics, and norms *all* play a role in explaining military conflict over independence. We tend to prefer stories with clear-cut endings, but the world is a messy place. Actors often neither follow the norm to the letter nor pursue self-interest to its limits. At least psychologically this seems quite common. Much of ethical theory is about when, where, and why compromises can be made. The relative importance of norms and self-interest vary. In a Cold War environment the US suppressed its human rights policies (except of course toward the Soviet bloc) and support of democracy, but in a post-Cold War world these issues are now on the agenda of institutions such as the World Bank and US AID. It may not be that these norms are now stronger but that the barrier suppressing them has been removed.

In a world that appears to be becoming more peaceful (though not less conflictual) the rules and norms that nations and other international actors define for themselves seem likely to play a larger role. The drive to protect national interests will not disappear but will be subject to more and more constraints of a normative character. Thus substantive contexts and the modes of context will become more important in the analysis of world politics.

13 POSTFACE: INTERACTING CONTEXTS AND EXPLAINING CONTEXTS

Seek simplicity and distrust it.
Alfred North Whitehead

Bivariate hypotheses may be too simple for understanding world politics. One response is to add more variables. If the goal is to explain a particular event then this is quite reasonable given that few events in the physical and human world have but one or two causes. The emphasis on context suggests that the mere "addition" of variables does not suffice, new kinds of relationships are necessary as well. Context as changing meaning and context as barrier are two different kinds of relationship that may be added to a conceptual tool box. In this book I have tried to construct a standard contextual tool and illustrate its use in a particular problem(s). But it is quite clear that customized tools work much better for specialized tasks.

Boyd and Iverson (1979) have already discussed a large number of statistical variations on the context as changing meaning tool, but there has been little corresponding theoretical development of the concept (hence the more theoretical nature of my discussion). The possibilities of the barrier mode remain to be exploited. Context as changing meaning models remain comfortably within the framework of general linear models (regression); barrier models seem to require different kinds of modeling techniques. In particular dynamic models appear appropriate; or perhaps with adaptation models could be stolen from hydraulics (after all the natural home of the metaphor). Different categories of barriers may exist, each with its own particular characteristics. Given how frequently the language of constraint, barrier, snowballing, waves, etc., occurs the potential applications of barrier models seem wide (though closer inspection may reveal that this is just casualness in language more than anything else).

Are there other modes of context, other conceptual tools that are useful for understanding how a state interacts with its environment? I suspect there are. Other substantive problems may suggest other modes. Expanding the conceptual tool box constitutes an area for future reflection.

While I have examined several contexts individually, I have not considered how contexts interact with each other. The central focus has been on the state–context (not context*s*) relationship. Obviously in any given situation there are multiple relevant contexts; history, norms, power structures are all present in differing degrees. How do these contexts relate to each other? In the case of oil nationalization the Cold War context clearly influenced how, when, and the extent to which the US government would back the major US oil companies. In all my figures context appears only as one element, a more complete picture would include multiple contexts.

One way contexts interact is by reinforcing each other. A number of factors working in conjunction contributed to the successful working of the international oil system until 1970. Contexts can also work in opposition, essentially canceling each other out: one context may be a cause, another a barrier. This was the case in barrier models where social pressure caused states to nationalize while oil companies and major powers put up barriers to nationalization.

Often there are well-established international norms that permit conflicting behavior, the GATT charter provides one example. Which norm will prevail? In domestic society a major role of the courts is to adjudicate in these cases. How is this done internationally where there are few recognized arenas for juridic review?

Contexts may arrange themselves into an hierarchical order. For example, norms are frequently divided into two categories, procedural and substantive. The former refers to rules about how to make rules (e.g., Constitutions) the latter are the specific rules that the rule-making process produces (e.g., laws voted by parliaments). Another form of hierarchy is priority ordering. Krasner (1978) claimed that the US foreign policy priorities in the raw material domain were hierarchical in this sense. If the conflict over oil fell into the Cold War then this context had priority over the defense of US oil companies, if the conflict fell outside then priority went to defending US economic interests.

If I were to define the concept of a regime, I would simply call it a structure of norms: regimes are systems of interacting and hierarchical norms. The character of these structures remains an open question. Are the norms contradictory or reinforcing? What are the systematics (in the biological sense) of these organisms? Do similar functions produce similar regime structures? I have tried to outline the elements of a theory of norms; using them I suggested some different building-block norms that might constitute regime structures. But how these blocks fit together and the properties of the resulting structures remain projects for further research.

Hierarchy, priority, contradiction, and reinforcement are all different structures of contexts. They come easiest to mind but there are certainly others. This is a rich vein for further exploration.

Just like economists who assume that opportunity structures are exogenous and given, I have been principally occupied with context as an independent variable. Context creation is a minor theme that has run throughout this volume. Mankind creates most of the environments that are important for states. This is of course not to say that any group can control or easily change these environments, but that like language they are creations of society. A vital part of any complete contextual theory consists in explaining contexts, taking state actions as independent variables and context as dependent ones. My procedure has been the converse: context as exogenous and state action as endogenous. A complete theory of context will include figures like the ones I have used, but with the causal arrows reversed. For example, hegemonic and coordination norms are effects of state action. Instead of context influencing the interaction of two states, states by their interaction create contexts.

The explanation of context creation has been a part of the discussion of the structure of a barrier as well as the creation of international norms. In both these cases there were feedback loops whereby the actions of individual states weakened or strengthened the context. Successful oil nationalization increased the pressure on the barrier and accelerated its decay. Successful decolonization increased the support and legitimacy of the norm of decolonization.

As a discipline we are very strong on causal arrows, but very weak on feedback loops. The major thrust of this book follows in that tradition. I have stressed that context is the interaction of individual and context, but in practice I have emphasized one direction of that interaction at the expense of the other. Much needs to be done to deepen our understanding of the structure and function of individual action as a context-creating force.

The emphasis on feedback loops has almost always coincided with the mention of the importance of the historical context. This is because contexts are large, inertial entities that normally change slowly. Barriers and norms change and evolve, but except in extraordinary times they change under the cumulative impact of many interactions. Explaining contexts almost always means explaining their change over time. Including feedback loops historicizes (by my definition of historical theories) the model as well as making it more dynamic.

Reviewing the substantive contexts discussed here I am made aware that all too often arguments or assertions have been made in a couple of lines that would have been more adequately defended in a paragraph. Often I have made a passing allusion to large bodies of research assuming that the reader was familiar with them. For example, to treat theoretically and empirically norms in a mere two chapters borders on folly. I hope the reader's forbearance has not been too strained by the lack of development and the failure to defend many of the claims of this book; as the French say I hope that *on n'est pas resté sur sa faim*, that the reader is not hungry for further explanation. In fact the need for further explanation is pushing me to elaborate and develop a number of topics, which have evolved into major projects in their own right. Paul Diehl and I are working on the problem of enduring rivalries. We hope eventually to provide more theoretical and empirical light on this problem than I have been able to give here. Similarly my interest in norms has expanded beyond what I could say here into another large project. I would like to examine other norms and to develop in more detail the methodology and theory of international norms.

Nevertheless, I hope that this sketchy account of how nations interact and are intertwined with their environments has provided food for thought. This problem is likely to get more and more important as relations between nations become more and more tight and complex. The notion of an anarchical system is even less valid today than it ever was, but as long as there exists no centralized international decision-making and sanctioning body many of the fundamental problems facing students of world politics will remain.

REFERENCES

Abel, E. 1990. *The shattered bloc: behind the upheaval in Eastern Europe*. Boston: Houghton Mifflin.

Adler, P. 1981. *Momentum: a theory of social action*. Beverly Hills: Sage Publications.

Akins, J. 1973. The oil crisis: this time the wolf is here. *Foreign Affairs* 51: 462–90.

Allan, P. 1983. *Crisis bargaining and the arms race: a theoretical model*. Cambridge, MA: Ballinger.

Allison, G. 1969. Conceptual models and the Cuban Missile Crisis. *American Political Science Review* 63: 689–718.

Altfeld, M. and Bueno de Mesquita, B. 1979. Choosing sides in war. *International Studies Quarterly* 23: 87–112.

Anderson, P. 1981. Justifications and precedents as constraints in foreign policy decision-making. *American Journal of Political Science* 25: 738–61.

Andreski, S. 1968. *Military organization and society*, 2nd edition. Berkeley: University of California Press.

Asher, H. 1976. *Causal modeling*. Beverly Hills: Sage Publications.

Austin, J. 1954. *The province of jurisprudence determined* and *The uses of the study of jurisprudence*. London: Weidenfeld & Nicolson.

Axelrod, R. 1984. *The evolution of cooperation*. New York: Basic Books.

1986. An evolutionary approach to norms. *American Political Science Review* 80: 1095–111.

Bairoch, P. 1976. Europe's GNP 1800–1975. *Journal of European Economic History* 5: 273–340.

Banks, A. 1971. *Cross-polity time-series data*. Cambridge, MA: The MIT Press.

Barkun, M. 1968. *Law without sanctions: order in primitive societies and the world community*. New Haven: Yale University Press.

Bartholomew, D. 1982. *Stochastic models for social processes*, 3rd edition. New York: John Wiley & Sons.

Bates, D. and Watts, D. 1988. *Nonlinear regression analysis and its applications*. New York: John Wiley & Sons.

Becker, L. 1986. *Reciprocity*. Chicago: University of Chicago Press.

Beer, F. 1979. The epidemiology of peace and war. *International Studies Quarterly* 23: 45–86.

Belsley, D., Kuh, E., and Welsh, R. 1980. *Regression diagnostics: identifying influential data and sources of collinearity*. New York: John Wiley & Sons.

Bem, D. and McConnell, H. 1970. Testing the self-perception explanation of dissonance phenomena: on the salience of premanipulation attitudes. *Journal of Personality and Social Psychology* 14: 23–31.

Benoit, E. and Lubell, H. 1967. The world burden of national defense. In Benoit, E. (ed.) *Disarmament and world economic interdependence*. New York: Columbia University Press.

Betts, R. 1985. *Uncertain dimensions: Western overseas empires in the twentieth century*. Minneapolis: University of Minnesota Press.

Blalock, H. 1961. *Causal inferences in nonexperimental research*. Chapel Hill: University of North Carolina Press.

Bollen, K. 1989. *Structural equations with latent variables*. New York: John Wiley & Sons.

Bollen, K. and Phillips, D. 1982. Imitative suicides: a national study of the effects of television news stories. *American Sociological Review* 47: 802–9.

Boulding, K. 1962. *Conflict and defense*. New York: Harper & Row.

Bourdieu, P. 1992. Le sociologue et la philosophie: Pierre Bourdieu répond à quelques questions. *La quinzaine littéraire* 593: 5–6.

Box, G. and Jenkins, G. 1976. *Time series analysis: forecasting and control*, revised edition. San Francisco: Holden-Day.

Boyd, L. and Iverson, G. 1979. *Contextual analysis: concepts and statistical techniques*. Belmont: Wadsworth.

Braithwaite, R. 1968. *Scientific explanations: a study of the function of theory, probability and law in science*. Cambridge University Press.

Bremer, S. 1992. Dangerous dyads: interstate war, 1816–1965. *Journal of Conflict Resolution* 36: 309–41.

Breslauer, G. and Tetlock, P. (eds.) 1991. *Learning in U.S. and Soviet foreign policy*. Boulder: Westview Press.

Bryk, A. and Raudenbush, S. 1992. *Hierarchical linear models: applications and data analysis methods*. Beverly Hills: Sage Publications.

Bueno de Mesquita, B. 1981. *The war trap*. New Haven: Yale University Press.

1985. Toward a scientific understanding of international conflict: a personal view. *International Studies Quarterly* 29: 121–36, 151–4.

1989. The contribution of expected-utility theory to the study of international conflict. In Midlarsky, M. (ed.) *Handbook of war studies*. Boston: Unwin Hyman.

Bueno de Mesquita, B. and Lalman, D. 1988. Empirical support for systemic and dyadic explanations of international conflict. *World Politics* 41: 1–20.

1992. *War and reason: domestic and international imperatives*. New Haven: Yale University Press.

Bull, H. 1966. International theory: the case for the classical approach. *World Politics* 18: 361–77.

Campbell, D. and Fiske, D. 1959. Convergent and discriminant validity by the multitrait-multimethod matrix. *Psychological Bulletin* 56: 81–105.

Cancian, F. 1975. *What are norms? A study of beliefs and actions in a Maya community.* Cambridge University Press.

Choucri, N. and North, R. 1975. *Nations in conflict: national growth and international violence.* San Francisco: W. H. Freeman.

Christensen, T. and Snyder, J. 1990. Chain gangs and passed bucks: predicting alliance patterns in multipolarity. *International Organization* 44: 138–68.

Cohen, J., Chesnick, E., and Haran, D. 1982. Evaluation of compound probabilities in sequential choice. In Kahneman, D., Slovic, P., and Tversky, A. (eds.) *Judgment under certainty: heuristics and biases.* Cambridge University Press.

Collingwood, R. 1940. *An essay on metaphysics.* Oxford University Press.

Cox, R. 1983. Gramsci, hegemony and international relations: An essay in method. *Millenium: Journal of International Studies* 12: 162–75.

Crank, J. 1975. *The mathematics of diffusion,* 2nd edition. Oxford University Press.

Cusack, T. and Stoll, R. 1990. *Exploring realpolitik: probing international relations theory with computer simulation.* Boulder: Lynne Rienner.

Cusack, T. and Ward, M. 1981. Military spending in the United States, Soviet Union, and the People's Republic of China. *Journal of Conflict Resolution* 25: 429–69.

Dahlberg, K. 1983. Contextual analysis: taking space and time seriously. *International Studies Quarterly* 27: 257–66.

David, P. 1986. Understanding the economics of QWERTY: the necessity of history. In Parker, W. (ed.) *Economic history and the modern economist.* Oxford: Basil Blackwell.

Davidson, D. 1980. *Essays on actions and events.* Oxford University Press.

Davis, W., Duncan, G., and Siverson, R. 1978. The dynamics of warfare: 1815–1965. *American Journal of Political Science* 22: 772–92.

Dawisha, K. 1984. *The Kremlin and the Prague Spring.* Berkeley: University of California Press.

1988. *Eastern Europe, Gorbachev and reform: the great challenge.* Cambridge University Press.

De Schweinitz, K. 1983. *The rise and fall of British India: imperialism as inequality.* London: Methuen.

Der Derian, J. and Shapiro, M. (eds.) 1989. *International/intertextual relations: postmodern readings of world politics.* Lexington: Lexington Books.

Deutsch, K. and Singer, J. D. 1964. Multipolar power systems and international stability. *World Politics* 16: 390–406.

Diehl, P. 1983. Arms races and the outbreak of war, 1816–1980. Ph.D. Dissertation, University of Michigan.

1985. Arms races to war: testing some empirical linkages. *Sociological Quarterly* 26: 331–49.

1985. Contiguity and military escalation in major power rivalries, 1816–1980. *Journal of Politics* 47: 1203–11.

1992. What are they fighting for? The importance of issues in international conflict research. *Journal of Peace Research* 29: 333–44.

Diehl, P. and Goertz, G. 1985. Trends in military allocation since 1816: what goes up does not always come down. *Armed Forces and Society* 12: 134–44.

1992. Entering international society: military conflict and national independence, 1816–1980. *Comparative Politics* 23: 497–518.

1993. The initiation and termination of enduring rivalries: the impact of political shocks. Workshop on Processes of Enduring Rivalries, Bloomington, IN.

Donnelly, J. 1989. *Universal human rights in theory and practice*. Ithaca: Cornell University Press.

Duncan, G. and Siverson, R. 1982. Flexibility of alliance partner choice in a multipolar system. *International Studies Quarterly* 26: 511–38.

Durkheim, E. 1937. *Les règles de la méthode sociologique*. Paris: Presses Universitaires de France.

Dworkin, R. 1986. *Law's empire*. Cambridge, MA: Harvard University Press.

Echikson, W. 1990. *Lighting the night: revolution in Eastern Europe*. New York: William Morrow.

Eckhardt, B. and Azar, E. 1978. Major world conflicts and interventions, 1945 to 1975. *International Interactions* 5: 79–110.

Edgerton, R. 1985. *Rules, exceptions and the social order*. Berkeley: University of California Press.

Eells, E. 1991. *Probabilistic causality*. Cambridge University Press.

Eells, E. and Sober, E. 1983. Probabilistic causality and the question of transitivity. *Philosophy of Science* 50: 35–57.

Eggertsson, T. 1990. *Economic behavior and institutions*. Cambridge University Press.

Eldredge, N. 1985. *Time frames: the evolution of punctuated equilibria*. Princeton: Princeton University Press.

Eldredge, N. and Gould, S. J. 1972. Punctuated equilibria: an alternative to phyletic gradualism. In Schopf, T. and Thomas, J. (eds.) *Models in paleobiology*. San Francisco: Freeman, Cooper.

Elias, N. 1969. *Über den Prozeß der Zivilisation*, 2 vols. Frankfort: Suhrkamp.

Elster, J. 1976. A note on hysteresis in the social sciences. *Synthèse* 33: 371–91.

1978. *Logic and society: contradictions and possible worlds*. New York: John Wiley & Sons.

1979. *Ulysses and the sirens*. Cambridge University Press.

1983. *Sour grapes: studies in the subversion of rationality*. Cambridge University Press.

1989a. *The cement of society: a study of social order*. Cambridge University Press.

1989b. *Nuts and bolts for the social sciences*. Cambridge University Press.

1989c. *Solomonic judgments: studies in the limitations of rationality*. New York: Cambridge University Press.

1990. Norms of revenge. *Ethics* 100: 862–85.

Elster, J. (ed.) 1986. *The multiple self*. Cambridge University Press.

Entwisle, B. and Mason, W. 1985. Multilevel effects of socioeconomic development and family planning programs on children ever born. *American Journal of Sociology* 91: 616–49.

Eulau, H. 1987. Book review of Political science: the science of politics, edited by H. Weisberg. *American Political Science Review* 81: 253–7.

Fearon, J. 1991. Counterfactuals and hypothesis testing in political science. *World Politics* 43: 169–95.

Feinberg, J. 1970. *Doing and deserving: essays in the theory of responsibility*. Princeton: Princeton University Press.

Feller, W. 1967. *Introduction to probability theory and its applications*, 3rd edition. New York: John Wiley & Sons.

Finlayson, J. and Zacher, M. 1983. The GATT and the regulation of trade: the sources and effects of regimes. In Krasner, S. (ed.) *International regimes*. Ithaca: Cornell University Press.

Fodor, J. 1979. *The language of thought*. Cambridge, MA: Harvard University Press.

Frank, R. 1985. *Choosing the right pond: human behavior and the quest for status*. Oxford University Press.

1988. *Passions within reason: the strategic role of the emotions*. New York: W. W. Norton.

Freeman, J. and Hannan, M. 1975. Growth and decline processes in organizations. *American Sociological Review* 40: 215–28.

Freeman, J. and Job, B. 1979. Scientific forecasts in international relations: problems of definition and epistemology. *International Studies Quarterly* 23: 113–44.

Garton Ash, T. 1989. *The uses of adversity: essays and the fate of Central Europe*. New York: Random House.

Gauthier, D. 1986. *Morals by agreement*. Oxford University Press.

Geller, D. 1992. Power transition and conflict initiation. *Conflict Management and Peace Science* 12: 1–16.

1993. Power transitions and war in rival dyads. *International Studies Quarterly* 37: 173–94.

Ghiselli, E. , Campbell, J., and Zedeck, S. 1981. *Measurement theory for the behavioral sciences*. San Francisco: W. H. Freeman.

Giddens, A. 1984. *The constitution of society: outline of the theory of structuration*. Berkeley: University of California Press.

Gilovich, T. 1981. Seeing the past in the present: the effect of associations to familiar events on judgments and decisions. *Journal of Personality and Social Psychology* 40: 797–808.

Gilovich, T., Vallone, R., and Tversky, A. 1985. The hot hand in basketball: on the misperception of random sequences. *Cognitive Psychology* 17: 295–314.

Gilpin, R. 1987. *The political economy of international relations*. Princeton: Princeton University Press.

Gochman, C. and Maoz, Z. 1984. Militarized interstate disputes, 1816–1976: procedures, patterns and insights. *Journal of Conflict Resolution* 28: 585–615.

Goertz, G. and Diehl, P. 1986. Measuring military allocations: a comparison of different approaches. *Journal of Conflict Resolution* 30: 553–81.

1992a. *Territorial change and international conflict*. London: Routledge.

1992b. Towards a theory of international norms: some conceptual and measurement issues. *Journal of Conflict Resolution* 36: 634–64.

Goleman, D. 1985. *Vital lies, simple truths: the psychology of self-deception.* New York: Simon and Schuster.

Gould, S. 1980. Were dinosaurs dumb? In *The panda's thumb: more reflections in natural history.* New York: W. W. Norton.

1985. Losing the edge. In *The flamingo's smile: reflections in natural history.* New York: W. W. Norton.

1991. The streak of streaks. In *Bully for brontosaurus: reflections in natural history.* New York: W. W. Norton.

Griliches, Z. 1957. Hybrid corn: an exploration in the economics of technological change. *Econometrica* 25: 501–22.

Haas, E. 1989. Conflict management and international organizations. In Diehl, P. (ed.) *The politics of international organizations.* Chicago: The Dorsey Press.

Haas, M. 1974. *International conflict.* Indianapolis: Bobbs-Merrill.

Hacking, I. 1990. *The taming of chance.* Cambridge University Press.

Haggard, S. and Simmonds, B. 1987. Theories of international regimes. *International Organization* 41: 491–517.

Harman, G. 1986. *Change in view: principles of reasoning.* Cambridge, MA: The MIT Press.

Harsanyi, J. 1976. *Essays in ethics, social behavior and scientific explanation.* Dortrecht: Reidel.

Hart, H. L. A. 1961. *The concept of law.* Oxford University Press.

Hart, H. L. A. and Honori, T. 1985. *Causation in the law,* 2nd edition. Oxford University Press.

Hayduk, L. 1987. *Structural equation modeling with LISREL: essentials and advances.* Baltimore: Johns Hopkins University Press.

Heintz, P. 1976. On the change of parameters of the international system 1870–1970: an analytic review of some recent literature. *Journal of Conflict Resolution* 20: 173–84.

Heise, D. 1975. *Causal analysis.* New York: John Wiley & Sons.

Hicks, J. 1979. *Causality in economics.* Oxford: Basil Blackwell.

Hirschman, A. 1970. *Exit, voice and loyalty: responses to decline in firms, organizations and states.* Cambridge, MA: Harvard University Press.

1977. *The passions and the interests: political arguments for capitalism before its triumph.* Princeton: Princeton University Press.

Holland, J. *et al.* 1986. *Induction: processes of inference, learning and discovery.* Cambridge, MA: The MIT Press.

Hollis, M. and Smith, S. 1990. *Explaining and understanding international relations.* Oxford University Press.

Holsti, K. 1991. *Peace and war: armed conflicts and international order, 1648–1989.* Cambridge University Press.

Houweling, H. and Kune, J. 1984. Do outbreaks of war follow a Poisson-process? *Journal of Conflict Resolution* 28: 51–61.

Huckfeldt, R. 1979. Political participation and the neighborhood social context. *American Journal of Political Science* 23: 579–92.

1983. The social context of political change: durability, volatility and social influence. *American Political Science Review* 77: 929–44.

1986. *Politics in context: assimilation and conflict in urban neighborhoods*. New York: Agathon Press.

Huckfeldt, R. and Sprague, J. 1987. Networks in context: the social flow of political information. *American Political Science Review* 81: 1197–1216.

Hudson, V. (ed.) 1991. *Artificial intelligence and international politics*. Boulder: Westview Press.

Humphreys, P. 1989. *The chances of explanation: causal explanation in the social, medical and physical sciences*. Princeton: Princeton University Press.

Huntington, S. 1991. *The third wave: democratization in the late twentieth century*. Norman: University of Oklahoma Press.

Huth, P. 1988. *Extended deterrence and the prevention of war*. New Haven: Yale University Press.

Huth, P., Bennett, S., and Gelpi, C. 1992. System uncertainty, risk propensity, and international conflict among the great powers. *Journal of Conflict Resolution* 36: 478–517.

Huth, P. and Russett, B. 1984. What makes deterrence work: cases from 1900 to 1980. *World Politics* 36: 496–525.

1993. General deterrence between enduring rivals: testing three competing models. *American Political Science Review* 87: 61–73.

Ikenberry, G. and Kupchan, C. 1990. Socialization and hegemonic power. *International Organization* 44: 283–315.

International Monetary Fund 1982. *International financial statistics*. Washington: IMF.

Jacoby, N. 1974. *Multinational oil: a study in industrial dynamics*. London: Macmillan.

Jervis, R. 1976. *Perception and misperception in international politics*. Princeton: Princeton University Press.

1983. Security regimes. In Krasner, S. (ed.) *International regimes*. Ithaca: Cornell University Press.

Jervis, R., Lebow, R., and Stein, J. 1985. *Psychology and deterrence*. Baltimore: Johns Hopkins University Press.

Jervis, R. and Synder, J. (eds.) 1991. *Dominoes and bandwagons: strategic beliefs and great power competition in the Eurasian rimland*. Oxford University Press.

Job, B. 1976. An appraisal of the methodological and statistical procedures of the Correlates of War Project. In Zinnes, D. and Hoole, F. (eds.) *Quantitative international politics: an appraisal*. New York: Praeger.

Johnston, J. 1972. *Econometric methods*, 2nd edition. New York: McGraw-Hill.

Jones, D. 1991. Enduring rivalries, dispute escalation and interstate war. North American Peace Science Conference, Columbus, Ohio.

Jordan, T. and Rowntree, L. 1982. *The human mosaic: a thematic introduction to human geography*, 3rd edition. New York: Harper & Row.

Jöreskog, K. 1979. Analyzing psychological data by structural analysis of covariance matrices. In Magidson, J. (ed.) *Advances in factor analysis and structural equation Rmodels*. Lanham: University Press of America.

Judge, G. *et al.* 1985. *The theory and practice of econometrics*, 2nd edition. New York: John Wiley & Sons.

Kahneman, D. and Tversky, A. 1982. On the study of statistical intuitions. In Kahneman, D., Slovic, P. and Tversky, A. (eds.) *Judgment under certainty: heuristics and biases*. Cambridge University Press.

Kegley, C. (ed.) 1991. *The long postwar peace: contending explanations and projections*. New York: HarperCollins.

Kegley, C. and Raymond, G. 1990. *When trust breaks down: alliance norms and world politics*. Columbia: University of South Carolina Press.

Kegley, C., Richardson, N., and Richter, G. 1978. Conflict at home and abroad: an empirical extension. *Journal of Politics* 40: 742–52.

Kelsen, H. 1967. *The pure theory of law*. Berkeley: University of California Press.

Kenny, D. 1979. *Correlation and causality*. New York: John Wiley & Sons.

Keohane, R. 1980. The theory of hegemonic stability and changes in international regimes, 1967–1977. In Holsti, O., Siverson, R., and George, A. (eds.) *Changes in the international system*. Boulder: Westview Press.

1983. The demand for international regimes. In Krasner, S. (ed.) *International regimes*. Ithaca: Cornell University Press.

1984. *After hegemony: cooperation and discord in world political economy*. Princeton: Princeton University Press.

Khong, Y. 1992. *Analogies at war: Korea, Munich, Dien Bien Phu, and the Vietnam decisions of 1965*. Princeton: Princeton University Press.

Khrushchev, N. 1970. *Khrushchev remembers*. Boston: Little, Brown.

Kim, J. 1978. Supervenience and nomological incommensurables. *American Philosophical Quarterly* 15: 149–56.

Kim, W. 1992. Power transitions and great power war from Westphalia to Waterloo. *World Politics* 45: 153–72.

Klein, H. 1964. American oil companies in Latin America: the Bolivian case. *Inter-American Economic Affairs* 18: 47–72.

Knight, J. 1992. *Institutions and social conflict*. Cambridge University Press.

Kobrin, S. 1984. The nationalization of oil production: 1919–1980. In Pearce, D. *et al.* (eds.) *The political economy of natural resource development*. London: Macmillan.

1985. Diffusion as an explanation of oil nationalization: or the domino effect rides again. *Journal of Conflict Resolution* 29: 3–32.

Koford, K. and Miller, J. (eds.) 1991. *Social norms and economic institutions*. Ann Arbor: University of Michigan Press.

Krasner, S. 1978. *Defending the national interest: raw materials investments and U.S. foreign policy*. Princeton: Princeton University Press.

1983a. Structural causes and regime consequences: regimes as intervening variables. In Krasner, S. (ed.) *International regimes*. Ithaca: Cornell University Press.

Krasner, S. (ed.) 1983b. *International regimes*. Ithaca: Cornell University Press.

Kuran, T. 1991. Now out of never: the element of surprise in the East European revolution of 1989. *World Politics* 44: 7–48.

Lakoff, G. 1987. *Women, fire and dangerous things; what categories reveal about the mind*. Chicago: University of Chicago Press.

Latsis, S. 1972. Situational determinism in economics. *British Journal for the Philosophy of Science* 23: 207–45.

Lave, C. and March, J. 1975. *An introduction to models in the social sciences*. New York: Harper & Row.

Lebow, N. 1983. The Cuban missile crisis: reading the lessons correctly. *Political Science Quarterly* 98: 431–58.

Leng, R. 1983. When will they ever learn? Coercive bargaining in recurrent crises. *Journal of Conflict Resolution* 27: 379–419.

1984. Reagan and the Russians: crisis bargaining beliefs and the historical record. *American Political Science Review* 78: 338–55.

1988. Crisis learning games. *American Political Science Review* 82: 179–94.

Leng, R. and Singer, J. D. 1977. Toward a multi-theoretical typology of international action. In Bunge, M., Galtung, J., and Malitza, M. (eds.) *Mathematical approaches to international politics*. Bucharest: Romanian Academy of Social and Political Science.

Levy, B. 1982. World oil marketing in transition. *International Organization* 36: 113–33.

Levy, J. 1982. The contagion of great power war, 1495–1975. *American Journal of Political Science* 26: 60–74.

1983. *War in the modern great power system, 1495–1975*. Lexington: University of Kentucky Press.

Lewis, D. 1969. *Convention: a philosophical study*. Cambridge, MA: Harvard University Press.

1973a. Causation. *Journal of Philosophy* 70: 556–67.

1973b. *Counterfactuals*. Cambridge, MA: Harvard University Press.

1986. *On the plurality of worlds*. Oxford: Basil Blackwell.

Li, R. and Thompson, W. 1975. The "coup contagion" hypothesis. *Journal of Conflict Resolution* 19: 63–88.

Luce, R. and Raiffa, H. 1957. *Games and decisions*. New York: John Wiley & Sons.

Machlup, F. 1974. Situational determinism in economics. *British Journal for the Philosophy of Science* 25: 271–84.

MacIntyre, A. 1973. Is a science of comparative politics possible? In Ryan, A. (ed.) *The philosophy of social explanation*. Oxford University Press.

Mackie, J. 1974. *The cement of the universe: a study of causation*. Oxford University Press.

Mahajan, V. and Peterson, R. 1978. Innovation diffusion in a dynamic potential adaptor population. *Management Science* 24: 1589–97.

1985. *Models for innovation diffusion*. Newbury Park: Sage Publications.

Malhotra, K. 1983. A comparison of the predictive validity of procedures for analyzing binary data. *Journal of Business and Economic Statistics* 1: 326–36.

Manheim, J. and Rich, R. 1986. *Empirical political analysis.* New York: Longman.

Manning, P. 1974. Analyzing the costs and benefits of colonialism. *African Economic History Review* 1: 15–22.

Mansfield, E. 1993. Concentration, polarity, and the distribution of power. *International Studies Quarterly* 37: 105–28.

Maoz, Z. 1982. *Paths to conflict: international dispute initiation.* Boulder: Westview Press.

Maoz, Z. and Russett, B. 1991. Alliance, contiguity, wealth and political stability: is the lack of conflict between democracies a statistical artifact? *International Interactions* 17: 245–68.

March, J. and Olsen, J. 1984. The new institutionalism: organizational factors in political life. *American Political Science Review* 78: 734–49.

Margolis, H. 1990. Equilibrium norms. *Ethics* 100: 821–37.

Martin, L. 1992. *Coercive cooperation: explaining multilateral economic sanctions.* Princeton: Princeton University Press.

Mayr, E. 1982. *The growth of biological thought: diversity, evolution, and inheritance.* Cambridge, MA: Harvard University Press.

1988. *Toward a new philosophy of biology: observations of an evolutionist.* Cambridge, MA: Harvard University Press.

McDougal, M. and associates 1987. *Studies in world public order.* New Haven: Yale University Press.

McGinnis, M. 1990. A rational model of regional rivalry. *International Studies Quarterly* 34: 111–36.

McGowan, P. and Rood, R. 1975. Alliance behavior in balance of power systems: applying a Poisson model to nineteenth century Europe. *American Political Science Review* 69: 859–70.

Midlarsky, M. 1970. Mathematical models of instability and a theory of diffusion. *International Studies Quarterly* 14: 60–84.

1978. Analyzing diffusion and contagion effects: the urban disorders of the 1960s. *American Political Science Review* 72: 996–1008.

Mill, J. S. 1859. *System of logic, ratiocinative and inductive.* New York: Harper.

Minsky, M. 1986. *The society of mind.* New York: Simon & Schuster.

Mitchell, B. 1978. *European historical statistics, 1750–1970.* New York: Columbia University Press.

Mlynář, Z. 1980. *Nightfrost in Prague: the end of humane socialism.* New York: Karz Publishers.

Montesquieu, Charles-Louis de Secondat, baron de 1977 (1748). *The spirit of laws.* Berkeley: University of California Press.

Morgenthau, H. 1973. *Politics among nations: the struggle for power and peace,* 5th edition. New York: Knopf.

Morrow, J. 1989. Bargaining in repeated crises: a limited information model. In

Ordeshook, P. (ed.) *Models of strategic choice in politics*. Ann Arbor: University of Michigan Press.

Most, B. and Starr, H. 1980. Diffusion, reinforcement, geopolitics and the spread of war. *American Political Science Review* 74: 932–46.

1989. *Inquiry, logic, and international politics*. Columbia: University of South Carolina Press.

1990. Theoretical and logical issues in the study of international diffusion. *Journal of Theoretical Politics* 2: 391–412.

Most, B., Starr, H. and Siverson, R. 1989. The logic and study of the diffusion of international conflict. In Midlarsky, M. (ed.) *Handbook of war studies*. Boston: Unwin Hyman.

Mullins, A. 1975. Manpower data as a measure of arms race phenomena. Unpublished manuscript, Ann Arbor, MI.

Munif, A. 1984. *Cities of salt*. New York: Vintage Press.

Nagel, T. 1970. *The possibility of altruism*. Oxford University Press.

Nardin, T. 1983. *Law, morality, and the relations of states*. Princeton: Princeton University Press.

Nelson, R. and Winter, S. 1982. *An evolutionary theory of economic change*. Cambridge, MA: Harvard University Press.

Neustadt, R. and May, E. 1986. *Thinking in time: the uses of history for decision-makers*. New York: The Free Press.

Newcombe, A. 1969. Towards the development of an inter-nation tensiometer. *Peace Research Society International Papers* 13: 11–27.

Newcombe, A., Newcombe, N., and Landrus, G. 1974. The development of an inter-nation tensiometer. *International Interactions* 1: 3–18.

Newcombe, A. and Wert, J. 1973. The use of an inter-nation tensiometer for the prediction of war. *Peace Science Society International* 21: 73–83.

Newell, A. and Simon, H. 1972. *Human problem solving*. Englewood Cliffs: Prentice-Hall.

Nincic, M. 1983. Fluctuations in Soviet defense spending: a research note. *Journal of Conflict Resolution* 27: 648–60.

Nincic, M. and Cusack, T. 1979. The political economy of U.S. military spending. *Journal of Peace Research* 16: 101–15.

Nisbett, R. and Wilson, T. 1977. Telling more than we know: verbal reports on mental processes. *Psychological Review* 84: 231–59.

Noel-Baker, P. 1958. *The arms race: a programme for world disarmament*. New York: Oceana.

North, D. 1990. *Institutions, institutional change and economic performance*. Cambridge University Press.

Nossal, K. 1989. International sanctions as international punishment. *International Organization* 43: 301–22.

Nozick, R. 1974. *Anarchy, state and utopia*. Oxford: Basil Blackwell.

O'Loughlin, J. 1986. Spatial models of international conflicts: extending current theories of war behavior. *Annals of the Association of American Geographers* 76: 63–80.

O'Loughlin, J. and Anselin, L. 1991. Bringing geography back to the study of international relations: spatial dependence and regional context in Africa, 1966–78. *International Interactions* 17: 29–62.

Oakeshott, M. 1975. *On human conduct*. Oxford University Press.

Olson, M. 1965. *The logic of collective action: public goods and the theory of groups*. Cambridge, MA: Harvard University Press.

Organski, A. and Kugler, J. 1980. *The war ledger*. Chicago: University of Chicago Press.

Oster, G. and Wilson, E. 1984. A critique of optimization theory in evolutionary biology. In Sober, E. (ed.) *Conceptual issues in evolutionary biology: an anthology*. Cambridge, MA: The MIT Press.

Park, T. and Ward, M. 1979. Petroleum-related foreign policy: Analytic and empirical analyses of Iranian and Saudi behavior (1948–1974). *Journal of Conflict Resolution* 23: 481–512.

Parsons, T. 1968. *The structure of social action*. New York: The Free Press.

Pearson, F. 1974. Geographic proximity and foreign military intervention. *Journal of Conflict Resolution* 18: 432–60.

Pennwell 1986. *Energy statistics sourcebook*. Tulsa: Pennwell Books.

Pettit, P. 1990. *Virtus normativa*: rational choice perspectives. *Ethics* 100: 725–55.

Pitcher, B., Hamblin, R., and Miller, J. 1978. The diffusion of collective violence. *American Sociological Review* 43: 23–35.

Popper, K. 1950. *The open society and its enemies*. Princeton: Princeton University Press.

1957. *Poverty of historicism*. Boston: Beacon Press.

Przeworski, A. 1974. Contextual models of political behavior. *Political Methodology* 1: 27–61.

Przeworski, A. and Teune, H. 1970. *The logic of comparative social inquiry*. New York: John Wiley & Sons.

Puchala, D. and Hopkins, R. 1983. International regimes: lessons from inductive analysis. In Krasner, S. (ed.) *International regimes*. Ithaca: Cornell University Press.

Ragin, C. 1987. *The comparative method: moving beyond qualitative and quantitative strategies*. Berkeley: University of California Press.

Rathwald, A. 1989. Soviet–East European relations. *Current History* 88: 377–82.

Rawls, J. 1971. *A theory of justice*. Cambridge, MA: Harvard University Press.

Ray, J. 1989. The abolition of slavery and the end of international war. *International Organization* 43: 405–40.

Raz, J. 1980. *The concept of a legal system: an introduction to the theory of legal system*, 2nd edition. Oxford University Press.

1990. *Practical reason and norms*. Princeton: Princeton University Press.

Reisinger, W. 1983. East European military expenditures in the 1970s: collective good or bargaining offer? *International Organization* 37: 143–55.

Richardson, L. 1960a. *Arms and insecurity*. Pittsburgh: Boxwood Press.

1960b. *Statistics of deadly quarrels*. Pittsburgh: Boxwood Press.

Riker, W. 1962. *The theory of political coalitions*. New Haven: Yale University Press.

Rogers, E. 1983. *Diffusion of innovations*, 3rd edition. New York: The Free Press.

Roncaglia, A. 1985. *The international oil market: a case of trilateral oligopoly*. London: Macmillan.

Rosenau, J. 1969. *International politics and foreign policy: a reader in research and theory*, revised edition. New York: The Free Press.

1990. *Turbulence in world politics: a theory of change and continuity*. Princeton: Princeton University Press.

Rosenberg, A. 1984. The supervenience of biological concepts. In Sober, E. (ed.) *Conceptual issues in evolutionary biology: an anthology*. Cambridge, MA: The MIT Press.

Ross, M. and Homer, E. 1976. Galton's problem in cross-national research. *World Politics* 29: 1–28.

Ruggie, J. 1982. International regimes, transactions, and change: embedded liberalism in the postwar economic order. *International Organization* 36: 379–415.

Rummel, R. 1972. *The dimensions of nations*. Beverly Hills: Sage Publications.

Russell, B. 1924. *An analysis of mind*. New York: Macmillan.

Russett, B. 1964. Measures of military effort. *American Behavioral Scientist* 7: 26–9.

1970. *What price vigilance? The burdens of national defense*. New Haven: Yale University Press.

1985. The mysterious case of vanishing hegemony: or, is Mark Twain really dead? *International Organization* 39: 207–31.

Russett, B. and Starr, H. 1992. *World politics: the menu for choice*, 4th edition. San Francisco: W. H. Freeman.

Sabrosky, A. 1975. From Bosnia to Sarajevo: a comparative discussion of interstate crises. *Journal of Conflict Resolution* 19: 3–24.

1976. Why wide wars? Capability distribution, alliance aggregation, and the expansion of interstate war, 1820–1965. Ph.D. Dissertation, University of Michigan.

Sampson, A. 1975. *The seven sisters: the great oil companies and the world they created*. New York: Viking.

Schelling, T. 1960. *Strategy of conflict*. Cambridge, MA: Harvard University Press.

Schumpeter, J. 1934. *The theory of economic development: an inquiry into profits, capital, credit, interest, and the business cycle*. Cambridge, MA: Harvard University Press.

Scott, J. 1971. *Internalization of norms: a sociological theory of moral commitment*. Englewood Cliffs: Prentice-Hall.

Searle, J. 1969. *Speech acts: an essay in the philosophy of language*. Cambridge University Press.

Sen, A. 1977. Rational fools: a critique of the behavioral foundations of economic theory. *Philosophy and Public Affairs* 6: 317–44.

1987. *On ethics and economics*. Oxford: Basil Blackwell.

Shepsle, K. and Weingast, B. 1981. Structure-induced equilibrium and legislative choice. *Public Choice* 37: 503–19.

Sikkink, K. 1989. Codes of conduct for transnational corporations: the case of the WHO/UNICEF Code. In Diehl, P. (ed.) *The politics of international organizations: patterns and insights*. Chicago: The Dorsey Press.

Singer, J. D. 1969. The level-of-analysis problem. In Rosenau, J. (ed.) *International politics and foreign policy: a reader in research and theory*, revised edition. New York: The Free Press.

Singer, J. D., Bremer, S., and Stuckey, J. 1972. Capability distribution, uncertainty, and major power war, 1820–1965. In Russett, B. (ed.) *Peace, war, and numbers*. Beverly Hills: Sage Publications.

Singer, J. D. and Cusack, T. 1981. Periodicity, inexorability and steersmanship in major power war. In Merritt, R. and Russett, B. (eds.) *From national development to global community: essays in honor of Karl W. Deutsch*. Boston: Allen & Unwin.

Singer, J. D. and Small, M. 1974. Foreign policy indicators: prediction of war in history and the State of the World Message. *Policy Sciences* 5: 271–96.

Siverson, R. and King, J. 1979. Alliances and the expansion of war. In Singer, J. D. and Wallace, M. (eds.) *To augur well: early warning indicators in world politics*. Beverly Hills: Sage Publications.

Siverson, R. and Starr, H. 1991. *The diffusion of war: a study of opportunity and willingness*. Ann Arbor: University of Michigan Press.

Siverson, R. and Sullivan, M. 1983. The distribution of power and the onset of war. *Journal of Conflict Resolution* 27: 473–94.

Skocpol, T. 1979. *States and social revolutions: a comparative analysis of France, Russia, and China*. Cambridge University Press.

Small, M. and Singer, J. D. 1982. *Resort to arms: international and civil wars 1816–1980*, 2nd edition. Beverly Hills: Sage Publications.

Smith, T. 1980. Arms race instability and war. *Journal of Conflict Resolution* 24: 253–84.

Snidal, D. 1985. Coordination versus Prisoners' Dilemma: implications for international cooperation and regimes. *American Political Science Review* 79: 923–42.

Sober, E. 1983. Equilibrium explanation. *Philosophical Studies* 43: 201–10.

1984. *The nature of selection: evolutionary theory in philosophical perspective*. Cambridge, MA: The MIT Press.

1988. Apportioning causal responsibility. *Journal of Philosophy* 85: 303–18.

Sperber, D. and Wilson, D. 1986. *Relevance: communication and cognition*. Cambridge, MA: Harvard University Press.

Sprague, J. 1976. Estimating a Boudon type contextual model: some practical and theoretical problems of measurement. *Political Methodology* 3: 333–53.

1982. Is there a micro theory consistent with contextual analysis? In Ostrom, E. (ed.) *Strategies of political inquiry*. Beverly Hills: Sage Publications.

Sprout, H. and Sprout, M. 1965. *The ecological perspective on human affairs*. Princeton: Princeton University Press.

Staar, R. 1989. Poland: renewal or stagnation? *Current History* 88: 373–6.

Staddon, J. 1983. *Adaptive behavior and learning*. Cambridge University Press.

Stallings, B. 1987. *Banker to the Third World: U.S. portfolio investment in Latin America, 1900–1986*. Berkeley: University of California Press.

Starr, H. 1978. "Opportunity" and "willingness" as ordering concepts in the study of war. *International Interactions* 4: 363–87.

1991. Democratic dominoes: diffusion approaches to the spread of democracy in the international system. *Journal of Conflict Resolution* 35: 356–81.

Starr, H. and Most, B. 1976. The substance and study of borders in international relations research. *International Studies Quarterly* 20: 581–620.

1978. A return journey: Richardson's "frontiers" and wars in the 1946–1965 era. *Journal of Conflict Resolution* 22: 441–67.

Stein, A. 1983. Coordination and collaboration: regimes in an anarchic world. In Krasner, S. (ed.) *International regimes*. Ithaca: Cornell University Press.

Stevens, P. 1985. A survey of structural change in the international oil industry 1945–1984. In Hawdon, D. (ed.) *The changing structure of the world oil industry*. London: Croom Helm.

Stoll, R. 1984. From fire to frying pan: the impact of major power war involvement on major power dispute involvement 1816–1975. *Conflict Management and Peace Science* 7: 71–82.

Stoll, R. and Champion, M. 1977. Predicting the escalation of serious disputes to war: Some preliminary findings. North American Peace Science Conference, Philadelphia, PA.

Stoll, R. and Ward, M. (eds.) 1989. *Power in world politics*. Boulder: Lynne Reinner.

Sugden, R. 1986. *The economics of rights, co-operation and welfare*. Oxford: Basil Blackwell.

1990. Contractarianism and norms. *Ethics* 100: 768–86.

Sunstein, C. 1990. Norms in surprising places: the case of statutory interpretation. *Ethics* 100: 803–20.

Sylvan, D. and Chan, S. 1984. *Foreign policy decision making perception: perception, cognition, and artifical intelligence*. New York: Praeger.

Snyder, G. 1991. Alliances, balance, and stability. *International Organization* 45: 121–42.

Tate, R. 1984. Limitations of centering for interactive models. *Sociological Methods and Research* 13: 251–71.

Tate, R. and Wongbundhit, Y. 1983. Random versus nonrandom coefficient models for multilevel analysis. *Journal of Educational Statistics* 8: 103–20.

Thompson, W. 1988. *On global war: historical-structural approaches to world politics*. Columbia: University of South Carolina Press.

Tillema, H. and Van Wingen, J. 1982. Law and power in military intervention: major states after World War II. *International Studies Quarterly* 26: 220–50.

Tittle, C. and Hill, R. 1967. Attitude measurement and prediction of behavior. *Sociometry* 30: 199–213.

Tocqueville, A. de (Bonner, J. trans.) 1856. *The old regime and the French Revolution*. New York: Harper & Bros.

Tugwell, F. 1975. *The politics of oil in Venezuela*. Stanford: Stanford University Press.

Turner, L. 1978. *The oil companies in the international system*. London: Royal Institute of International Affairs.

Tversky, A. and Kahneman, D. 1981. The framing of decisions and the psychology of choice. *Science* 211: 453–8.

Ulč, O. 1989. Czechoslovakia: Realistic socialism? *Current History* 88: 389–92.

Ullmann-Margalit, E. 1977. *The emergence of norms*. Oxford University Press.

US Arms Control and Disarmament Agency 1983. *World military expenditures and arms transfers 1971–80*. Washington, DC: ACDA.

US Bureau of the Census 1975. *Historical statistics of the United States, colonial times to 1970*, bicentennial edition. Washington, DC: Bureau of the Census.

US Department of the Interior, Bureau of Mines 1950–1965. *Minerals yearbook*. Washington, DC: Government Printing Office.

US Department of Energy 1978. *International petroleum annual*. Washington, DC: Department of Energy.

Uvin, P. 1992. Regime, surplus, and self-interest: The international politics of food aid. *International Studies Quarterly* 36: 293–312.

Van Evera, S. 1984. The cult of the offensive and the origins of World War I. *International Security* 9: 58–107.

Van Wingen, J. and Tillema, H. 1980. British military intervention after World War II: Militance in a second-rank power. *Journal of Peace Research* 17: 291–303.

Vasquez, J. 1983. *The power of power politics: A critique*. New Brunswick: Rutgers University Press.

1993. *The war puzzle*. Cambridge University Press.

Vasquez, J. and Mansbach, R. 1984. The role of issues in global cooperation and conflict. *British Journal of Political Science* 14: 411–33.

Veblen, T. 1899. *The theory of the leisure class: An economic study in the evolution of institutions*. New York: Macmillan.

Veen, R. van der 1981. Meta-rankings and collective optimality. *Social Science Information* 20: 345–74.

Vernon, R. 1971. *Sovereignty at bay: The multinational spread of U.S. enterprises*. New York: Basic Books.

Volgyes, I. 1989. Hungary: Dancing in the shackles of the past. *Current History* 88: 381–4.

Wagner, R. 1989. Uncertainty, rational learning, and bargaining in the Cuban Missile Crisis. In Ordeshook, P. (ed.) *Models of strategic choice in politics*. Ann Arbor: University of Michigan Press.

Walker, R. 1990. History and structure in the theory of international relations. In Haglund, D. and Hawes, M. (eds.) *World politics: Power, interdependence, and dependence*. Toronto: Harcourt Brace Jovanovich.

Walt, S. 1987. *The origins of alliances*. Ithaca: Cornell University Press.

Waltz, K. 1964. The stability of a bipolar world. *Daedalus* 93: 881–909.

1979. *Theory of international relations*. Boston: Addison-Wesley.

Walzer, M. 1977. *Just and unjust wars: A moral argument with historical illustrations*. New York: Basic Books.

Ward, M. and Luterbacher, U. (eds.) 1985. *Dynamic models of international conflict.* Boulder: Lynne Rienner.

Wayman, F. 1982. War and power transition in enduring rivalries. Institute for the Study of Conflict Theory and International Conflict, Urbana IL.

1984. Bipolarity and war: The role of capability concentration and alliance patterns among major powers, 1816–1965. *Journal of Peace Research* 21: 61–78.

Wayman, F. and Diehl, P. 1994. *Reconstructing realpolitik.* Ann Arbor: University of Michigan Press.

Wayman, F. and Jones, D. 1991. Evolution of conflict during enduring rivalries. International Studies Association Meetings, Vancouver, BC.

Wayman, F., Singer, J. D., and Goertz, G. 1984. Capabilities, allocations, and success in militarized disputes and wars, 1816–1976. *International Studies Quarterly* 27: 497–515.

Weber, M. 1958. *The Protestant ethic and the spirit of capitalism.* New York: Scribners.

Weede, E. 1970. Conflict behavior of nation-states. *Journal of Peace Research* 3: 229–35.

1977. National position in world politics and military allocation ratios in the 1950s and 1960s. *Jerusalem Journal of International Relations* 2: 63–80.

1981. Preventing war by nuclear deterrence or by détente. *Conflict Management and Peace Science* 6: 1–18.

Weizsäcker, C. von 1971. Notes on endogenous change of tastes. *Journal of Economic Theory* 3: 345–72.

White, M. 1943. Historical explanation. *Mind* 52: 212–29.

Wildavsky, A. 1975. *Budgeting: a comparative theory of budgetary process.* Boston: Little, Brown.

Williams, J. and McGinnis, M. 1992. The dimension of superpower rivalry: a dynamic factor analysis. *Journal of Conflict Resolution* 36: 86–118.

Williams, T. 1969. *Huey Long.* New York: Knopf.

Winch, P. 1958. *The idea of social science and its relation to philosophy.* London: Routledge & Kegan Paul.

Wittgenstein, L. 1953. *Philosophical investigations.* London: Macmillan.

World Bank 1983. *China: socialist economic development,* Vol. I: *The economy, statistical system, and basic data.* Washington: World Bank.

Yamamoto, Y. 1974. Probability models of war expansion and peacetime alliance formation. Ph.D. Dissertation, University of Michigan.

Yergin, D. 1991. *The prize: the epic quest for oil, money, and power.* New York: Simon & Schuster.

Young, O. 1983. Regime dynamics: The rise and fall of international regimes. In Krasner, S. (ed.) *International regimes.* Ithaca: Cornell University Press.

Zacher, M. 1979. *International conflicts and collective security, 1946–1977.* New York: Praeger.

INDEX

22 KEITH KRAUSE
Arms and the state: patterns of military production and trade

21 ROGER BUCKLEY
US–Japan alliance diplomacy 1945–1990

20 JAMES N. ROSENAU and ERNST-OTTO CZEMPIEL (eds.)
Governance without government order and change in world politics

19 MICHAEL NICHOLSON
Rationality and the analysis of international conflict

18 JOHN STOPFORD and SUSAN STRANGE
Rival states, rival firms
Competition for world market shares

17 TERRY NARDIN and DAVID R. MAPEL (eds.)
Traditions of international ethics

16 CHARLES F. DORAN
Systems in crisis
New imperatives of high politics at century's end

15 DEON GELDENHUYS
Isolated states: a comparative analysis

14 KALEVI J. HOLSTI
Peace and war: armed conflicts and international order 1648–1989

13 SAKI DOCKRILL
Britain's policy for West German rearmament 1950–1955

12 ROBERT H. JACKSON
Quasi-states: sovereignty, international relations and the Third World

11 JAMES BARBER and JOHN BARRATT
South Africa's foreign policy
The search for status and security 1945–1988

10 JAMES MAYALL
Nationalism and international society

9 WILLIAM BLOOM
Personal identity, national identity and international relations

8 ZEEV MAOZ
National choices and international processes

7 IAN CLARK
The hierarchy of states
Reform and resistance in the international order

6 HIDEMI SUGANAMI
The domestic analogy and world order proposals

5 STEPHEN GILL
American hegemony and the Trilateral Commission

4 MICHAEL C. PUGH
The ANZUS crisis, nuclear visiting and deterrence

3 MICHAEL NICHOLSON
Formal theories in international relations

2 FRIEDRICH V. KRATOCHWIL
Rules, norms, and decisions
On the conditions of practical and legal reasoning in international relations and domestic affairs

1 MYLES L. C. ROBERTSON
Soviet policy towards Japan
An analysis of trends in the 1970s and 1980s